WHAT AM I
DOING HERE?

What Am I Doing Here?

BY ABNER DEAN

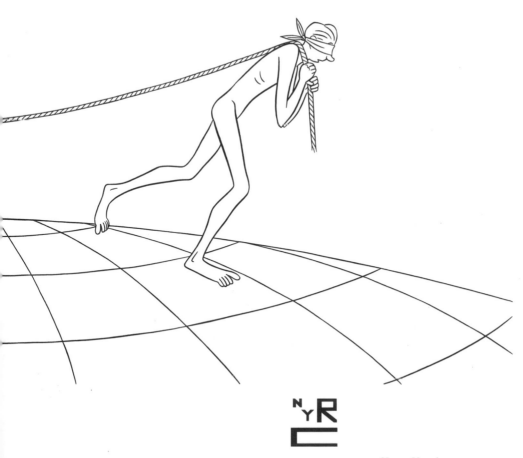

NYR

NEW YORK REVIEW COMICS · *New York*

THIS IS A NEW YORK REVIEW COMIC
PUBLISHED BY THE NEW YORK REVIEW OF BOOKS
435 Hudson Street, New York, NY 10014
www.nyrb.com

Copyright © 1947 by Abner Dean
Prefatory note published by arrangement with The Estate of Clifton Fadiman

All images courtesy of Dartmouth College Library except those on pages 23, 75, 80–81, and 102

A catalog record for this book is available from the Library of Congress

ISBN 978-1-68137-049-1
Available as an electronic book; ISBN 978-1-68137-050-7

Printed in China
10 9 8 7 6 5 4 3 2 1

TABLE OF

CONTENTS

A NOTE ABOUT

A NEW YORKER by birth and inclination, Abner Dean (1910–1982) attended the National Academy of Design and then Dartmouth College, which he graduated from in 1931. Out of school, he soon found success in commercial illustration, drawing covers, advertisements, and cartoons for the likes of *Collier's*, *The New Yorker*, *Newsweek*, *Esquire*, *Life*, *Time*, and other publications.

In 1941, he pursued the cartoonist's holy grail: a syndicated feature. He started a single-panel gag strip called *Funny Side Up* for United Features, and drew more than three hundred cartoons. But after ten months he abandoned the effort, noting that "the demands of commercial art are so great and lead so far away from the purer forms that I don't believe a compromise between the two is ever possible."

His commercial employment continued (including a series of illustrations of George Orwell's *1984* for *Life*), and in the hours of escape from persistent deadlines he completed his first book of more personal work, *It's a Long Way to Heaven*, published in 1945. Some received this venture cautiously. *The New York Times* said of it: "Whether Dean's conceptions are readily seized is a question for the individual, who should have a good time finding out." Others embraced it: Northrop Frye wrote that Dean's poetical cartoons "have a disturbingly haunting quality that one rarely finds in the more realistic captioned cartoons of the *New Yorker* school, and in fact are 'funny' only to the extent of making one giggle hysterically"; and the *Saturday Review*, noting the persistent nudity of Dean's characters, declared him "the Rembrandt of the buttock."

Dean continued to develop his unique style of comics with this book, *What Am I Doing Here?*, in 1947, and a string of other titles through the 1950s: *On the Eighth Day, Come As You Are* ("a book about people at parties"), *Cave Drawings for the Future*, *Wake Me When It's Over*, and *Not Far from the Jungle* (the last two featuring his verse alongside his drawings). In 1963 he released Abner Dean's *Naked People*, a deluxe selection of his previous work.

ABNER DEAN

Dean also pursued a variety of non-cartoon endeavors. He was a panelist on the television program *Draw to Win* in 1952 and the set designer for the 1963 Broadway production *Too Good to Be True*, which featured the silent-film star Lillian Gish. He also tried his hand at inventing and acquired two patents, one of which was for a multilevel folding table.

He lived in New York for the rest of his life. His papers, including the original drawings for *What Am I Doing Here?*, are in the Rauner Special Collections Library at Dartmouth College.

A PREFATORY NOTE

MUCH as he hates to admit it, the life of the average man (which means virtually all of us) tends to assume the form of a longish doze, interrupted by fits and starts of bewildered semi-alertness. We will invent a hundred ways of heading off self-awareness to one that may force us to ask ourselves who the devil we are. You cannot turn on your radio or unfold your newspaper without being offered all the answers. But where shall we go if we wish to be asked the questions?

The question-askers are usually of two kinds. There are, first, the men of true religion, the prophets, of whom only a few exist in any generation; and, second, the artists, among whom we should include, of course, all true scientists, educators, and philosophers. They are the ones who rowel us out of our sleep. They are the magnificent cockleburs of the human race.

Abner Dean is such a cocklebur. He disquiets us. He unsettles us. He takes us by the scruff of our unconscious and drops us all squealing right into the middle of his astonishing pictures. He asks us questions and makes us ask ourselves questions.

Is life more like making the 5:15 in which every commuter is meaningless? Or is it more like wandering in a wood where every tree is a mystery? Am I complete because I have a pocketbook, a Social Security number, a last will and testament? Or have I lost something I cannot put a name to? I am elated because I possess electric switches, clocks and watches, pants with zippers, clutchless automobiles, telephones, radio sets, and a civil servant in gray who brings me newspapers and magazines telling me I should acquire more electric switches, pants with zippers, etc. Am I a fool in my elation? Or do I really have reality reduced to a dial system and therefore licked? Do I know my way around—or don't I?

This naked little man created by Abner Dean wanders about among other naked men and women, full of good will and curiosity and fatuity. He gets into jams, but is always pretty certain that something can be done about them. He's proud of the idiot contraptions he's assembled. He's always

by CLIFTON FADIMAN

forgotten something, he's always looking for something. He tries hard to conform—that is to say, he preserves a bland detachment among the lunacies that strew his path. Then he breaks out of the pattern in maniac glee, and throws the shoes of his questionings into the machinery. He will stumble, he will fall, he will be beaten, he will be blindfolded, he will be disappointed—somehow he will survive.

It is pointless to try to "explain" Abner Dean. His pictures are trick mirrors in which we catch sight of those absurd fragments of ourselves that we never see in the smooth glass of habit. Formulae for the art of Abner Dean are irrelevant. What is important is the fact that it jolts you into sudden awareness of your own pathos, your own plight, your own unending and gigantic laughableness.

This book is a real book, and not a collection of cartoons. The naked wanderings of his eternally bemused, eternally hopeful hero trace an interesting pattern, full of ingenious echoes and returns, like a fugue. The macabre alternates with the wistful; the hero leaps from exaltation to pathetic self-reproach; he holds the truth in his hand—no, he has lost it; love is the answer—or isn't it? A hundred stray, flying strands of the inner life are woven into this visible odyssey of a latter-day Everyman.

The urge to call Dean bats will be strong; but that is only because we have so large a vested interest in being "normal" that we panic easily when this investment is threatened. We have always tried and always will try to laugh down those who question the value of this investment. But, sooner or later, such is their charm, such the subtle appeal they make to that repressed part of ourselves which knows that we are absurd and wonderful, we go back to them to receive the ration they offer us of disquietude. They cannot help us to accumulate three-dimensional objects, or to torment and kill others: the main objects of modern life. They can only help us to feel what it is to be human. There are few rich enough to offer this gift, and of these Abner Dean is one.

To Eleanor with love

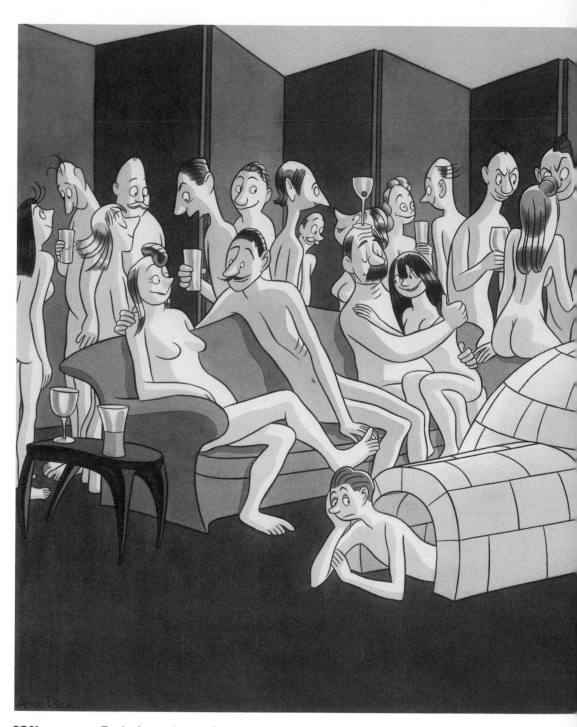

What am I doing here?

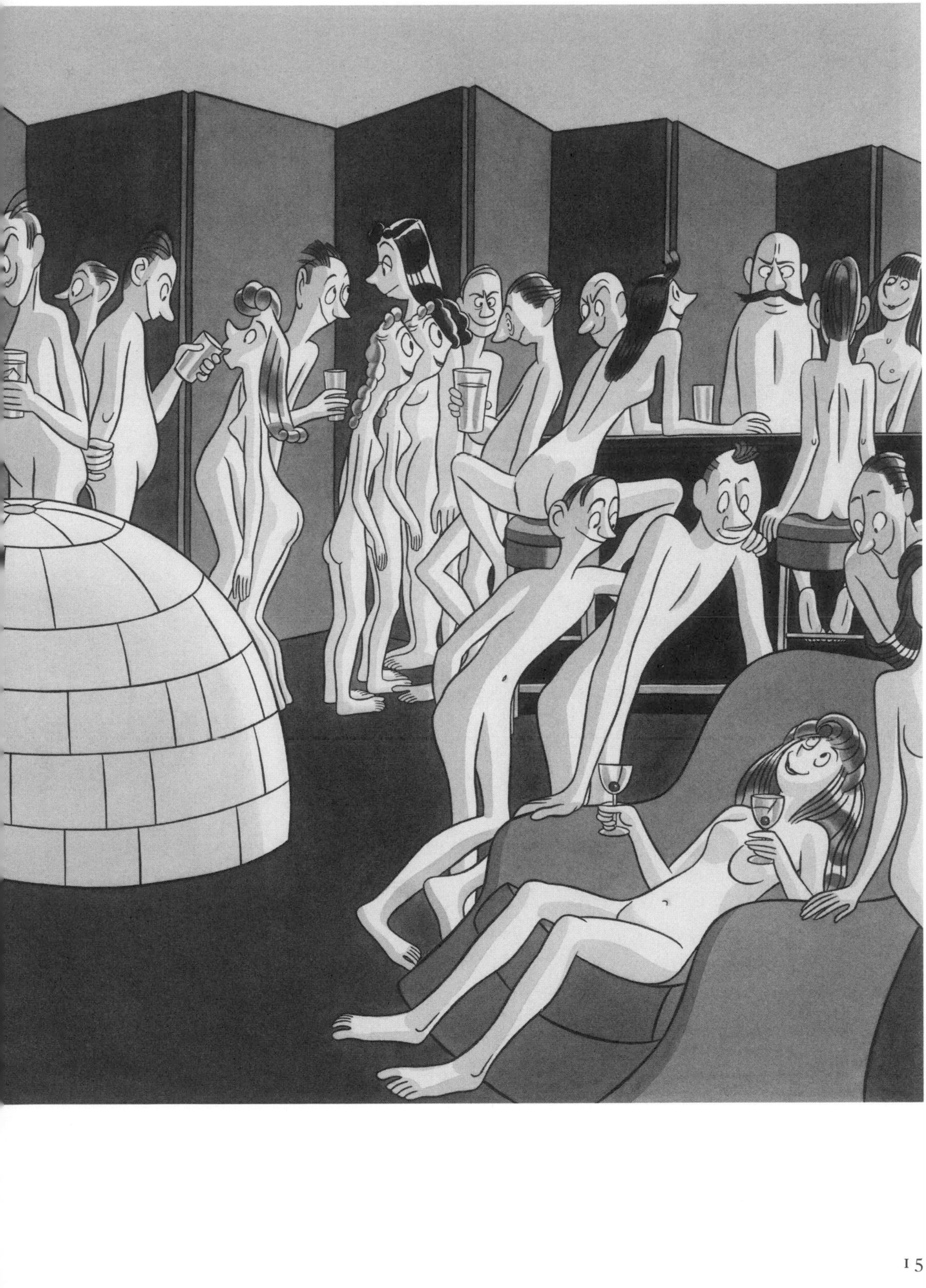

Everyone has a story

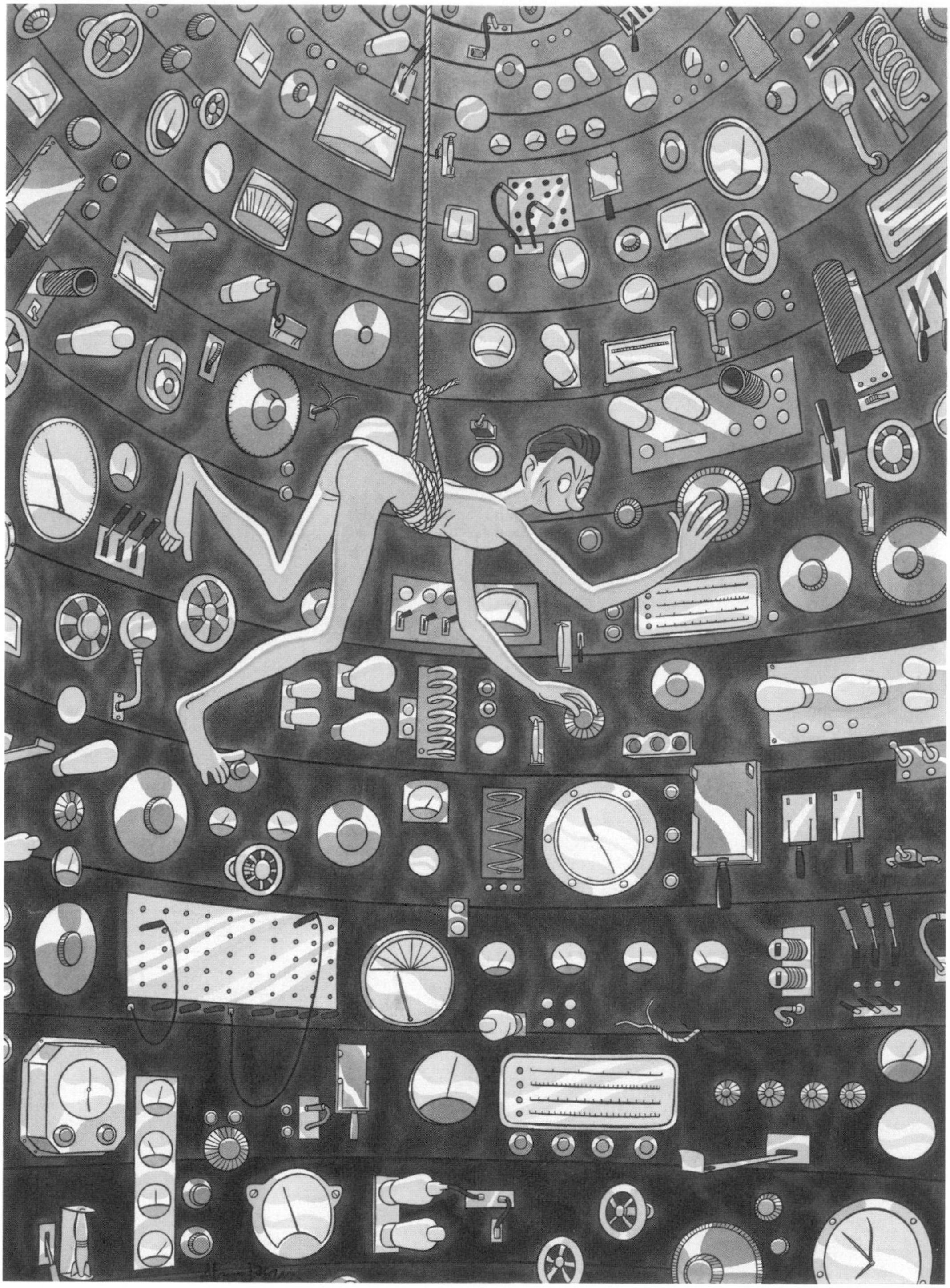

I have great power of selection

Let's talk in code

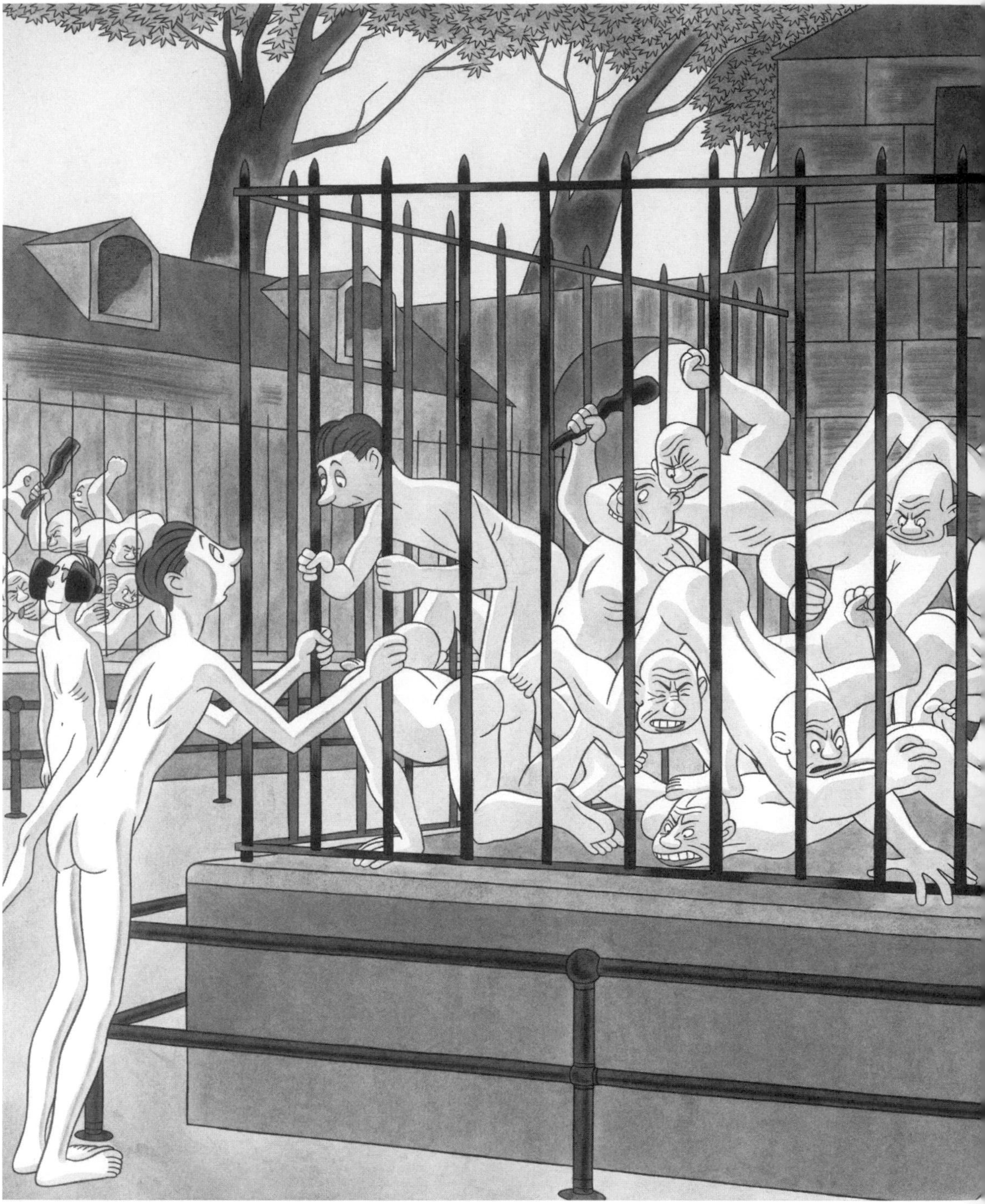

Do you shock easily?

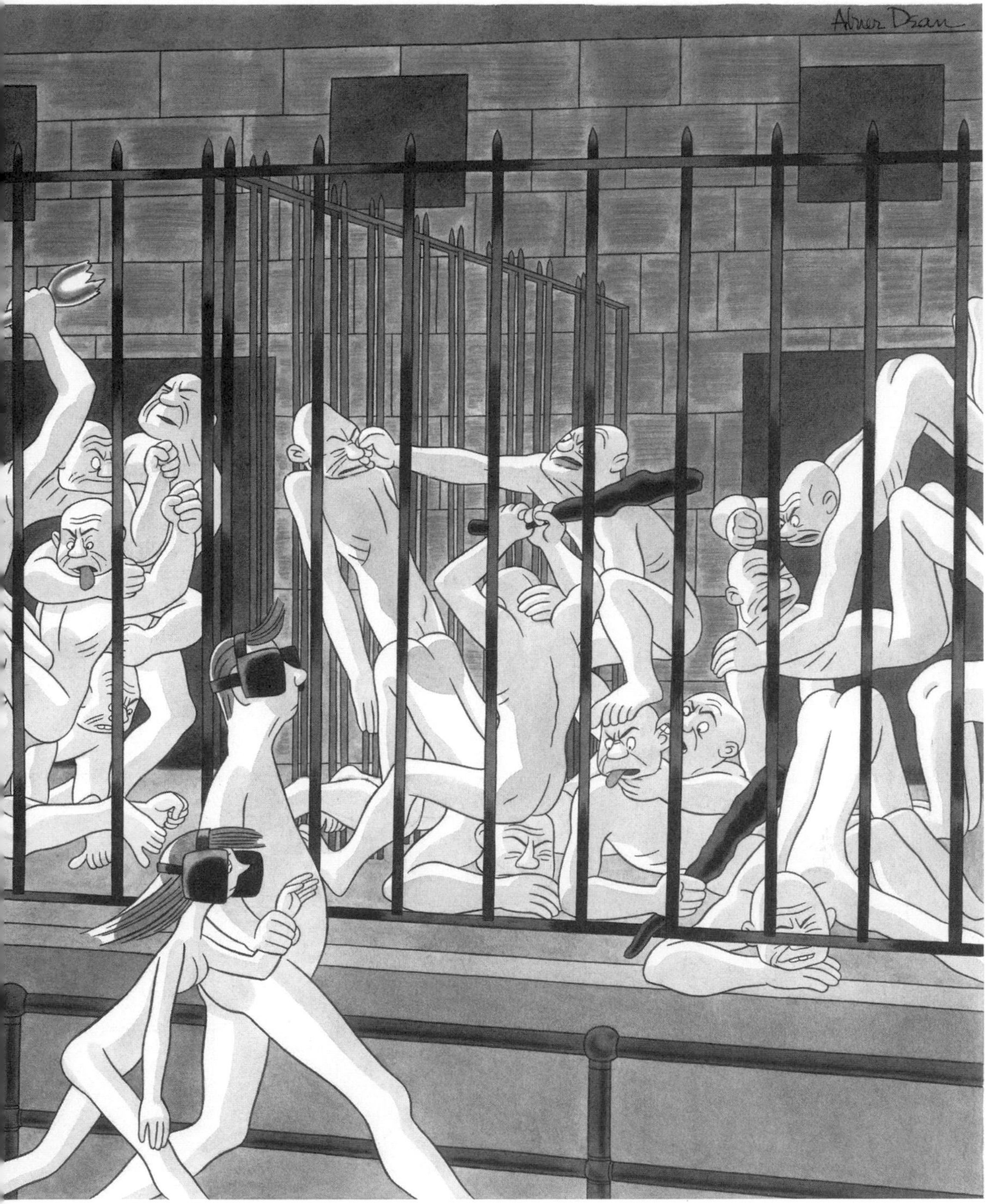
Abner Dean

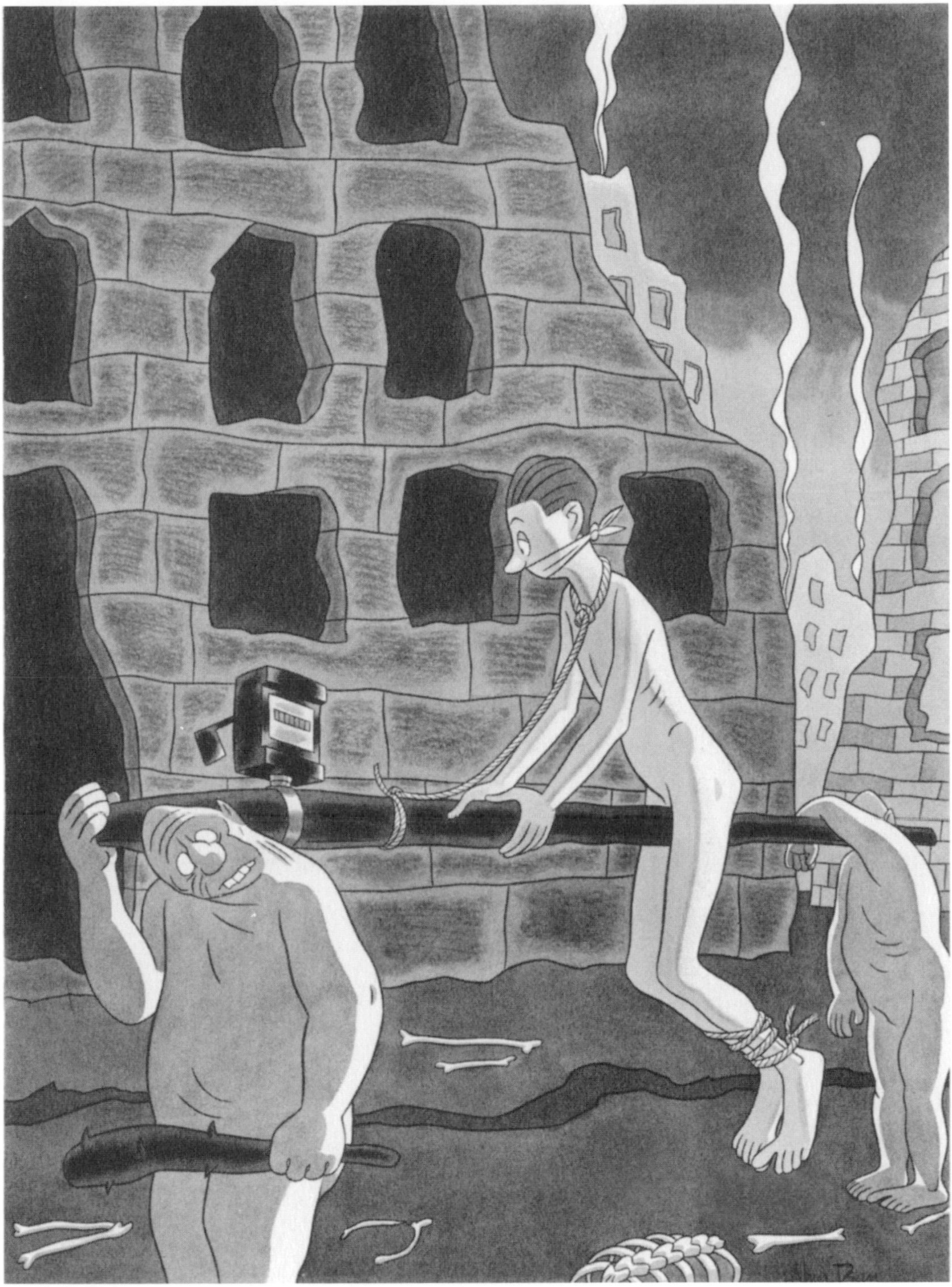

Where to, Buddy?

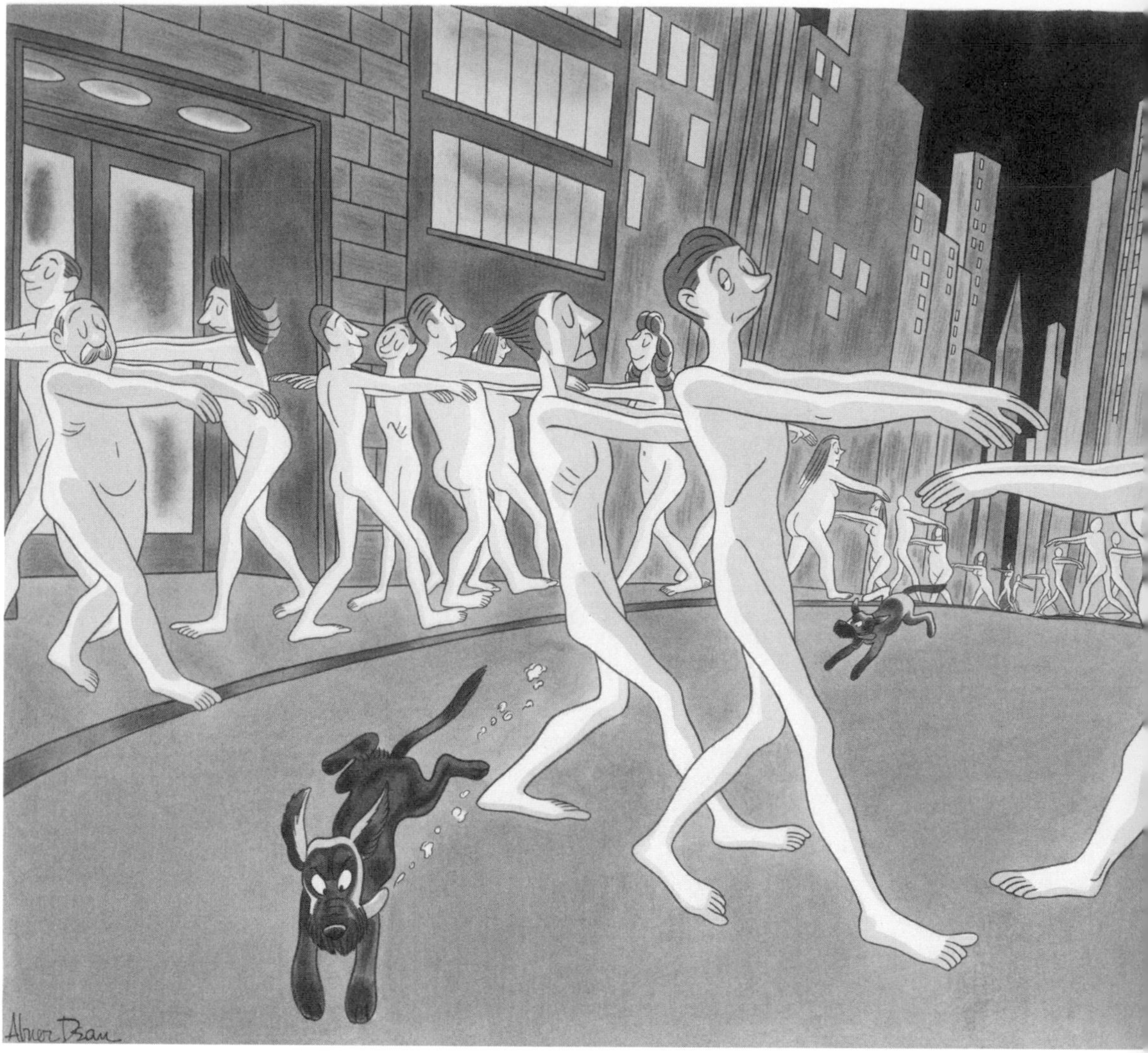
Abner Dean

We're all in it together

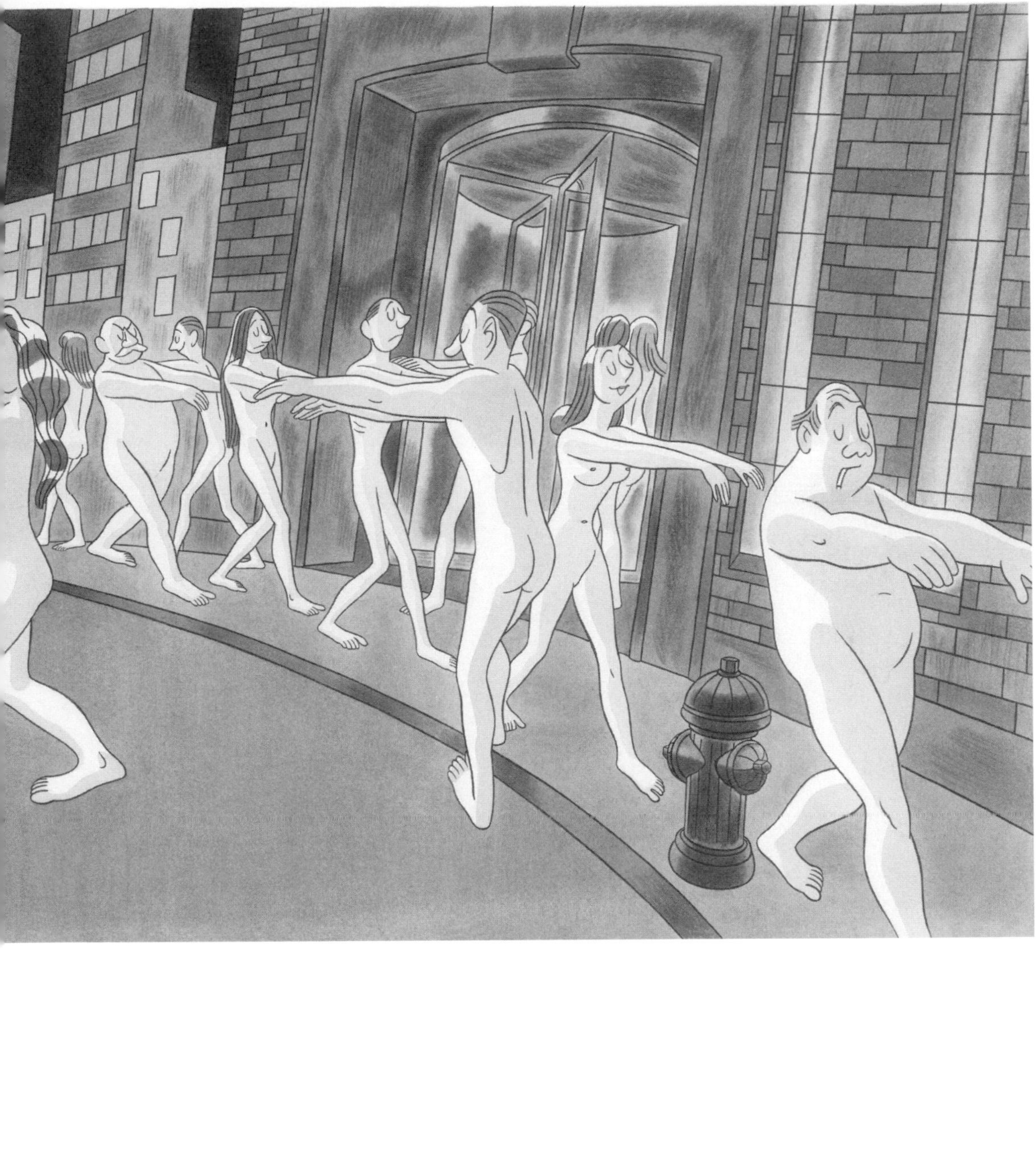

This thing has meaning

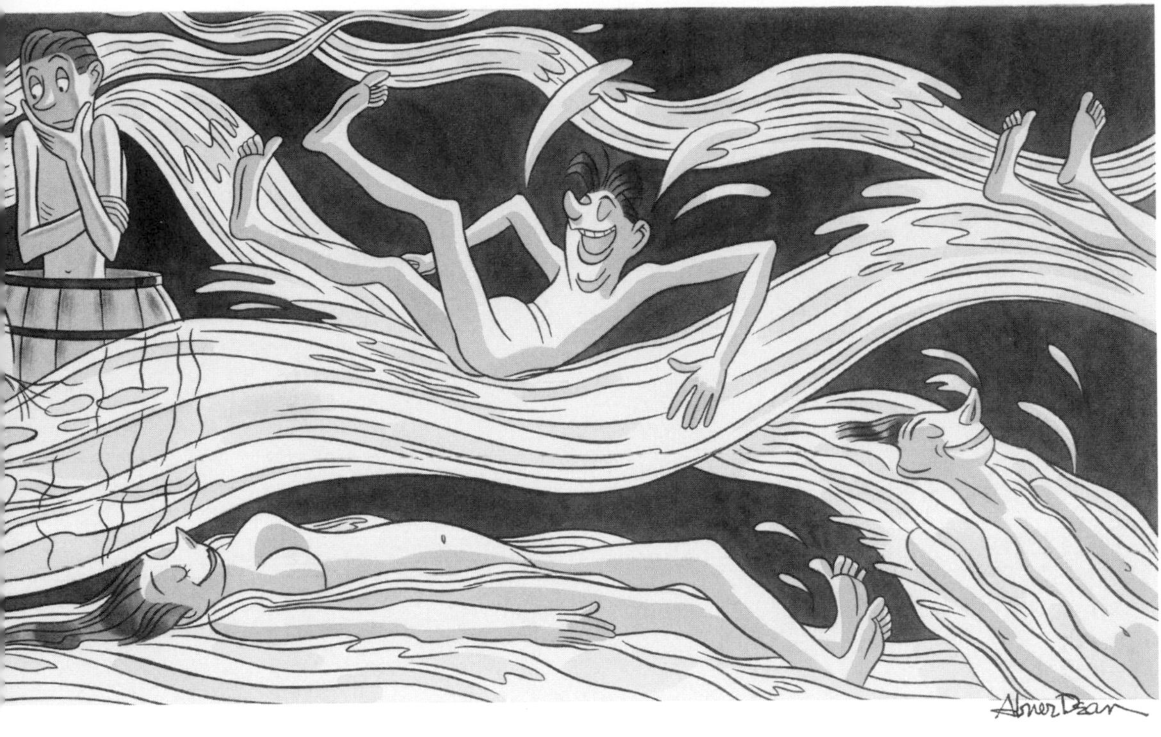
Abner Dean

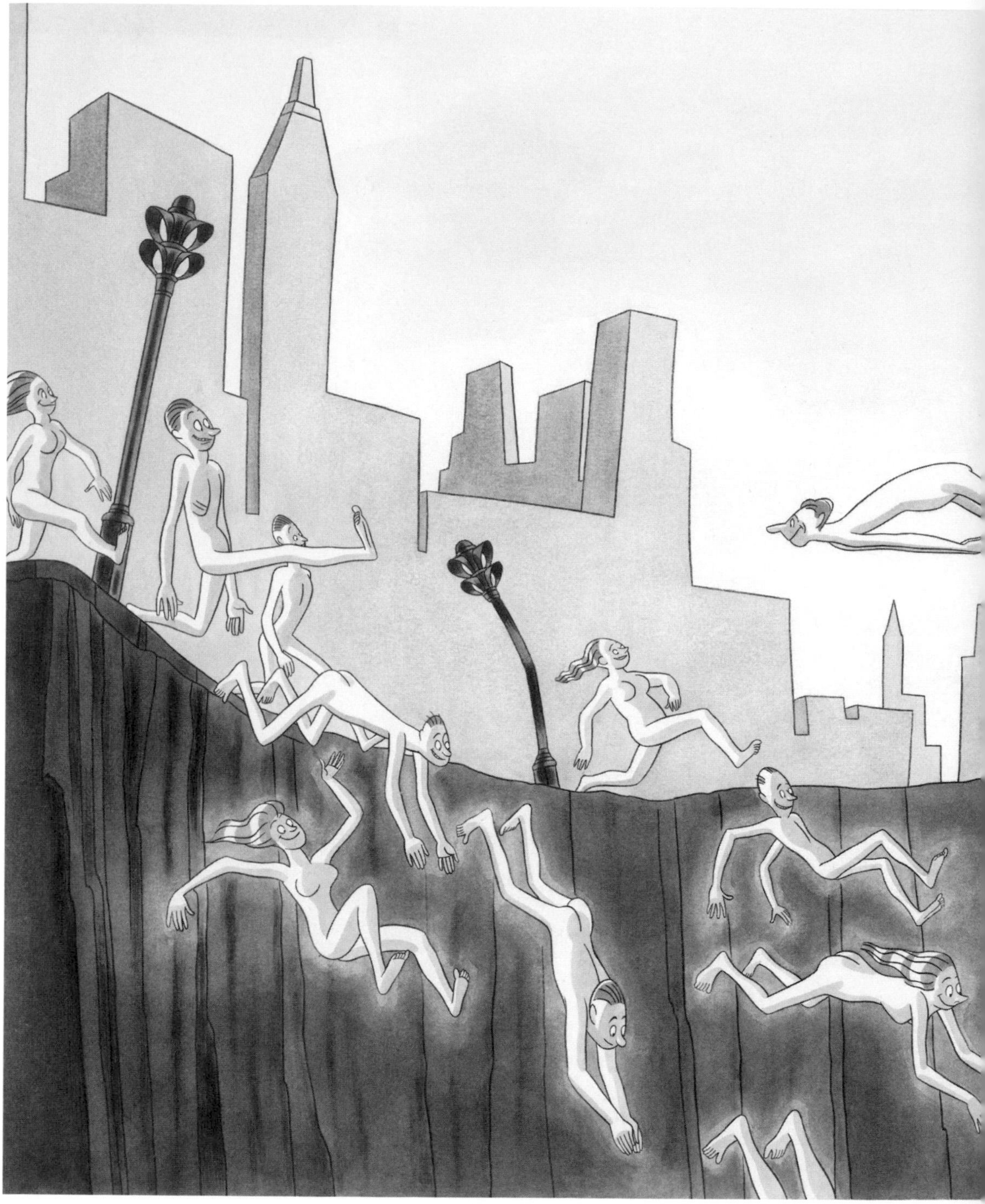

Other people are brave

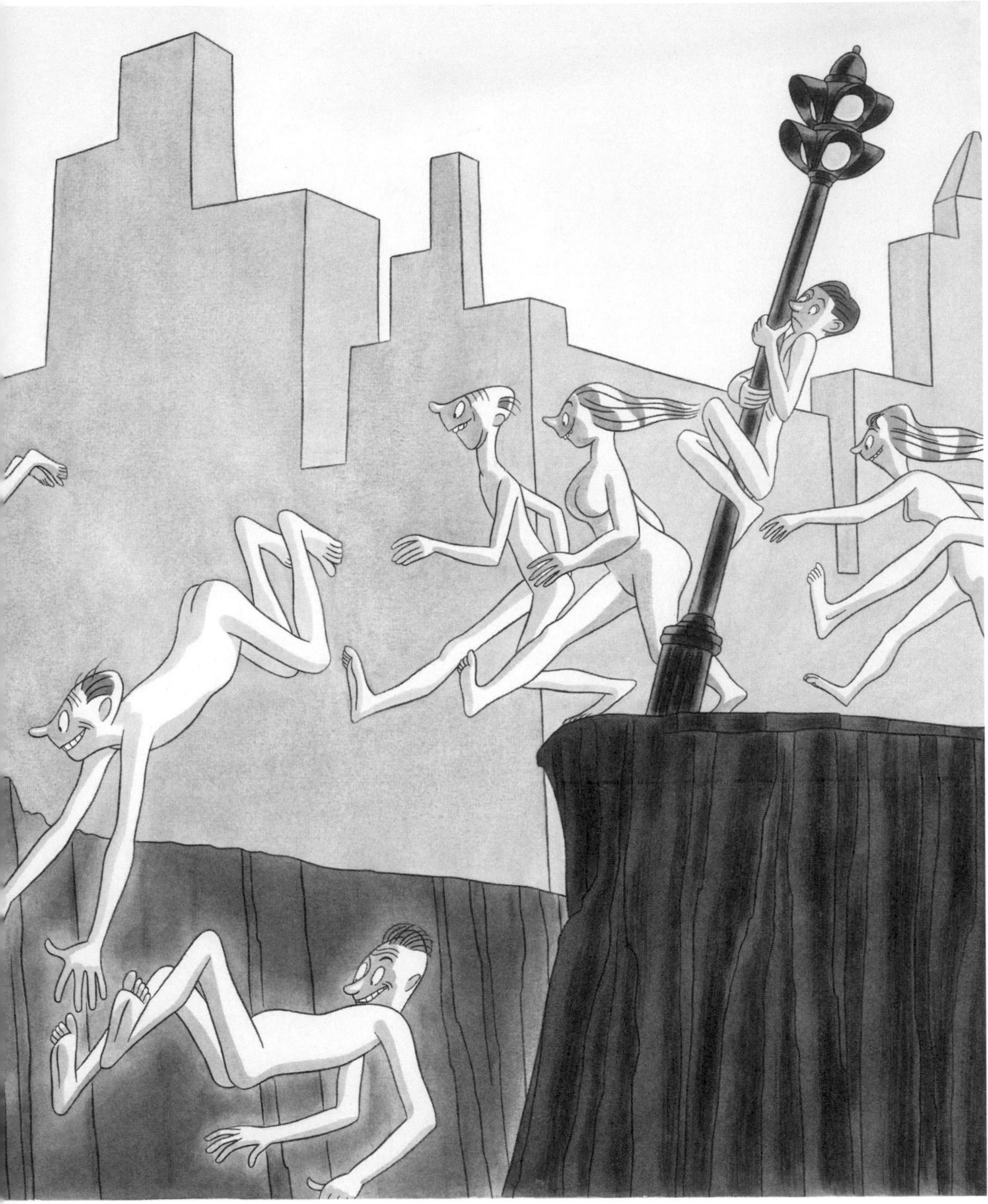

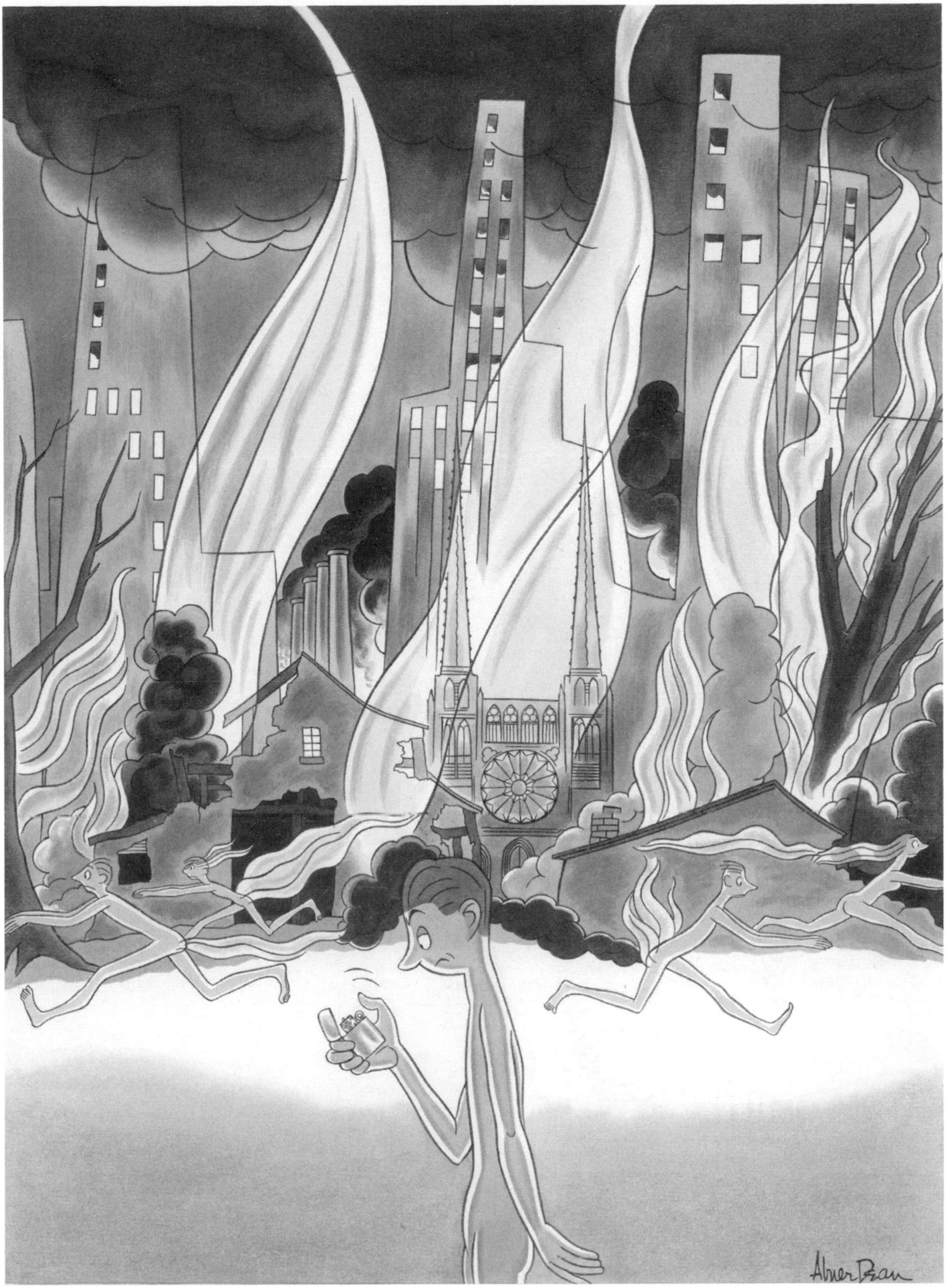
Abner Dean

I must remember to have it fixed

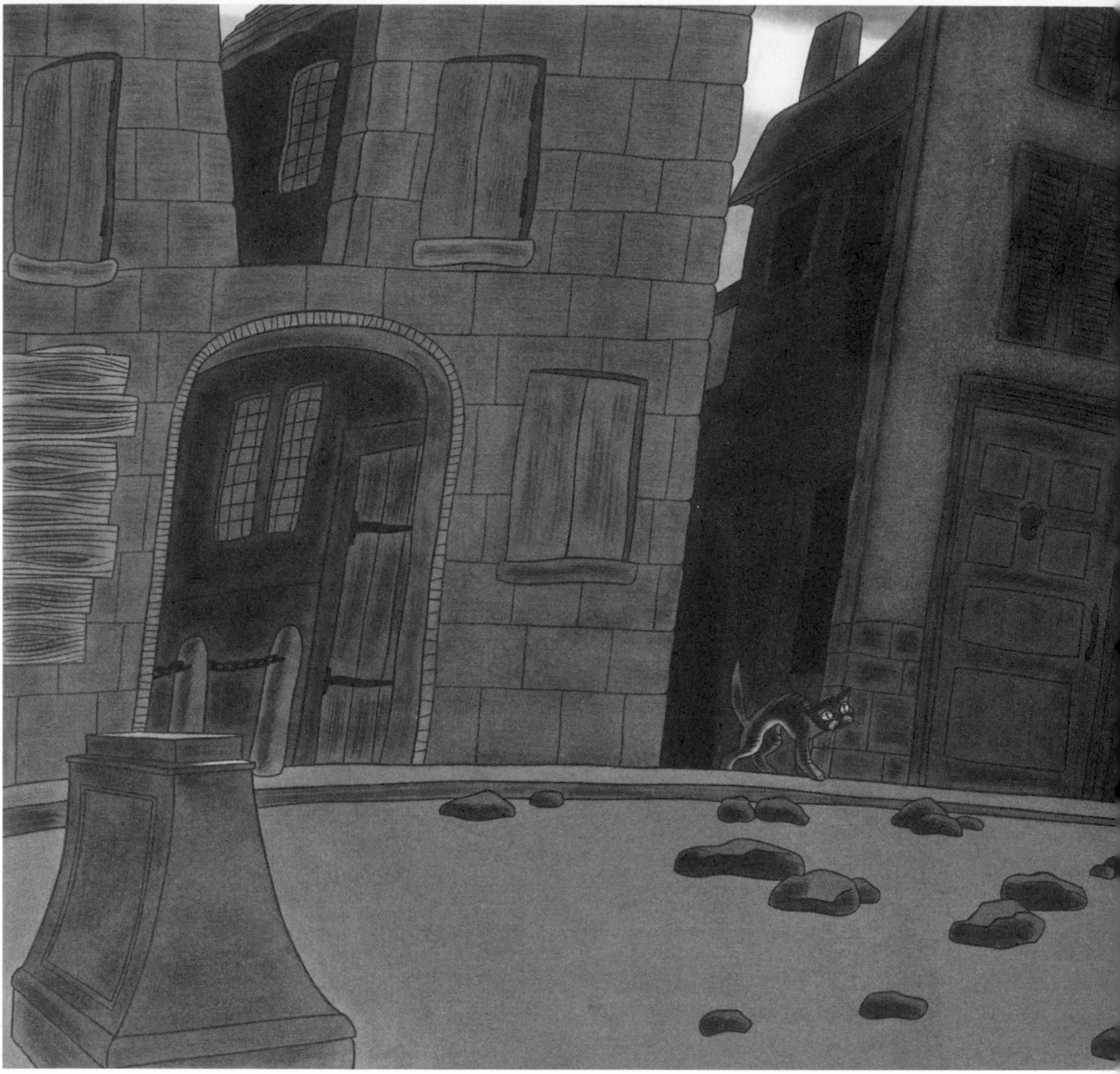

I'm looking for someone with a mole on her elbow

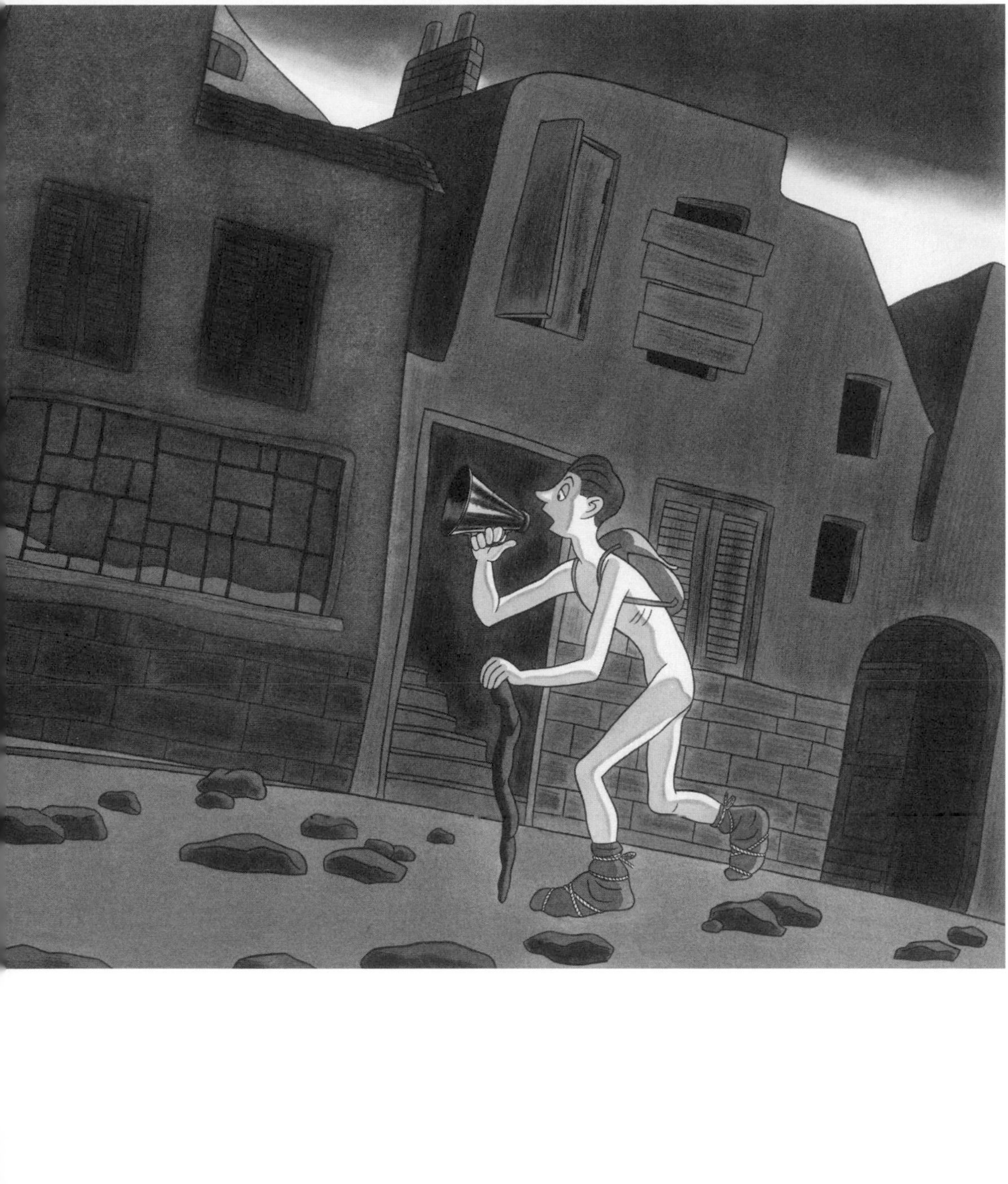

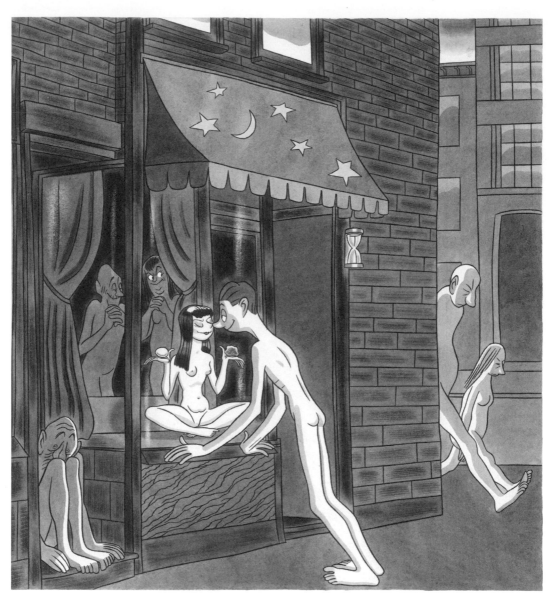

There's something here for me

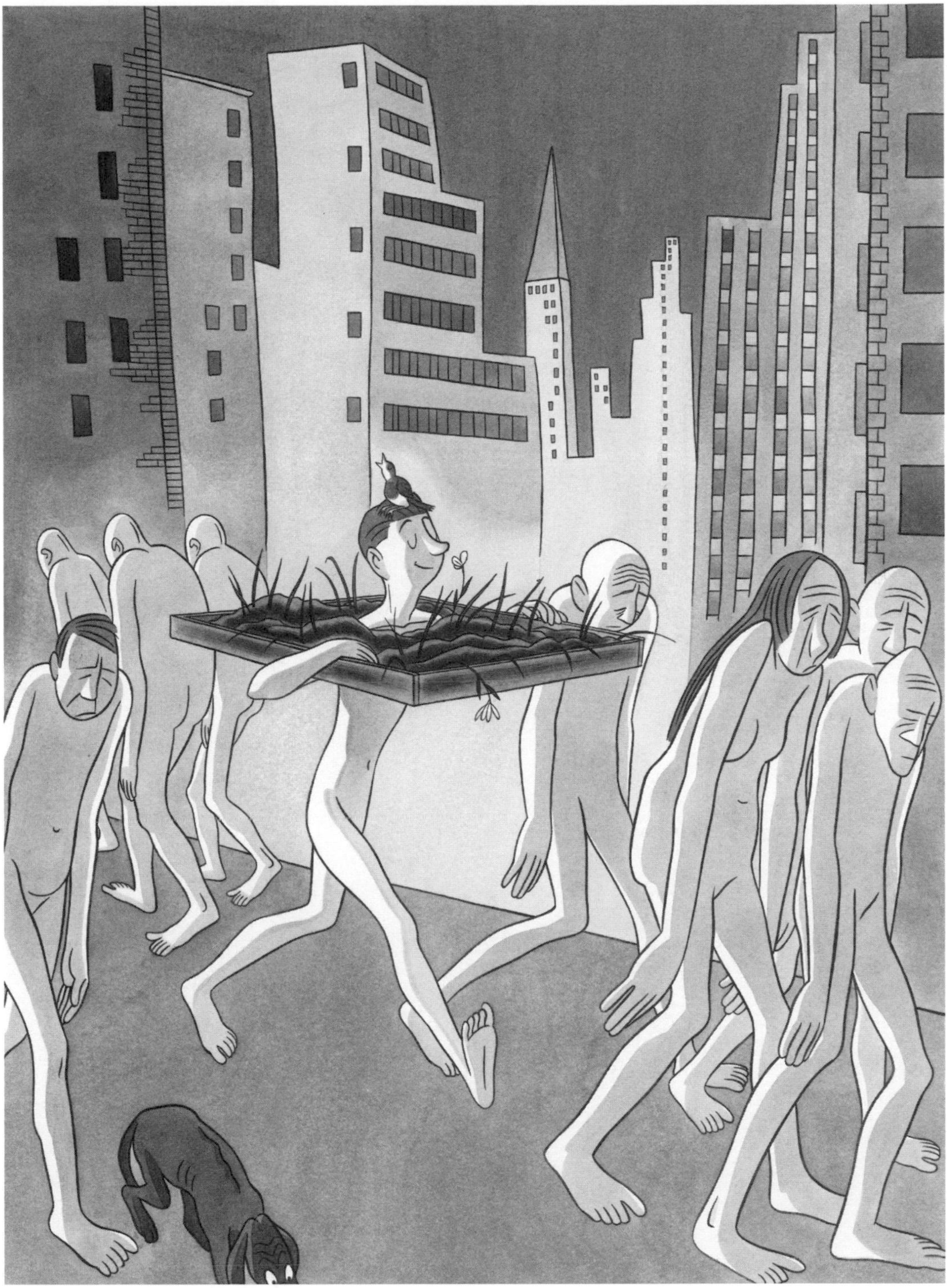

It's good to own a piece of land

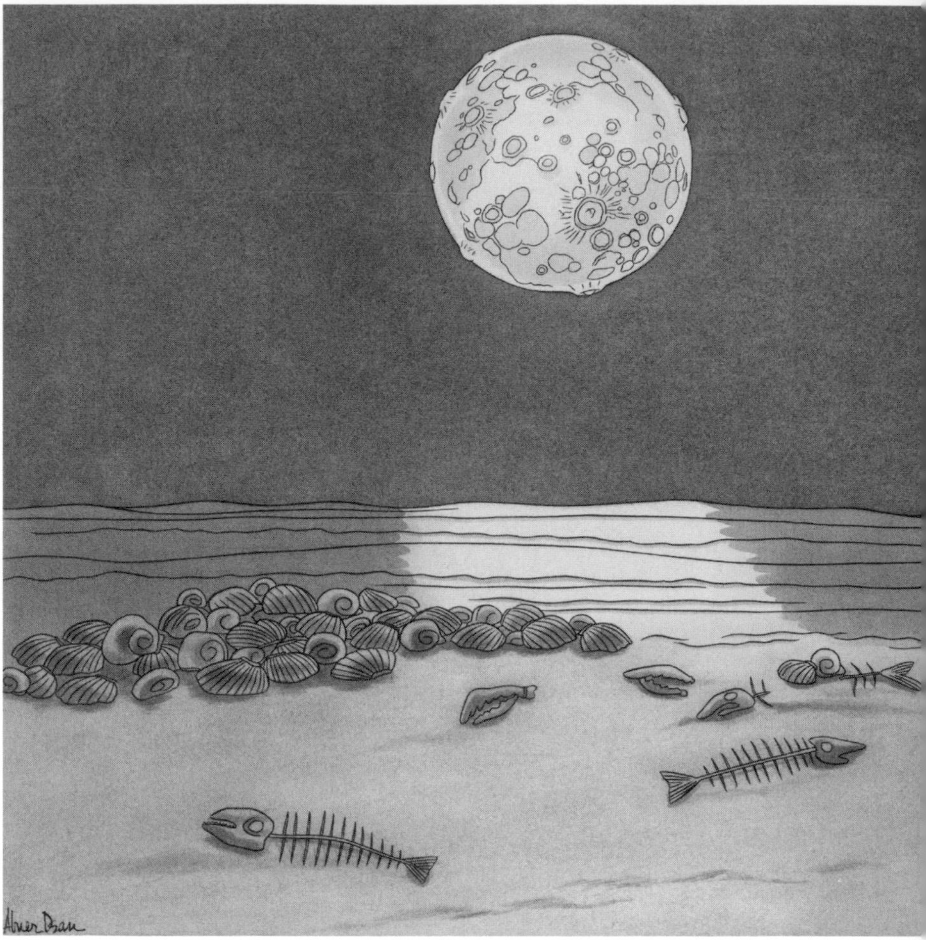
Abner Dean

Don't analyze . . . dream

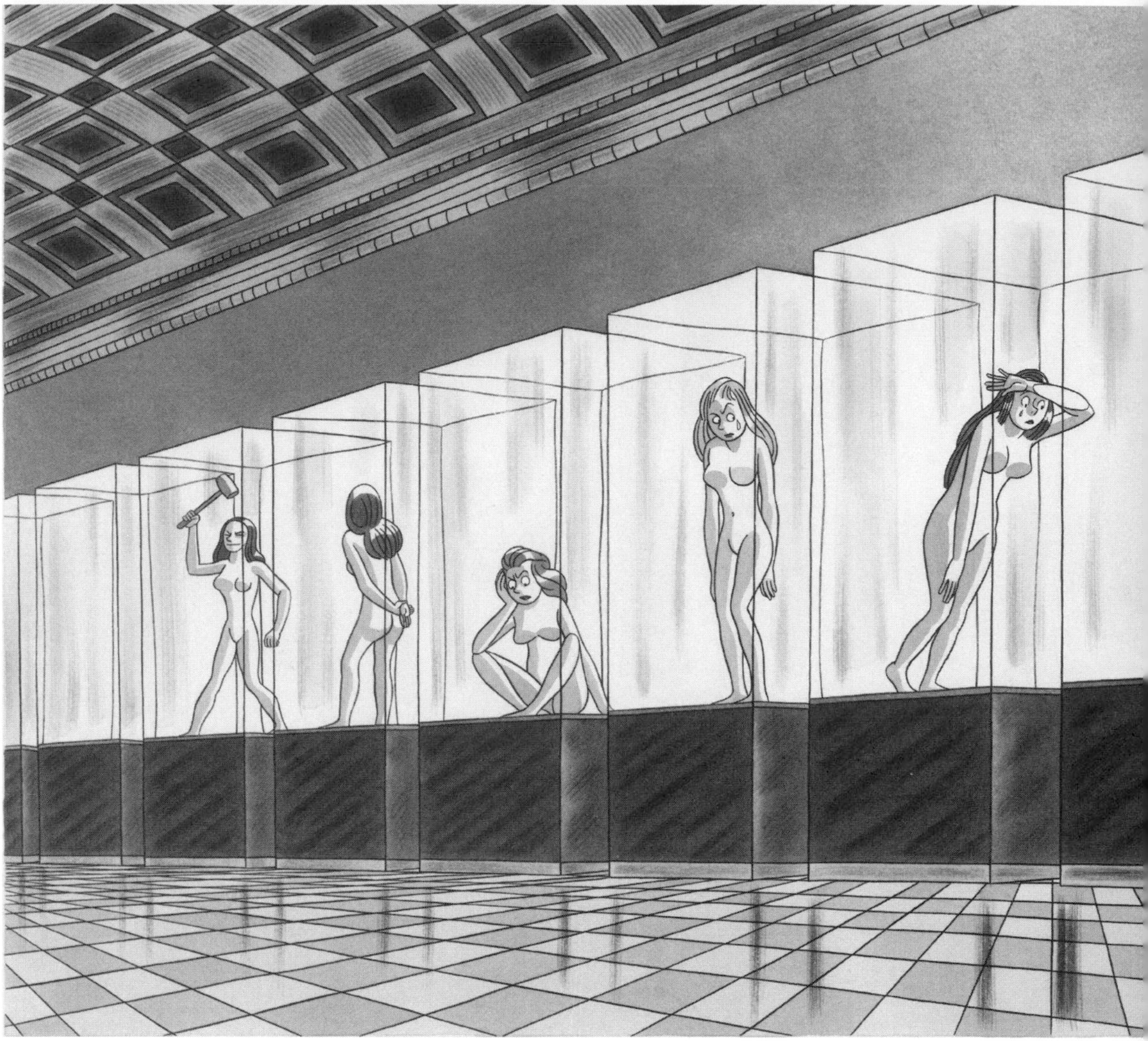

I'll write you

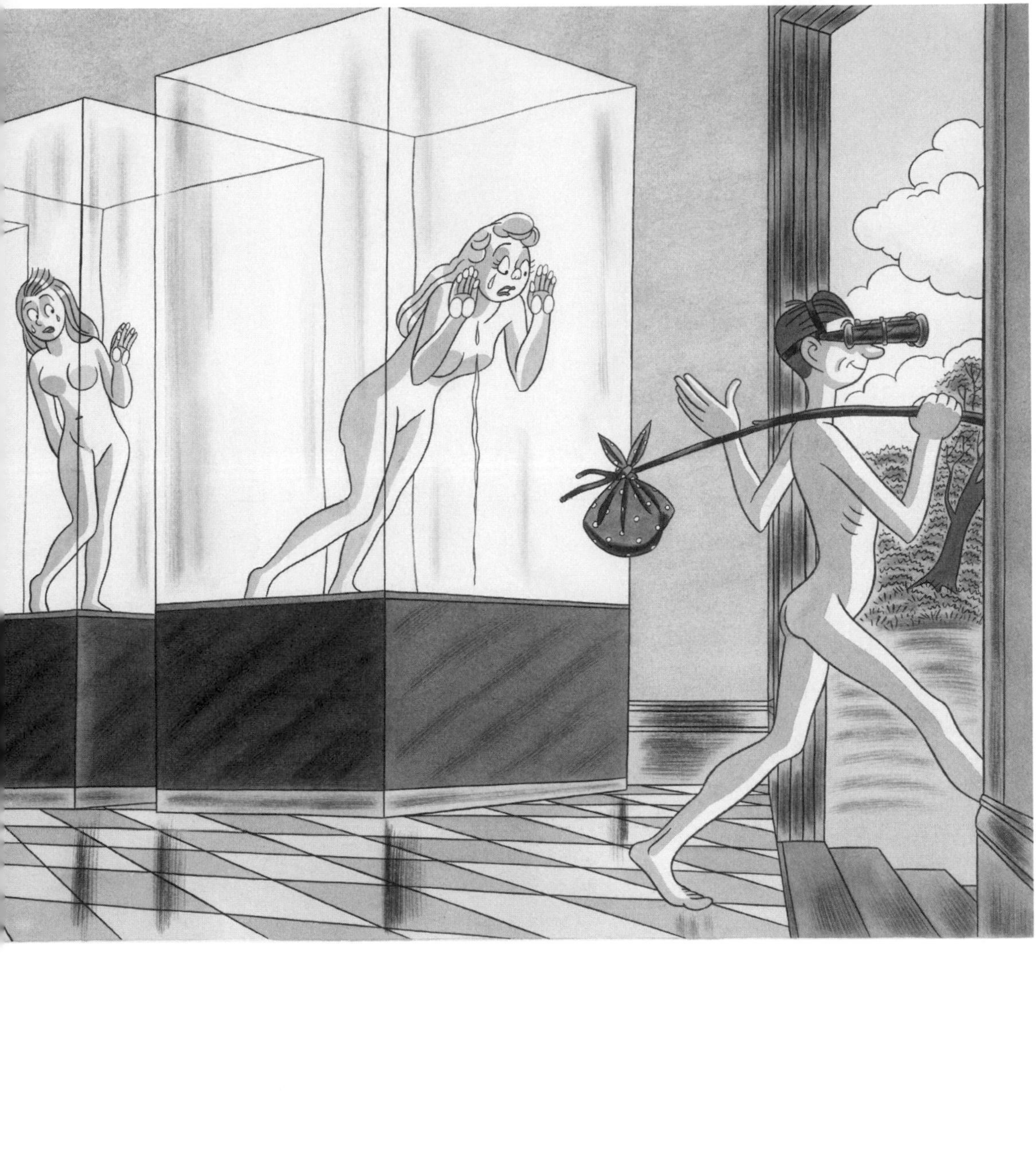

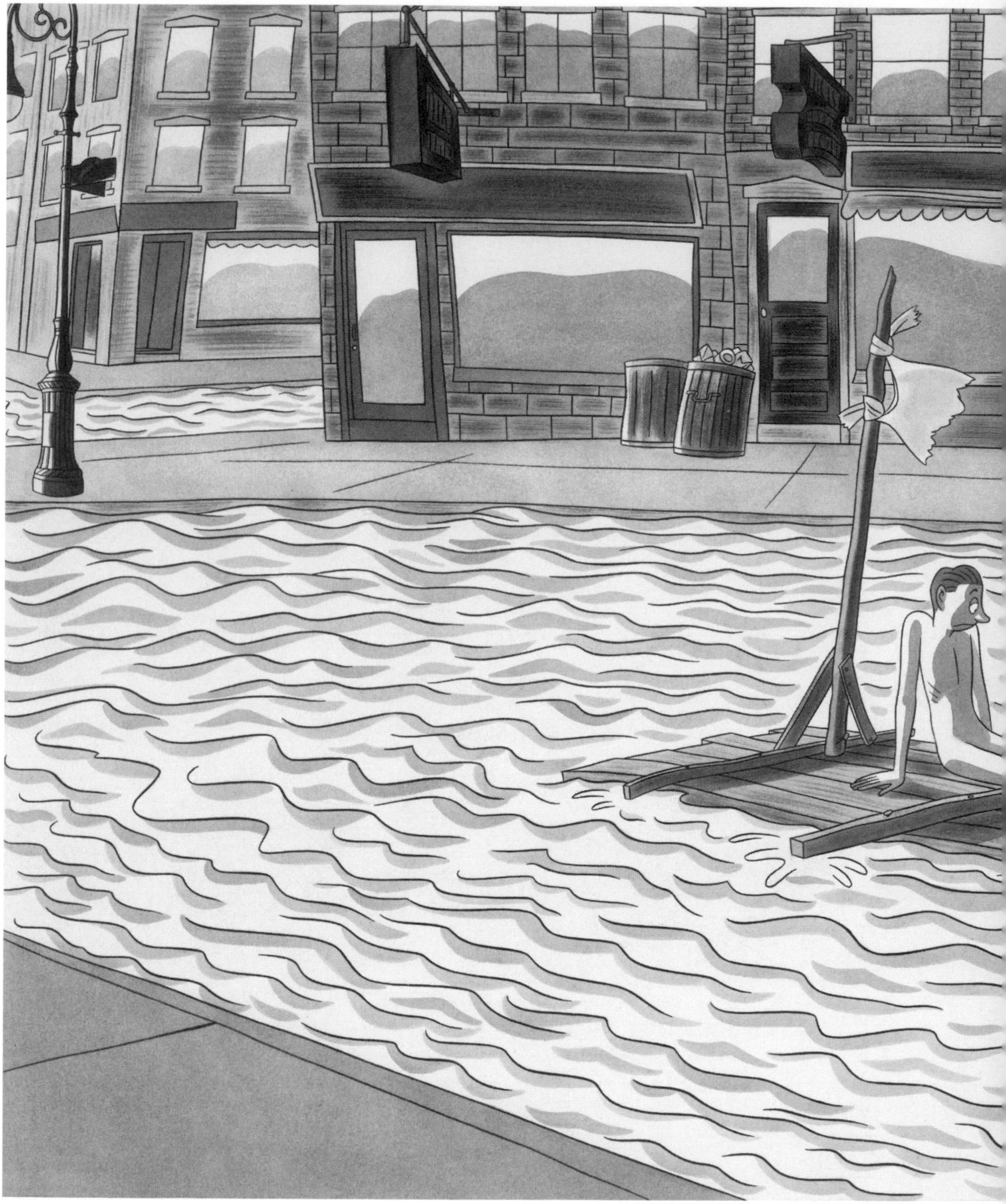

What am I doing here?

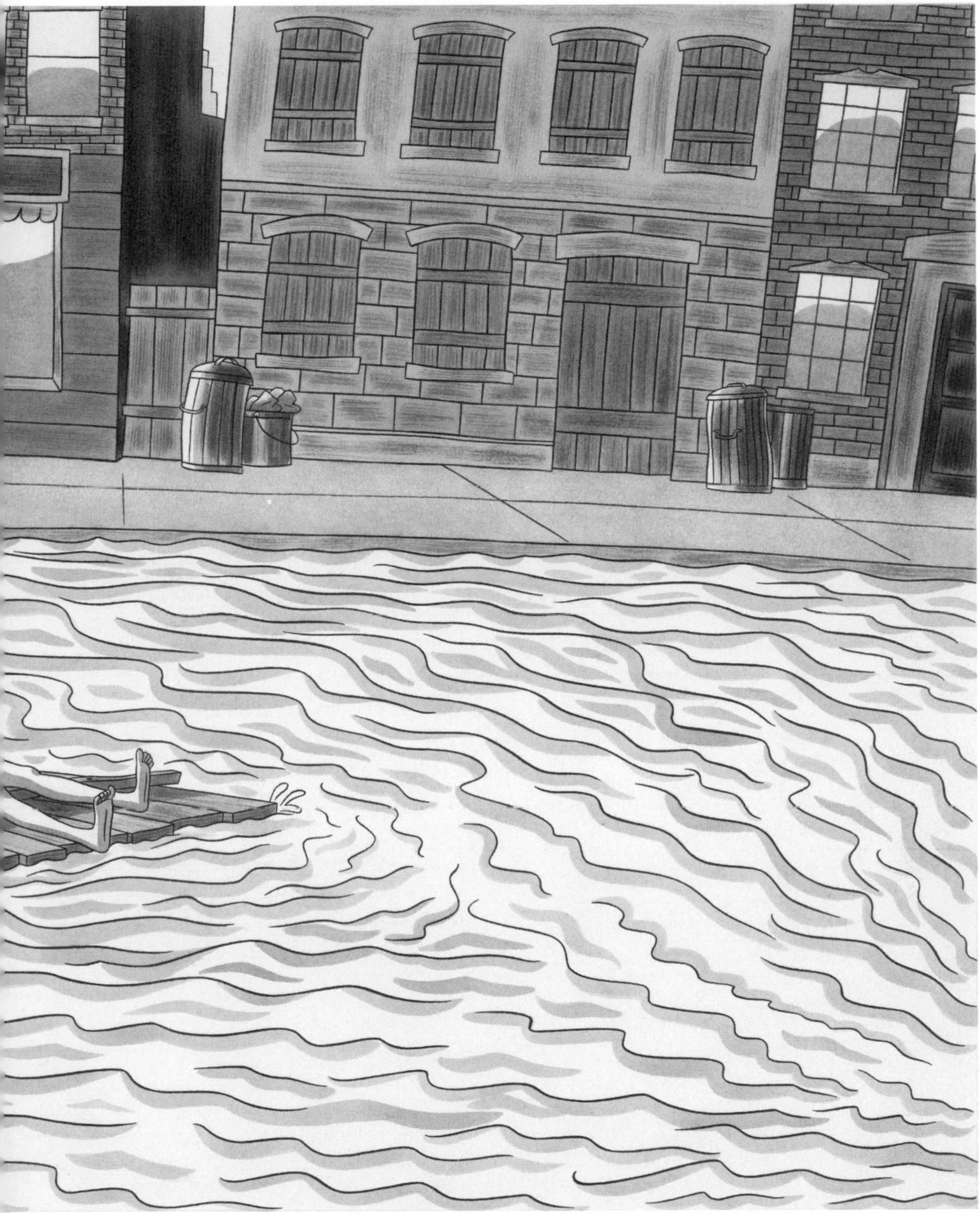

Not too many!

Sometimes everything's unreal

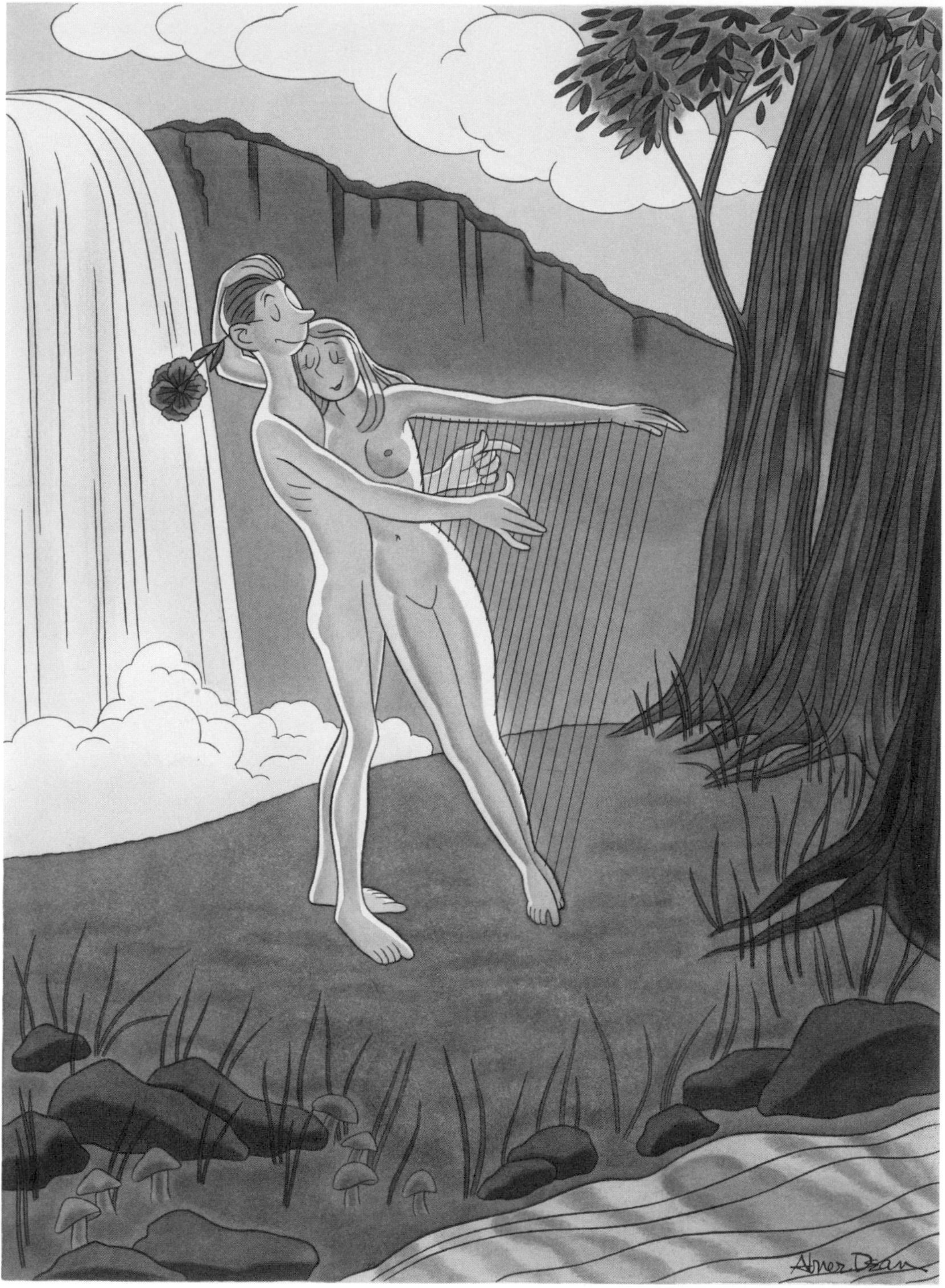
Abner Dean

Music is good

I really miss her

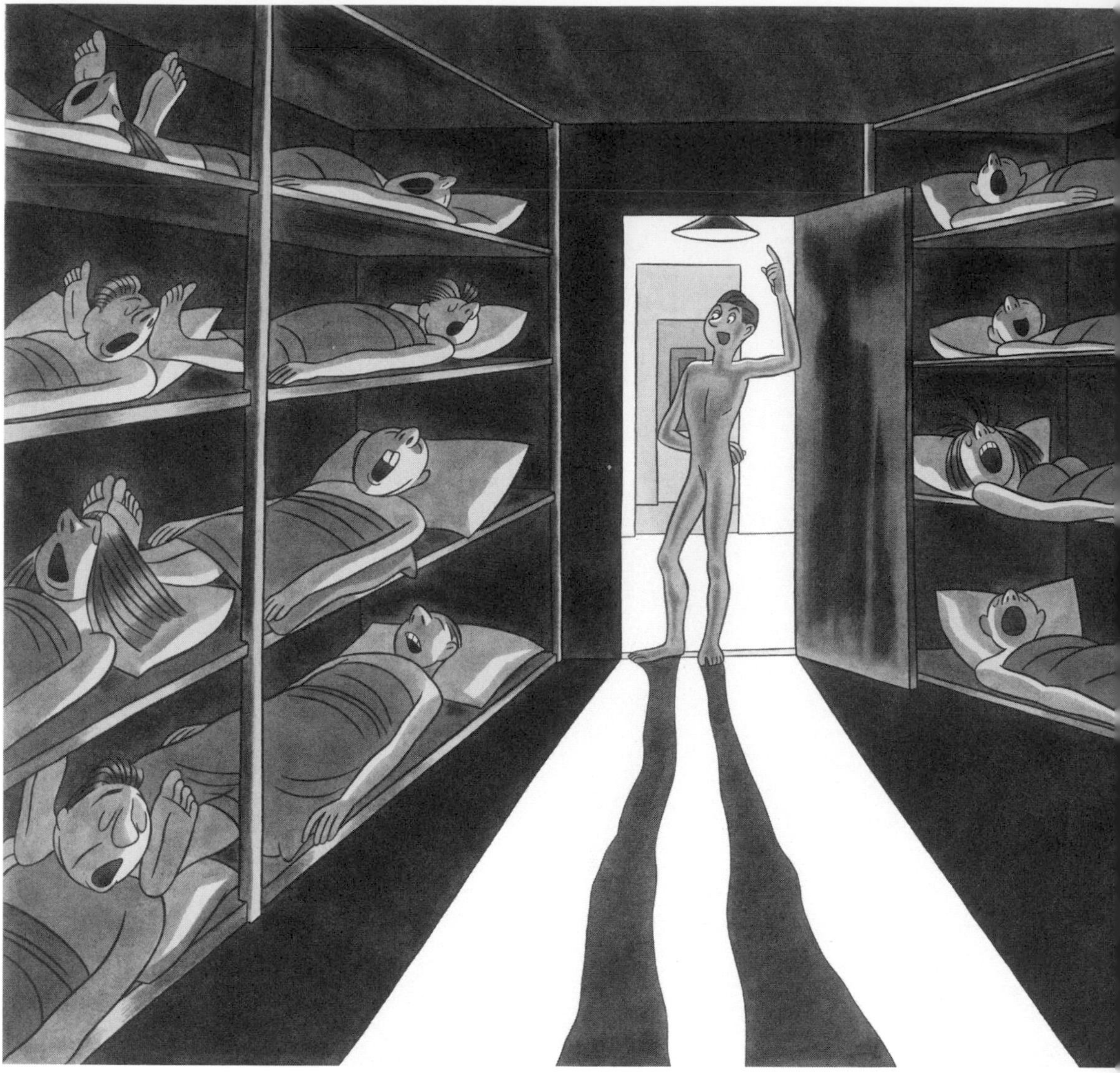

Let me give you a piece of advice

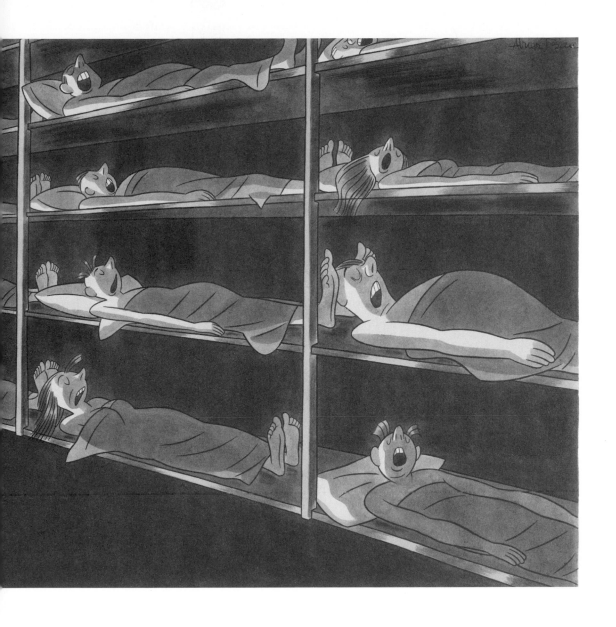

49

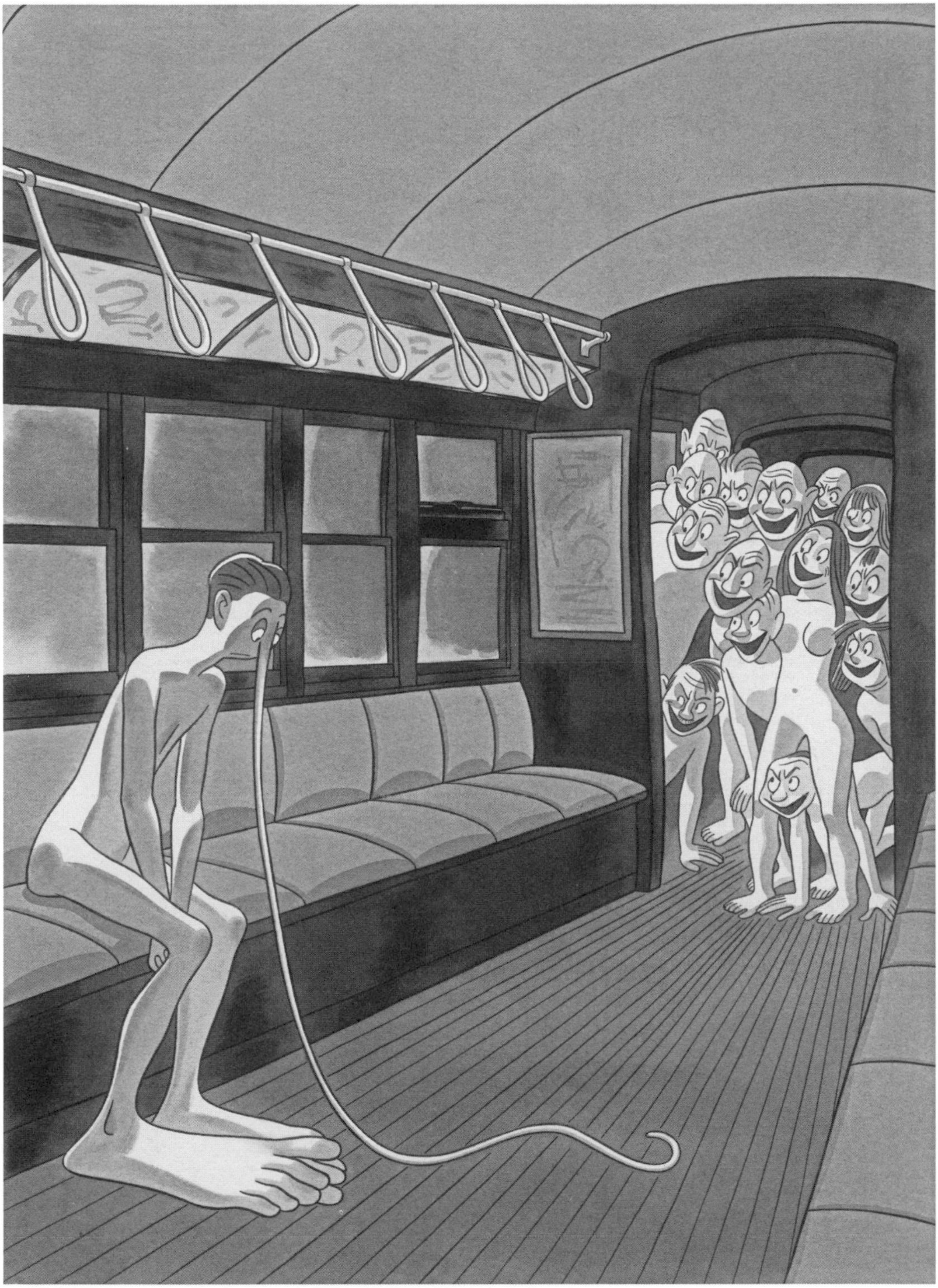

I made a fool of myself last night

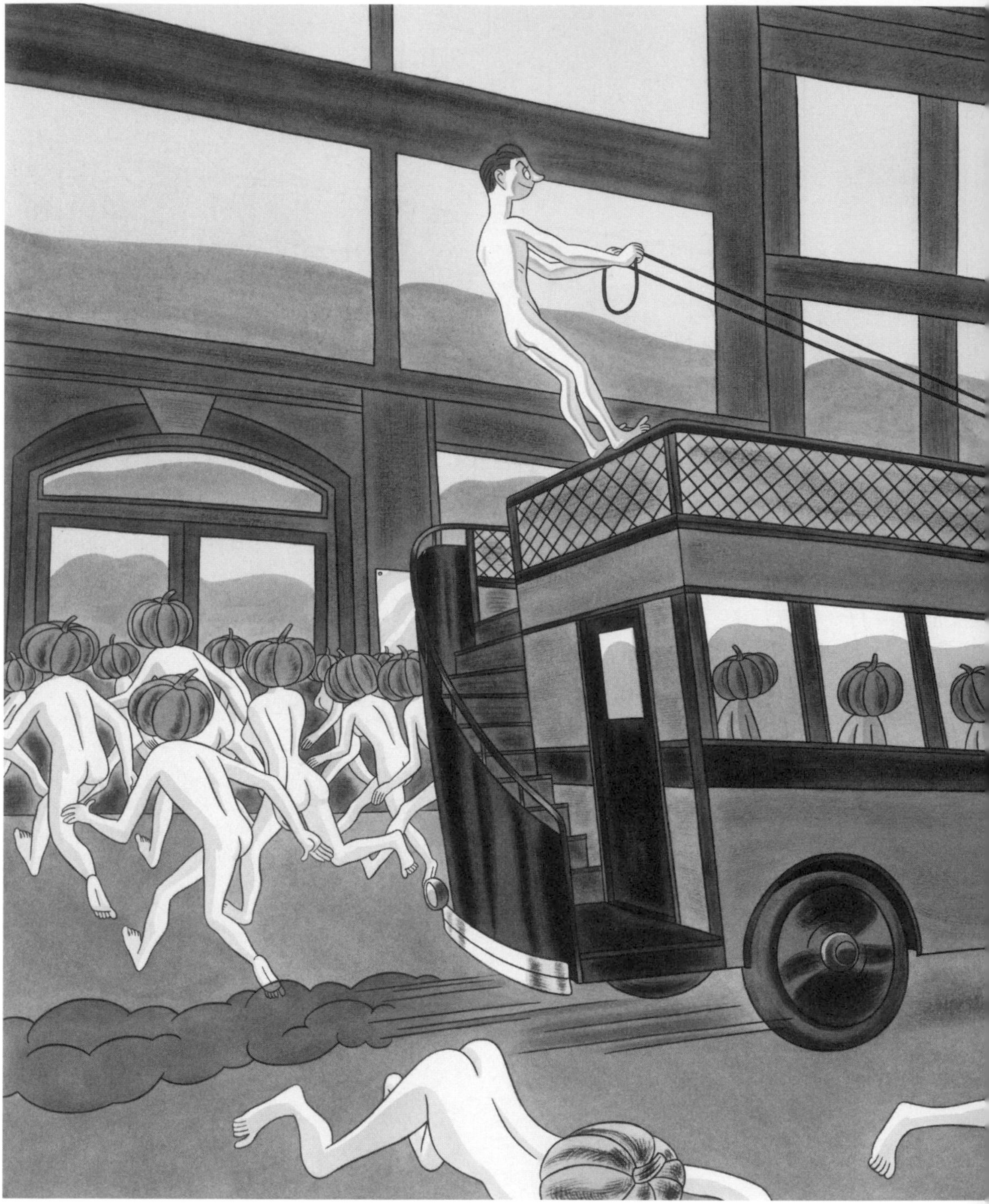

Some days I feel confident

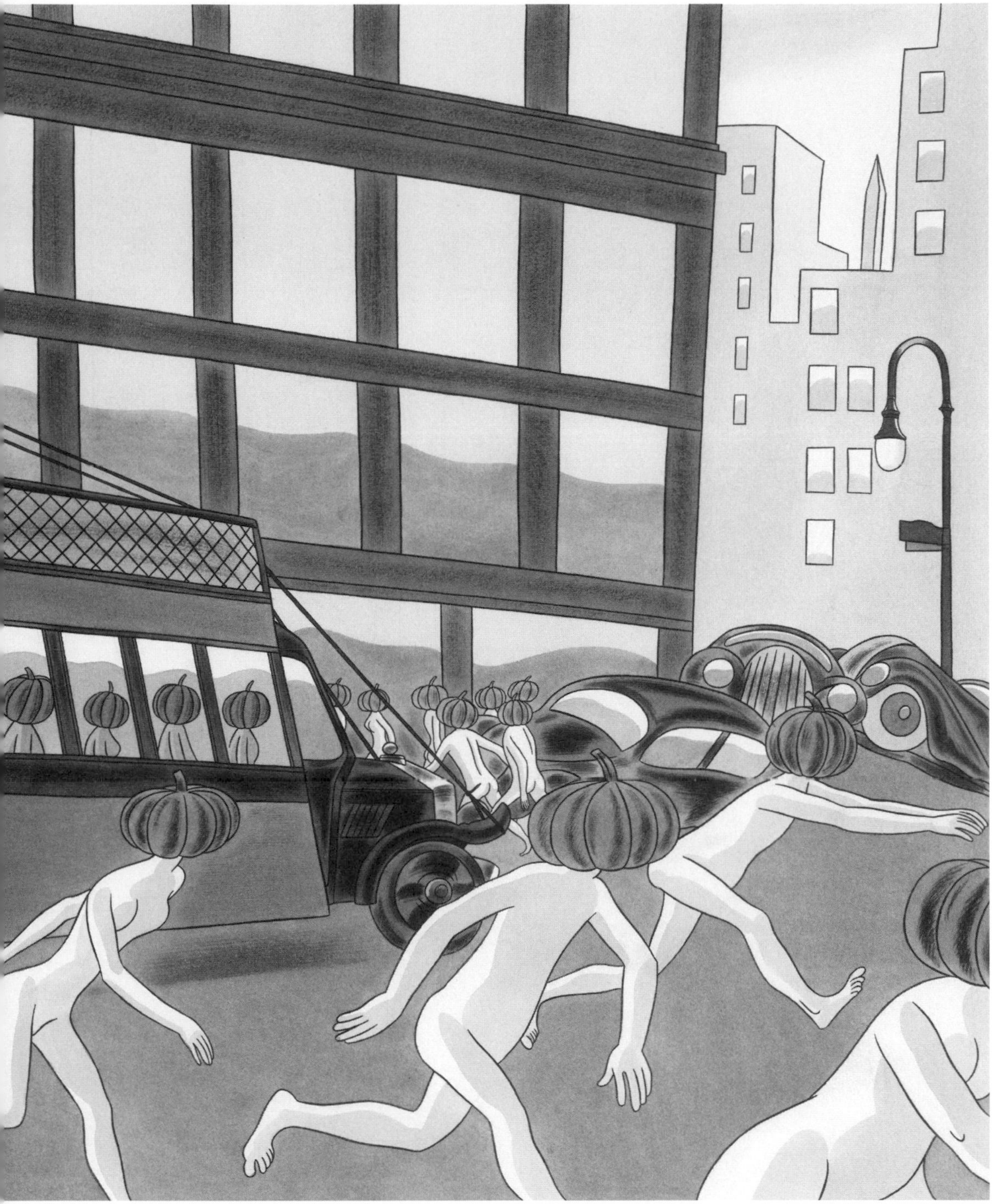

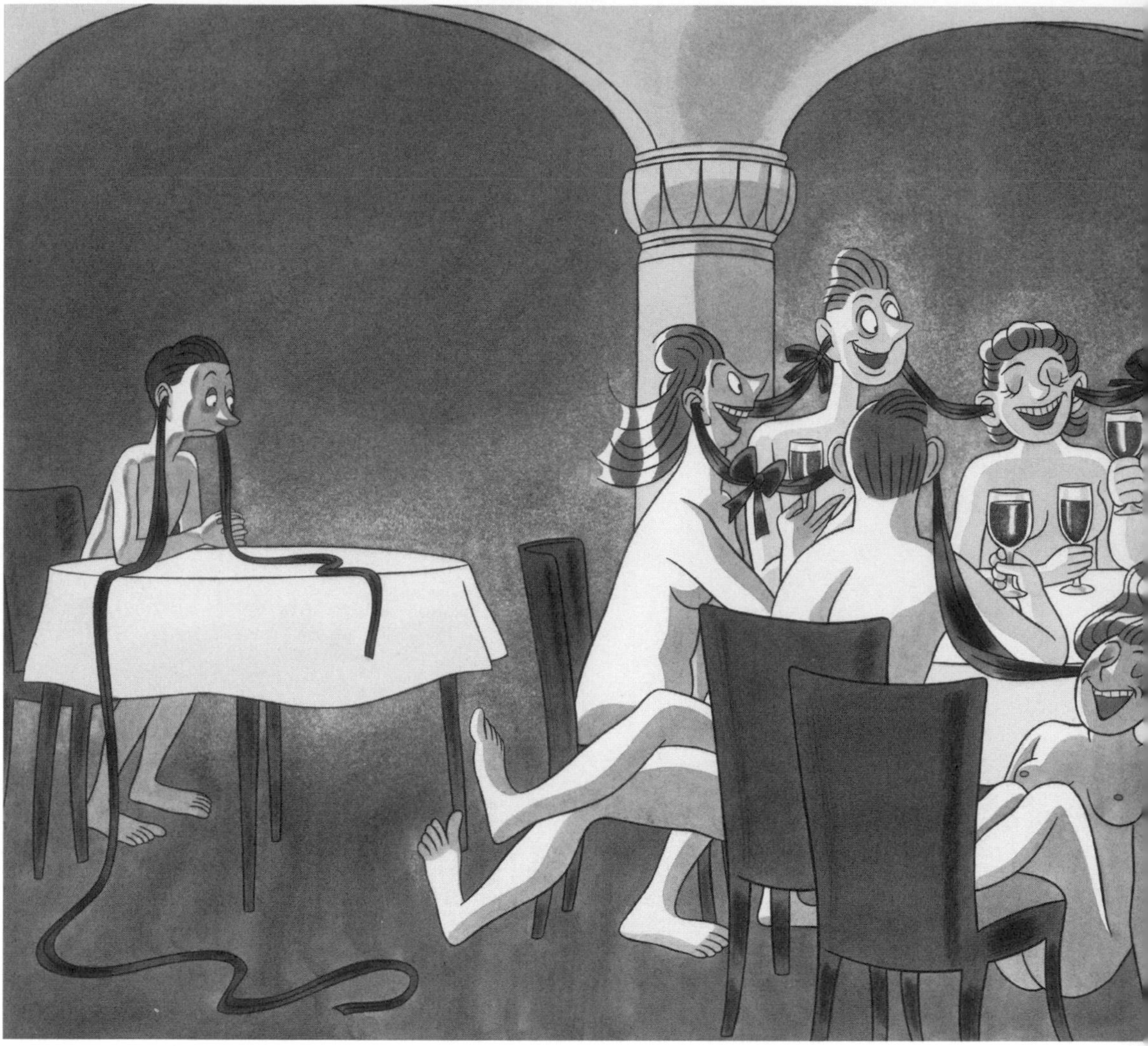

The people at the next table are all idiots

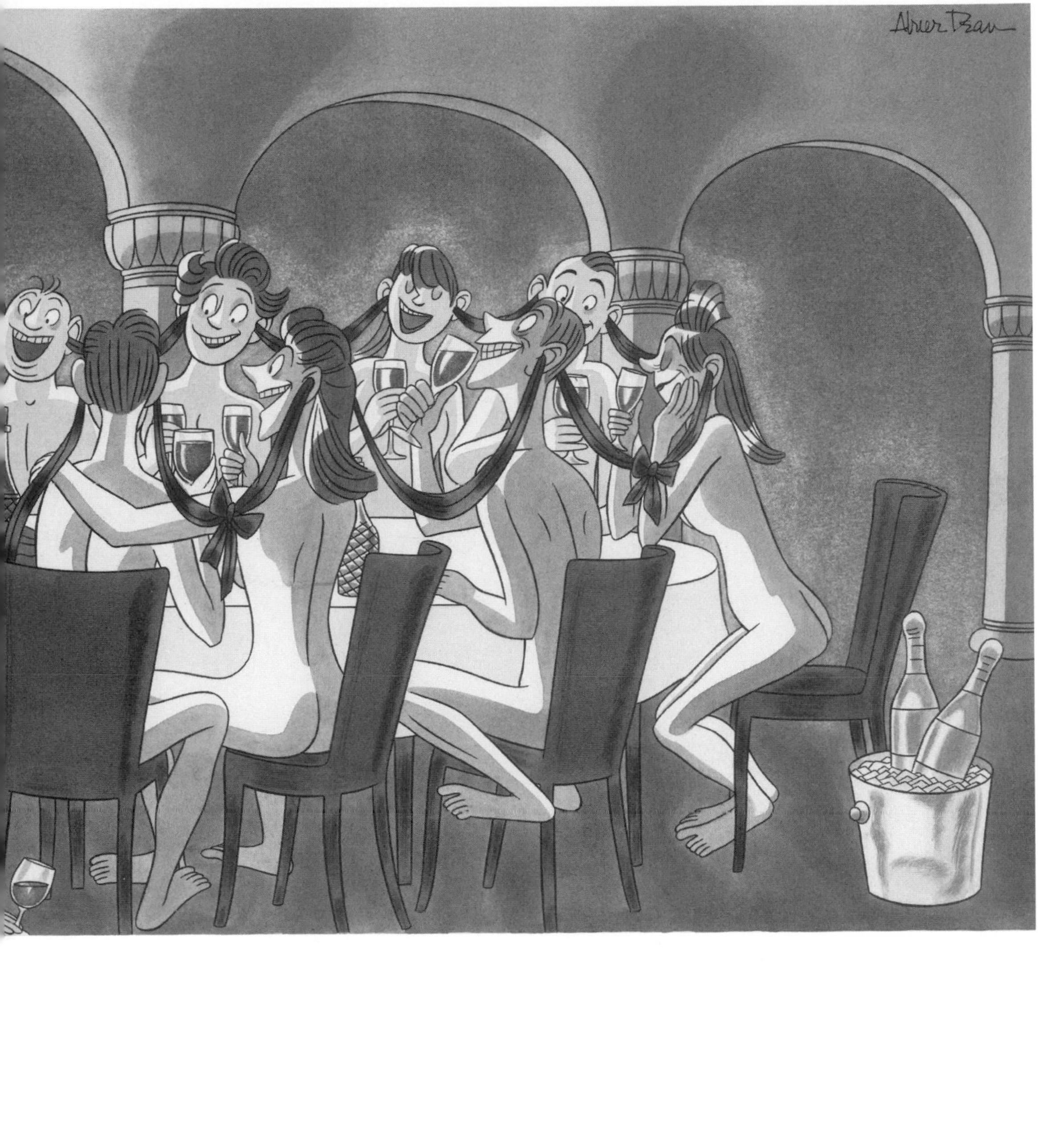

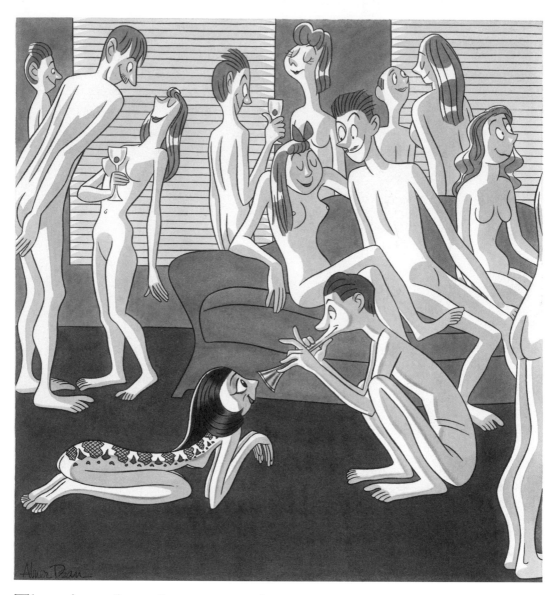

There's a place I want to take you to

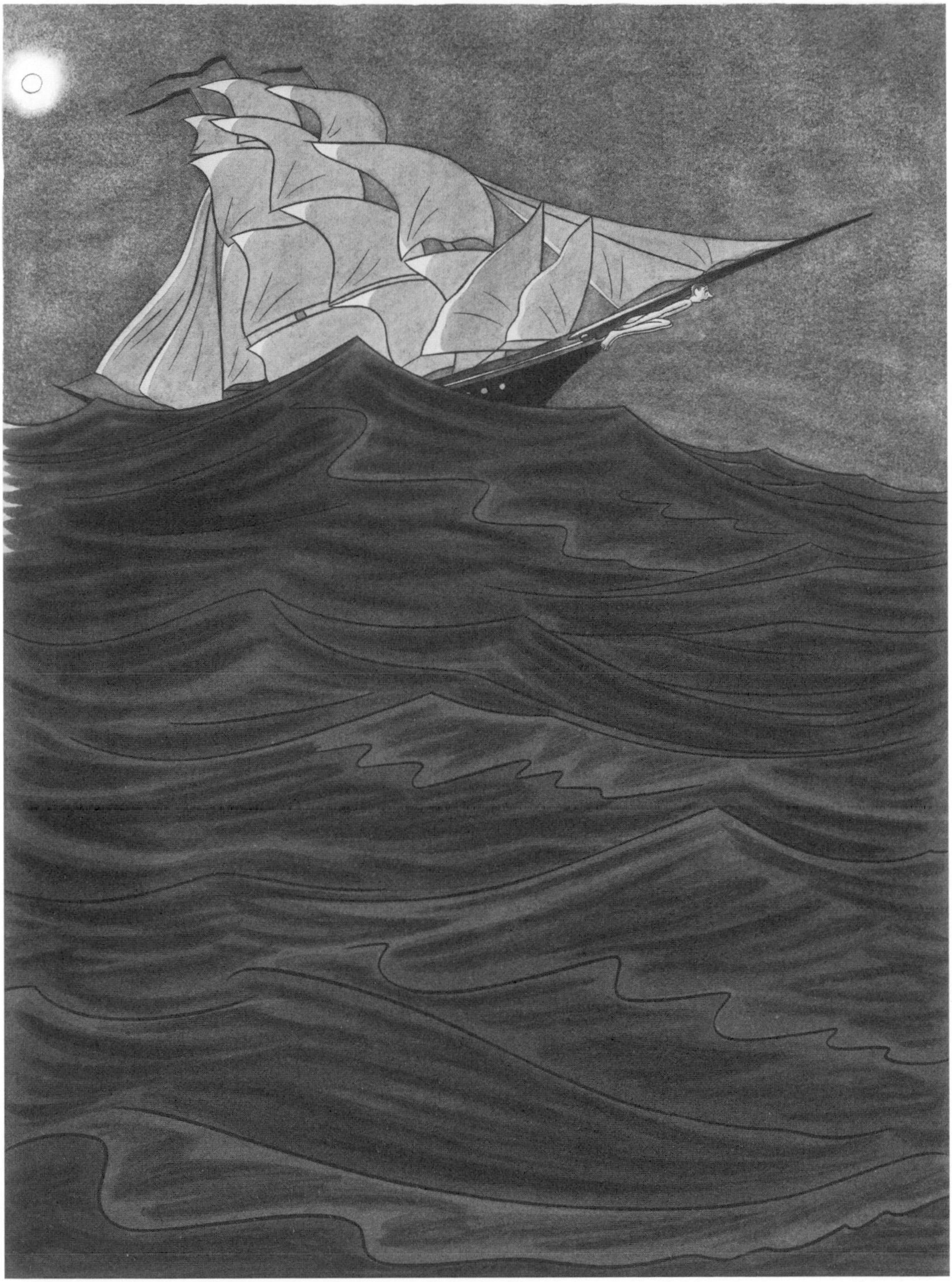

Sometimes I can almost hear it

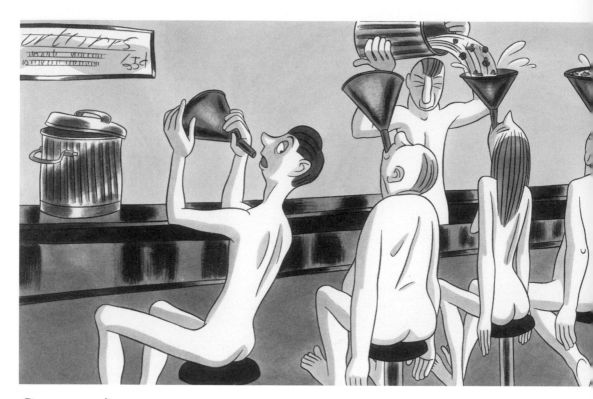

Gotta eat!

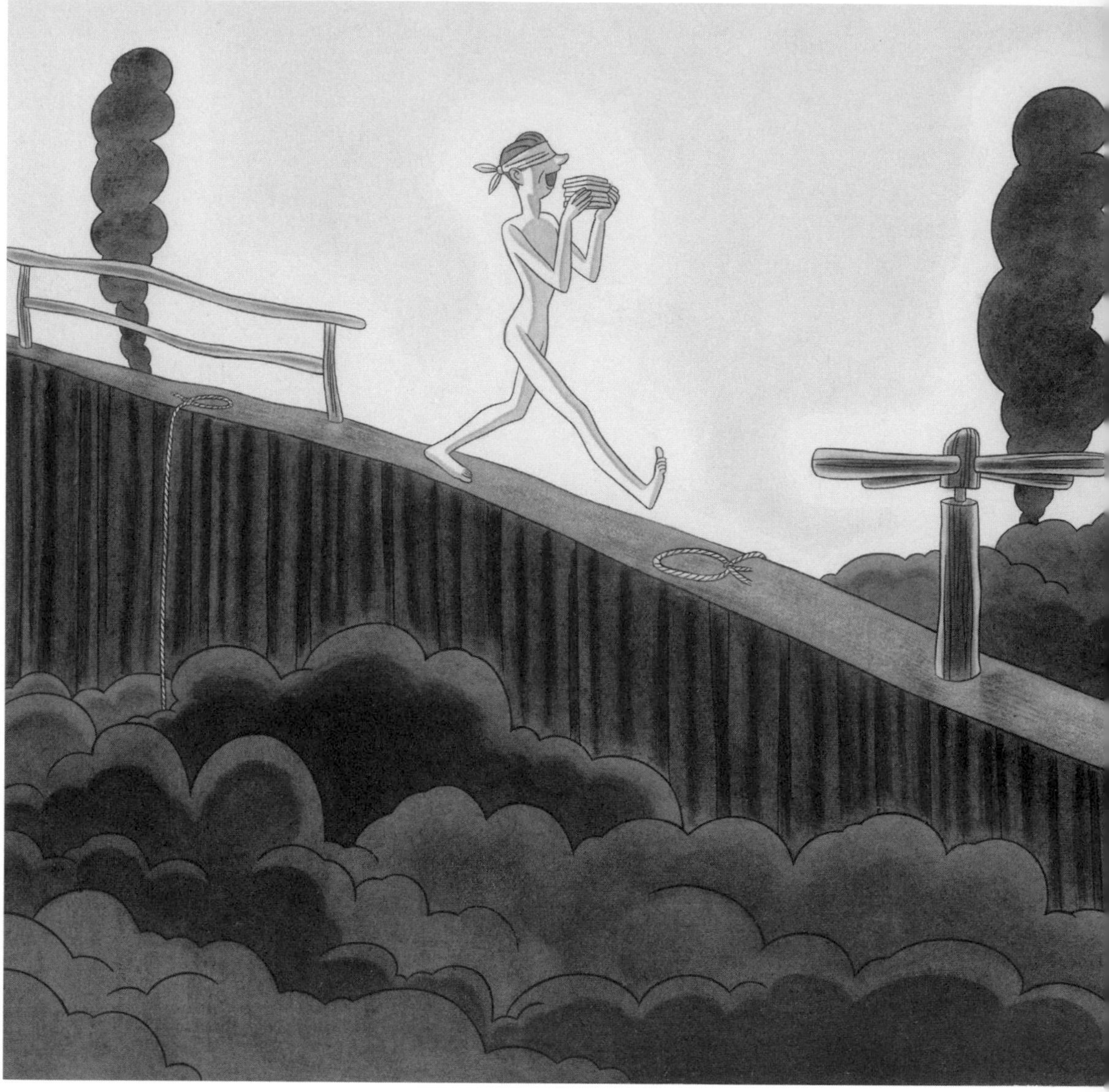

It's all true

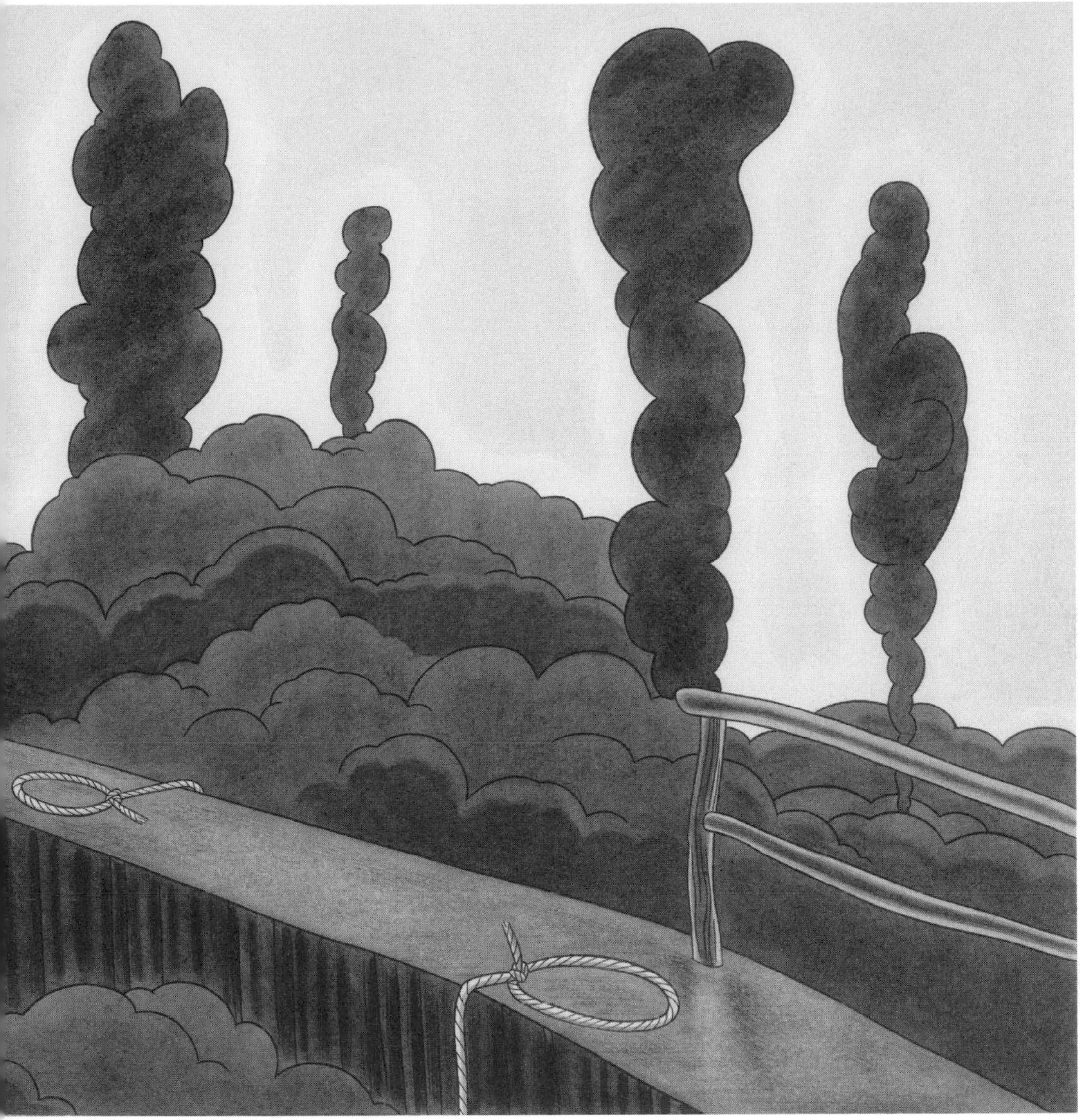

Everyone must have a label

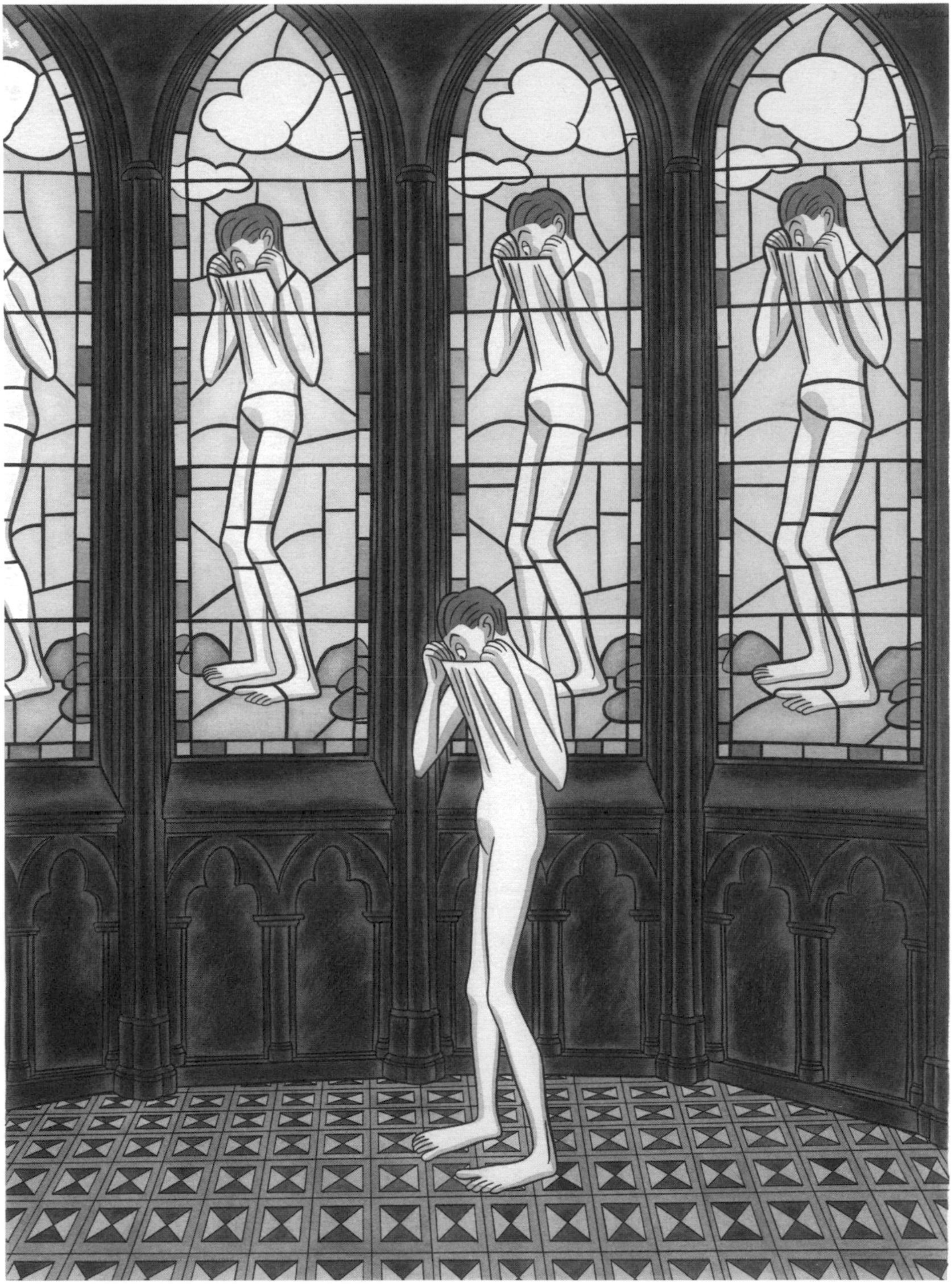

How much of me is me?

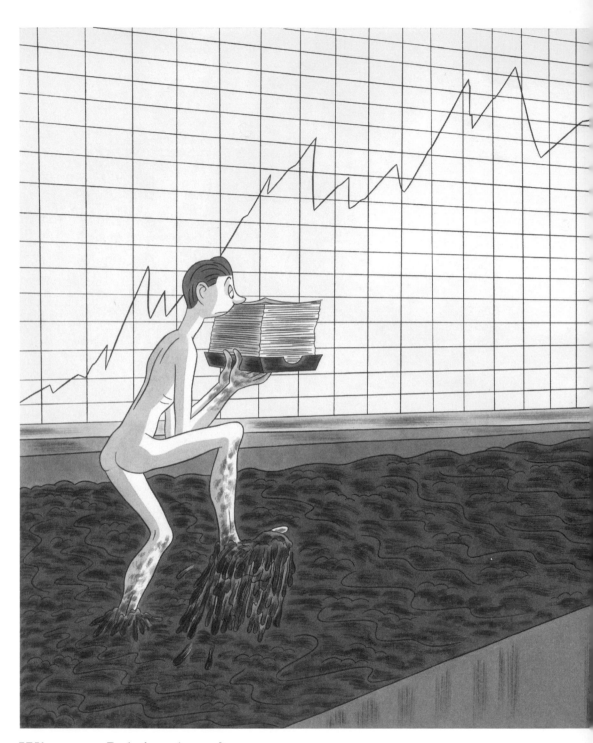

What am I doing here?

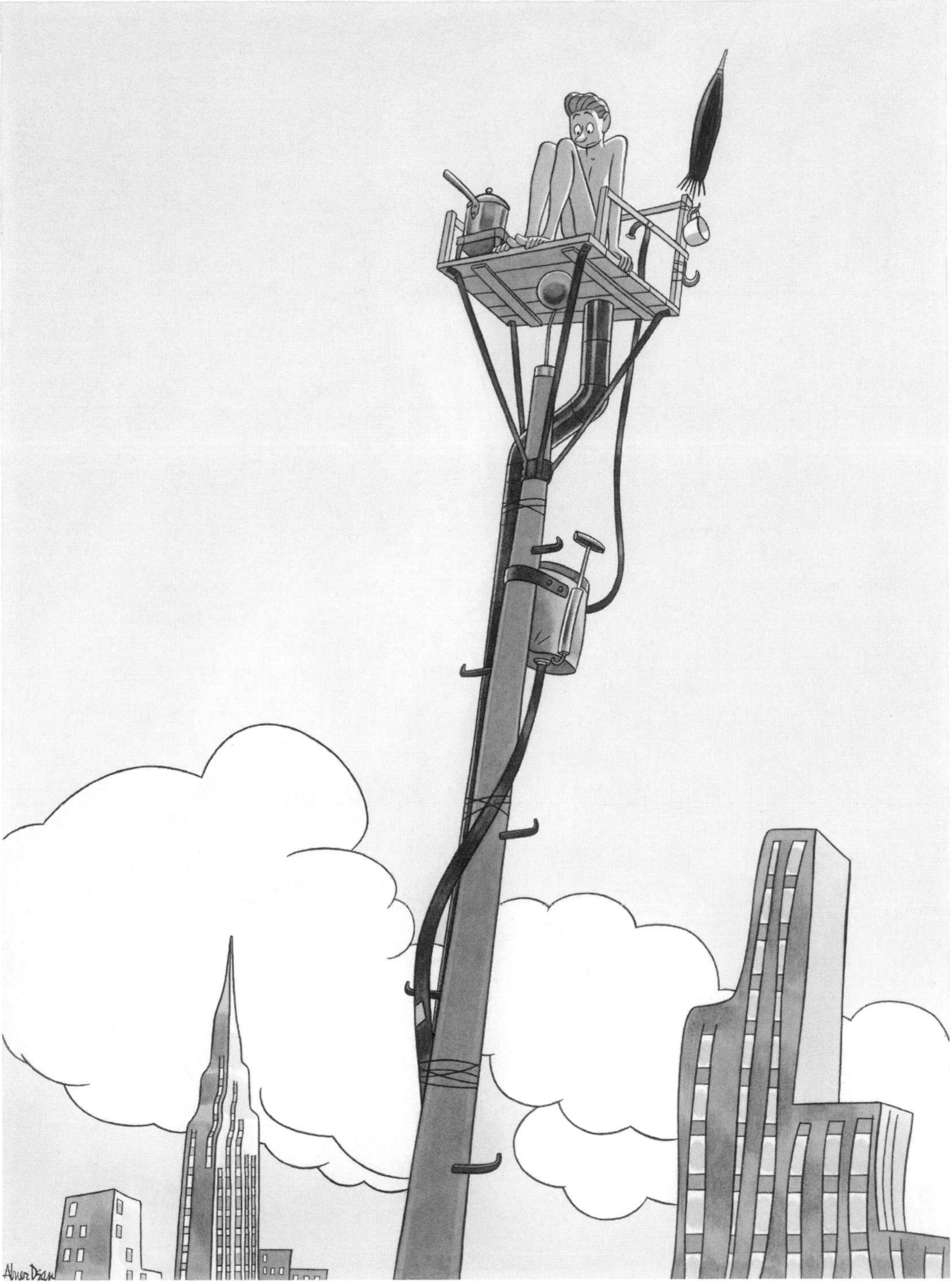

This isn't the way I planned it

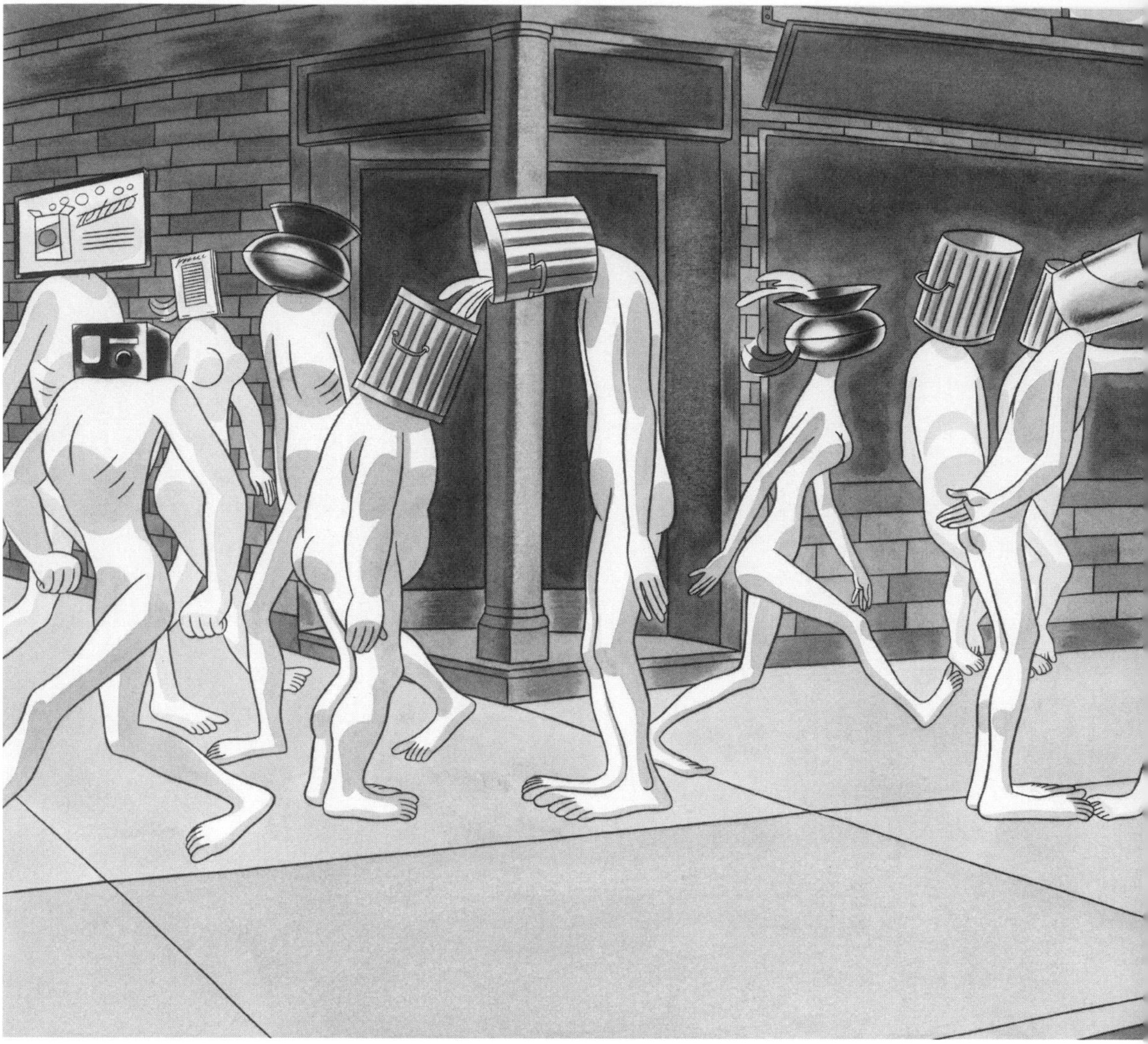

Let's clean up the place

I hate apple pie

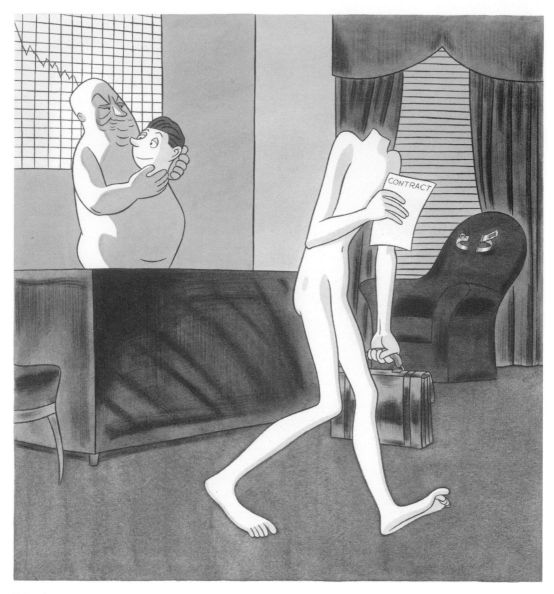

He's a better businessman than I am

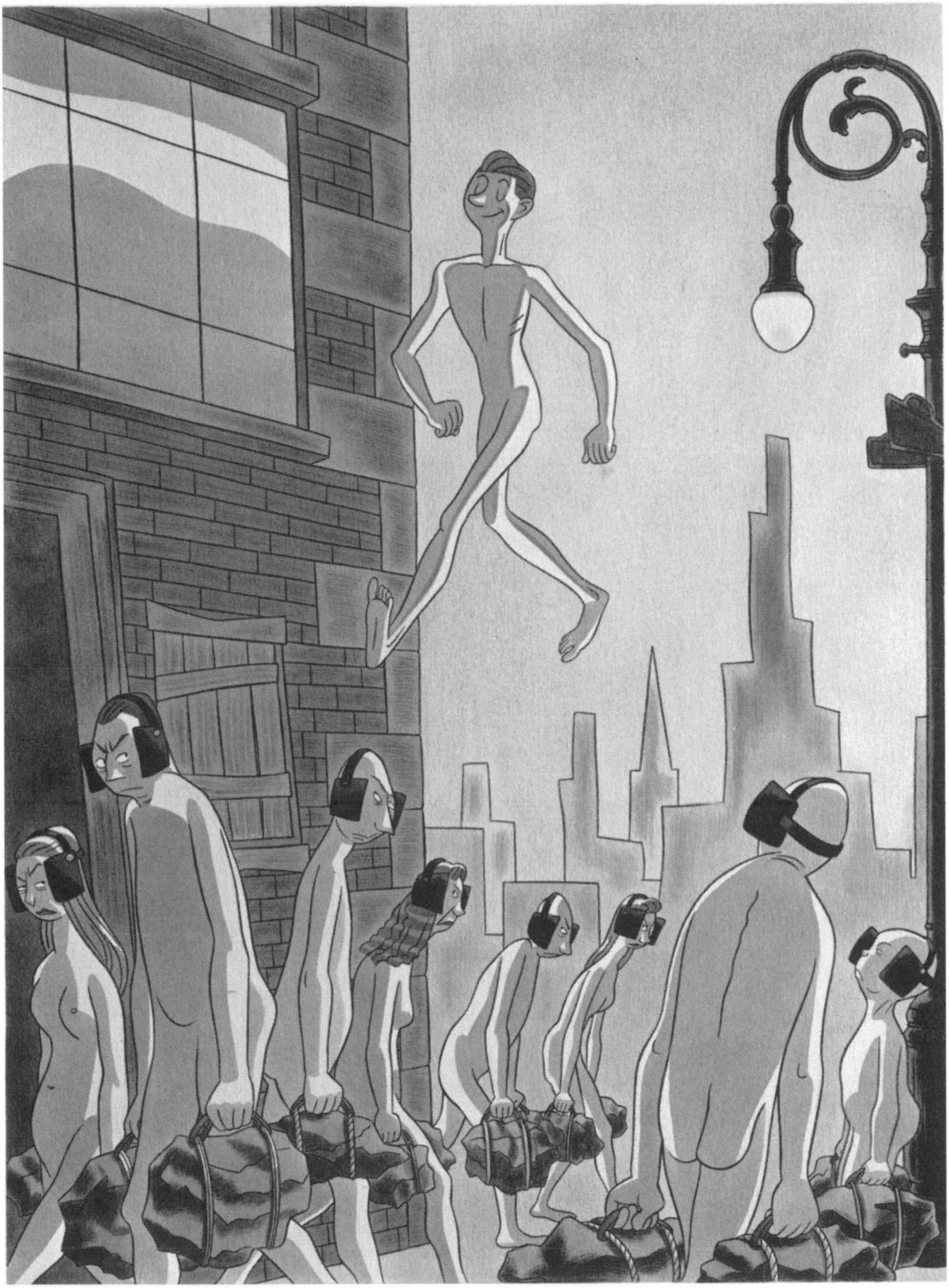

It's just a knack

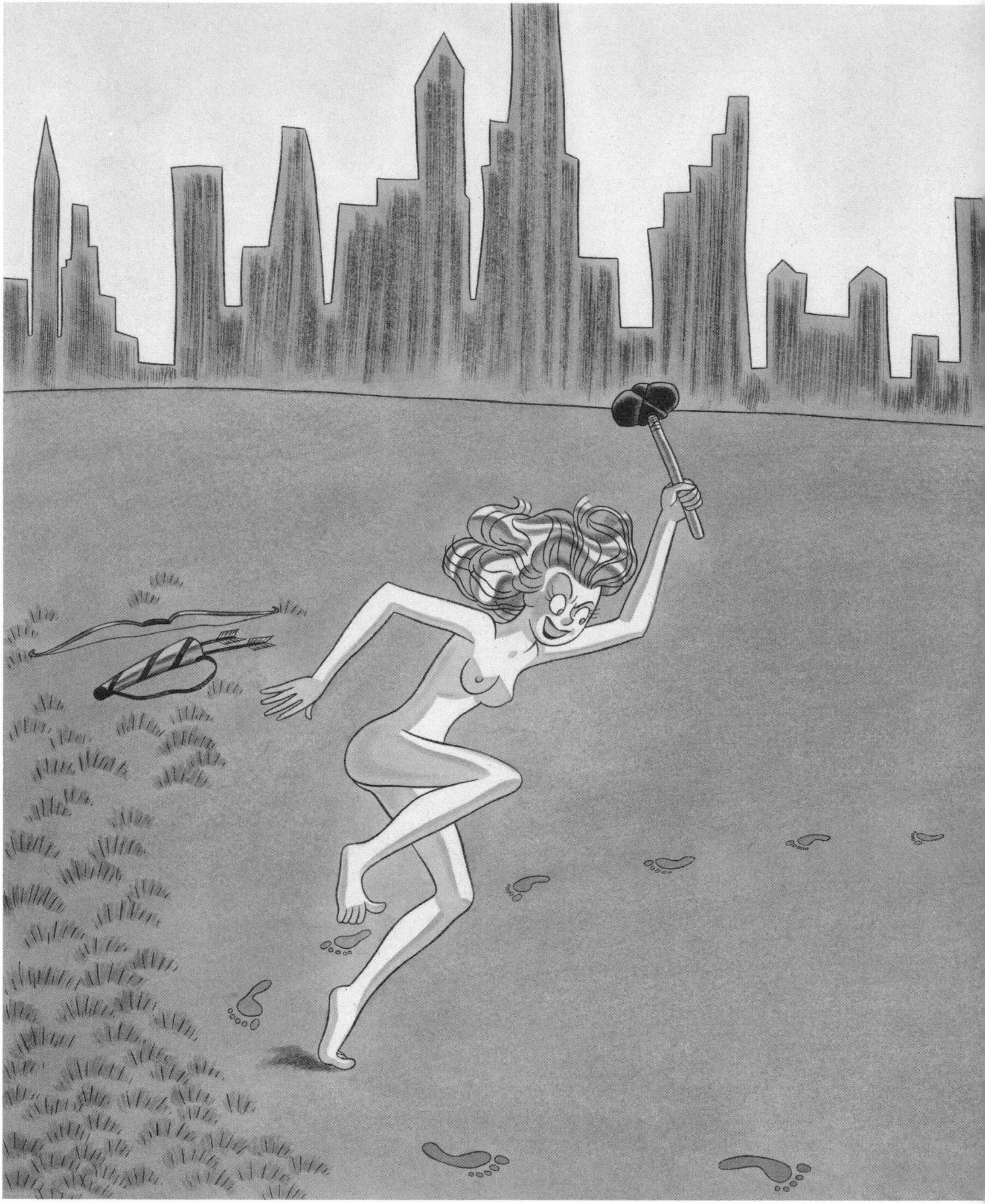

You used to be good

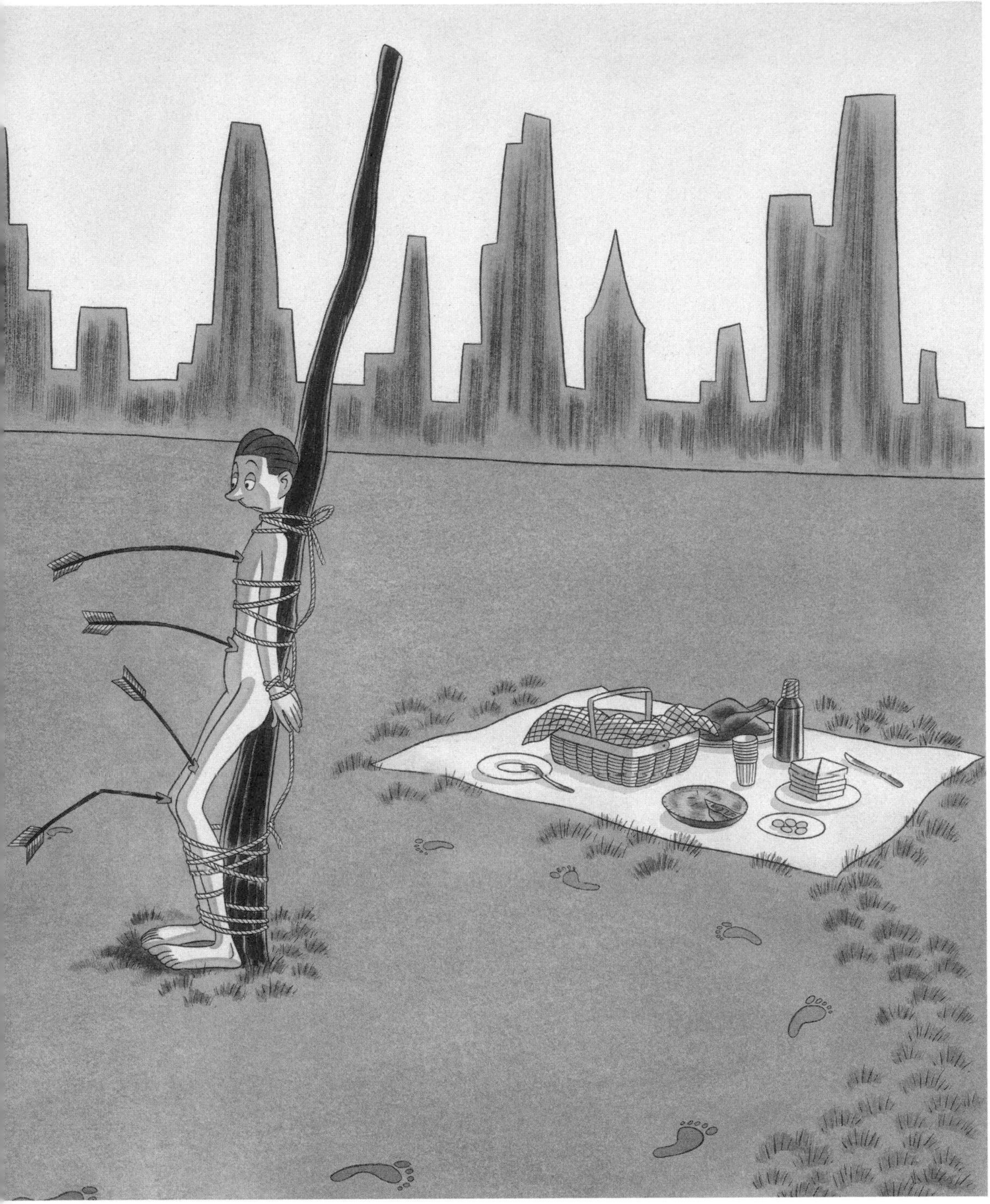

I have an important appointment

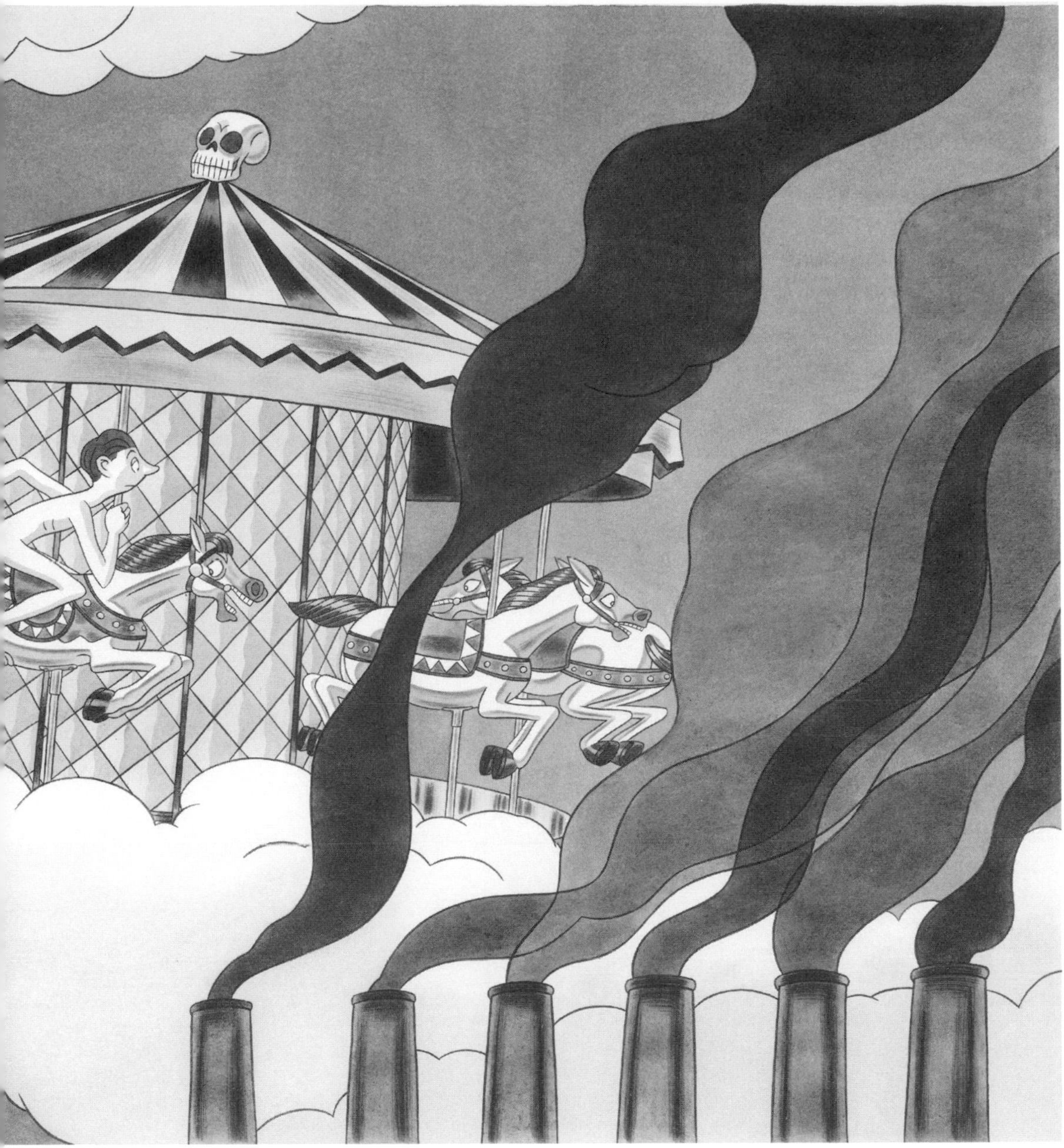

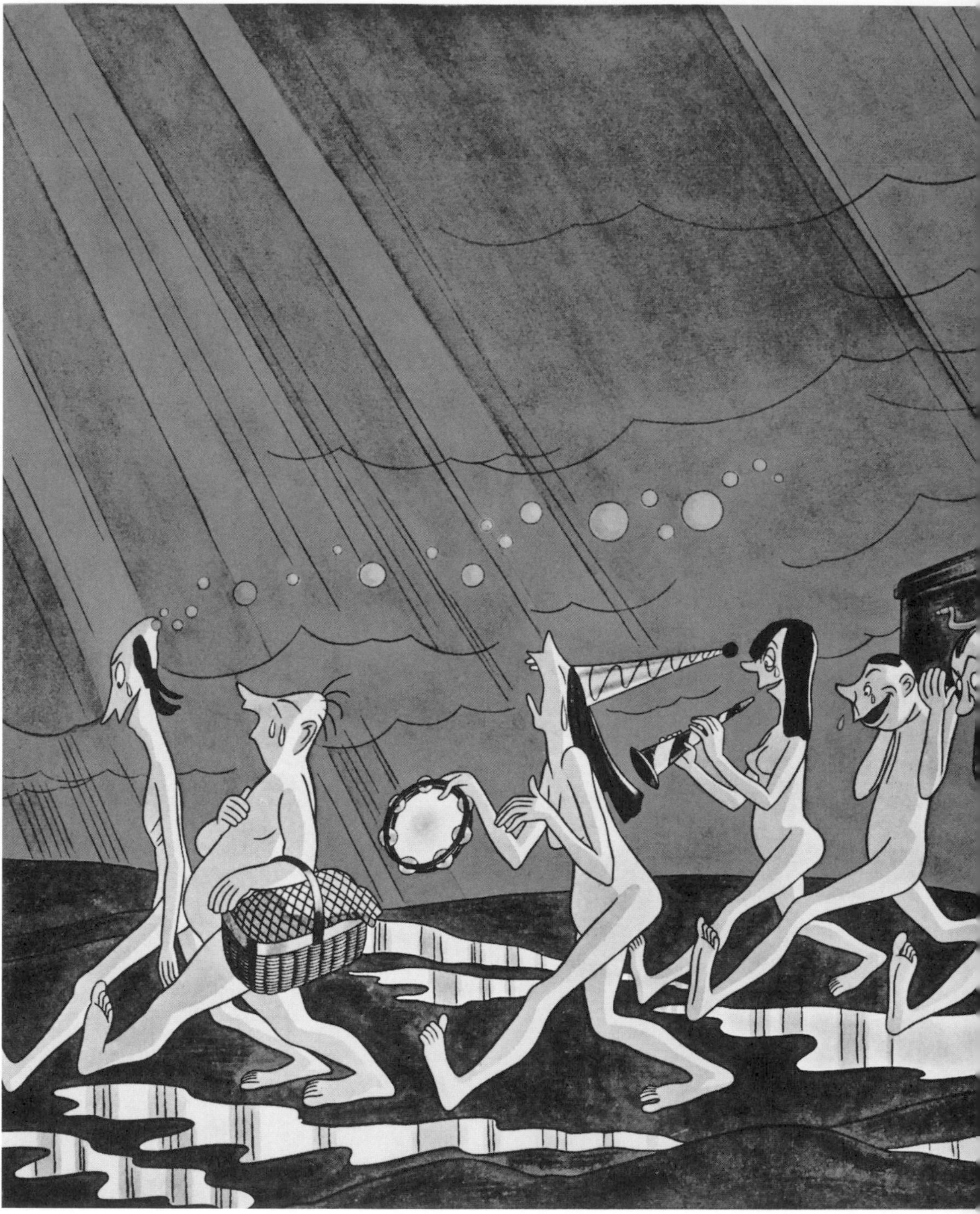

Now what was *that* all about?

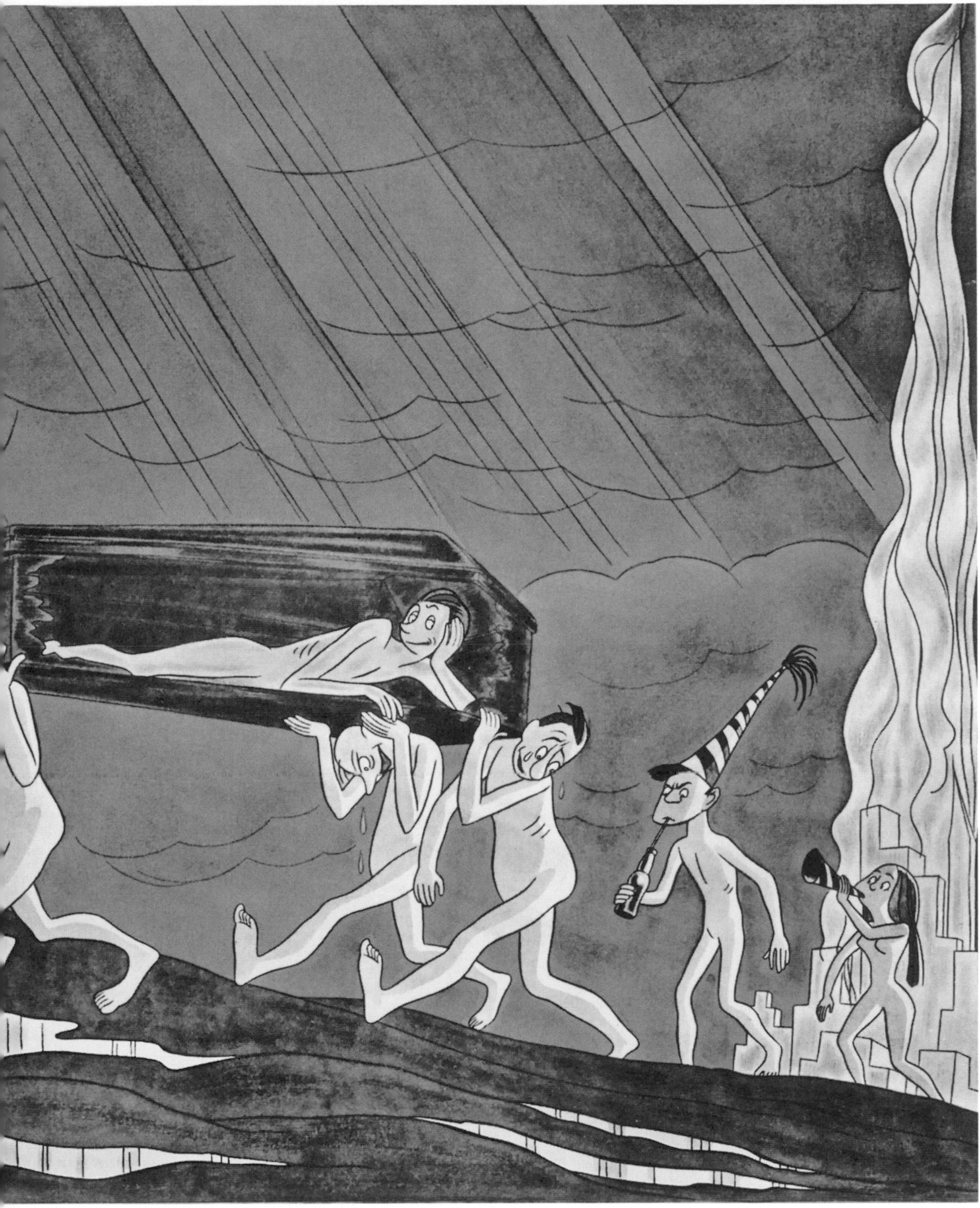

I wrote a stupid letter

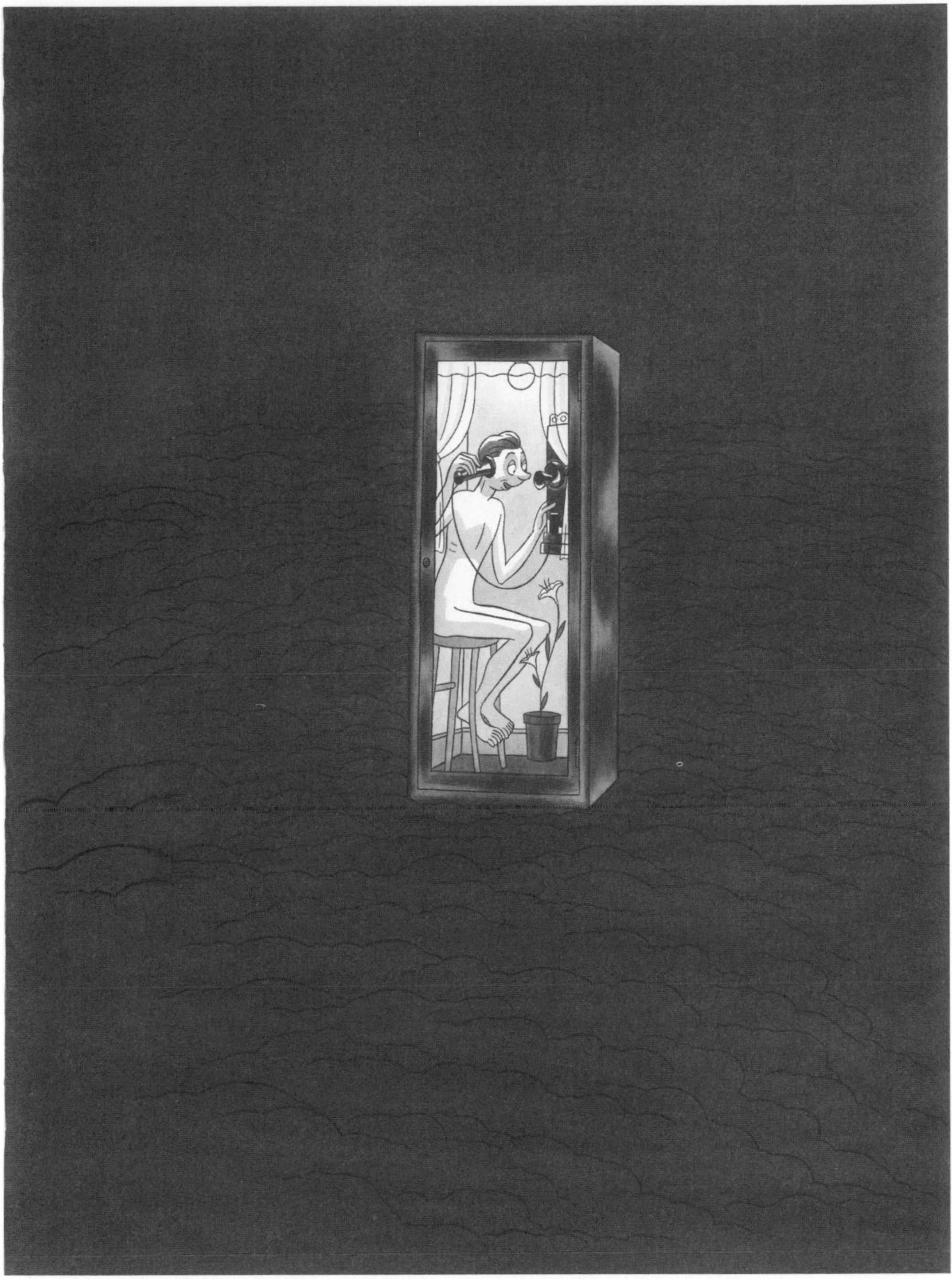

Tell me a story

I never did this before

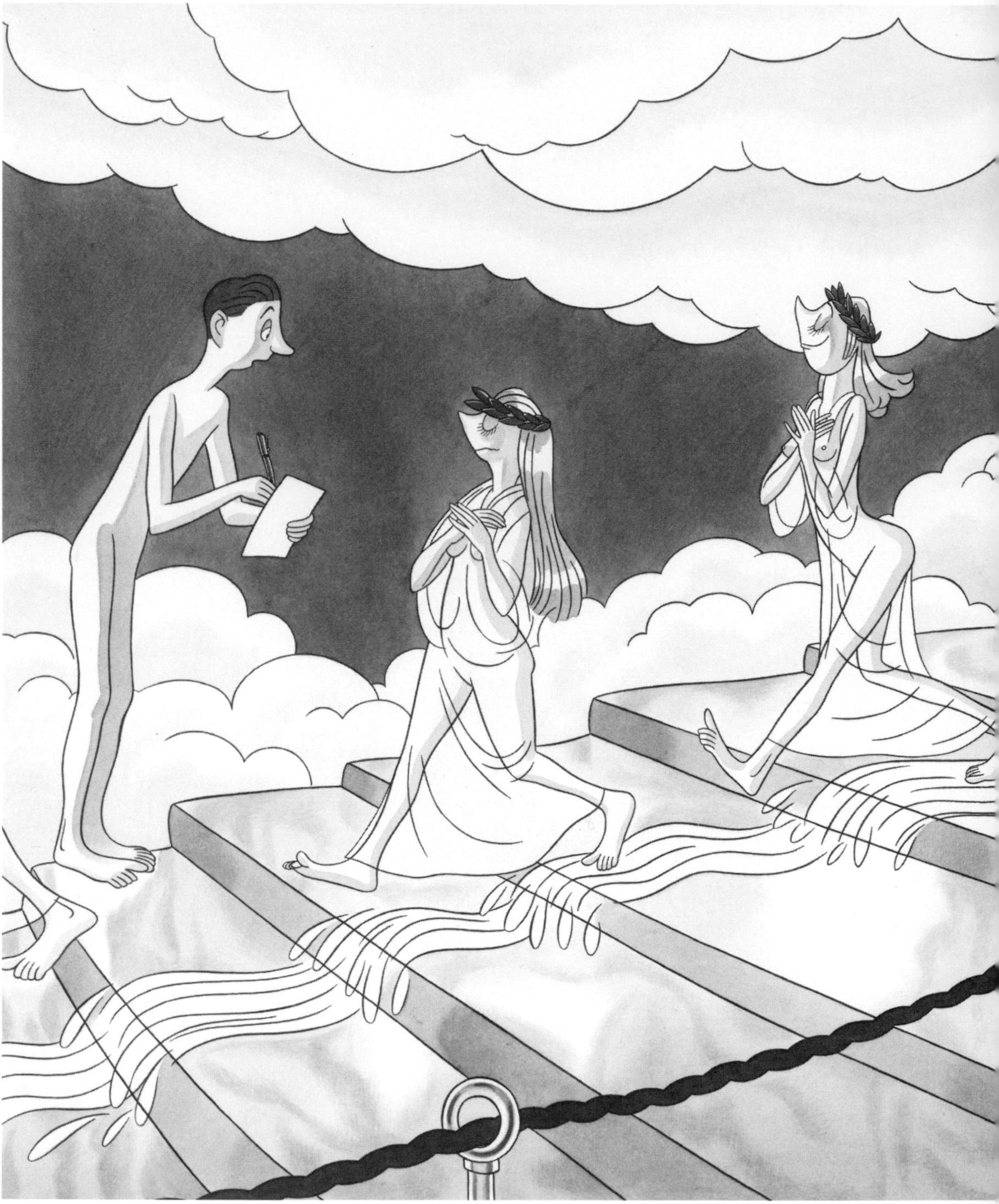

What was it like?

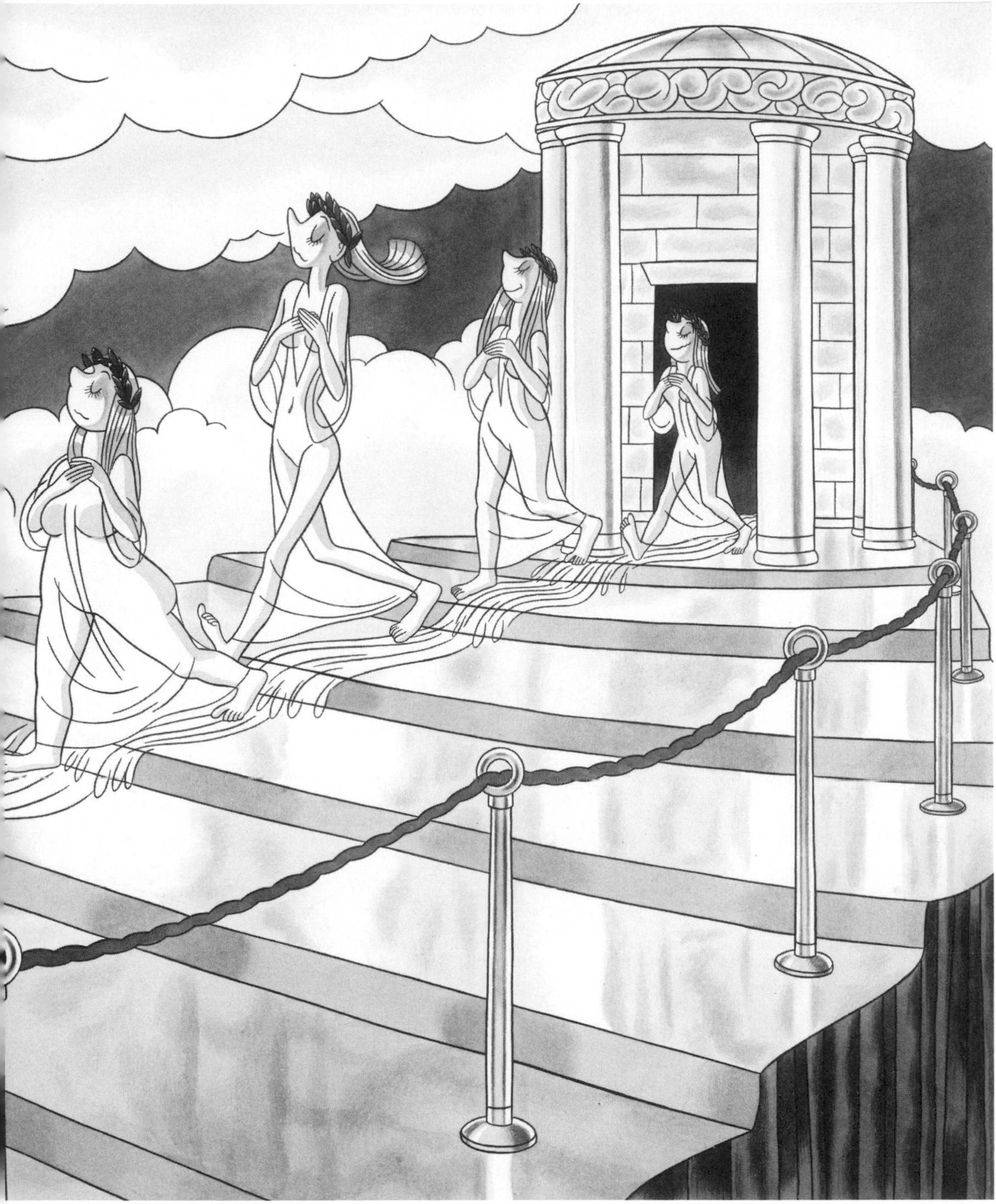

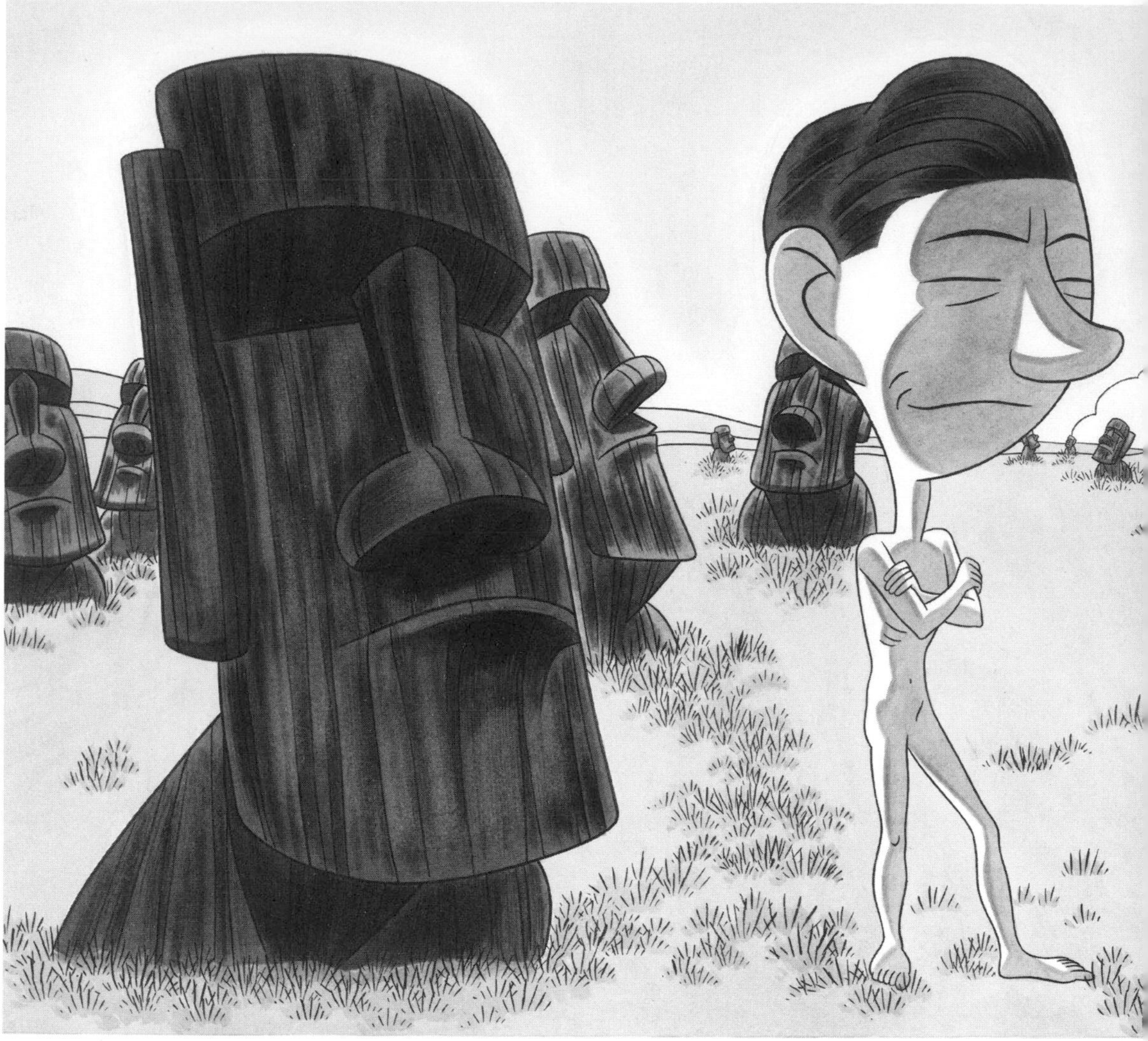

I'm important

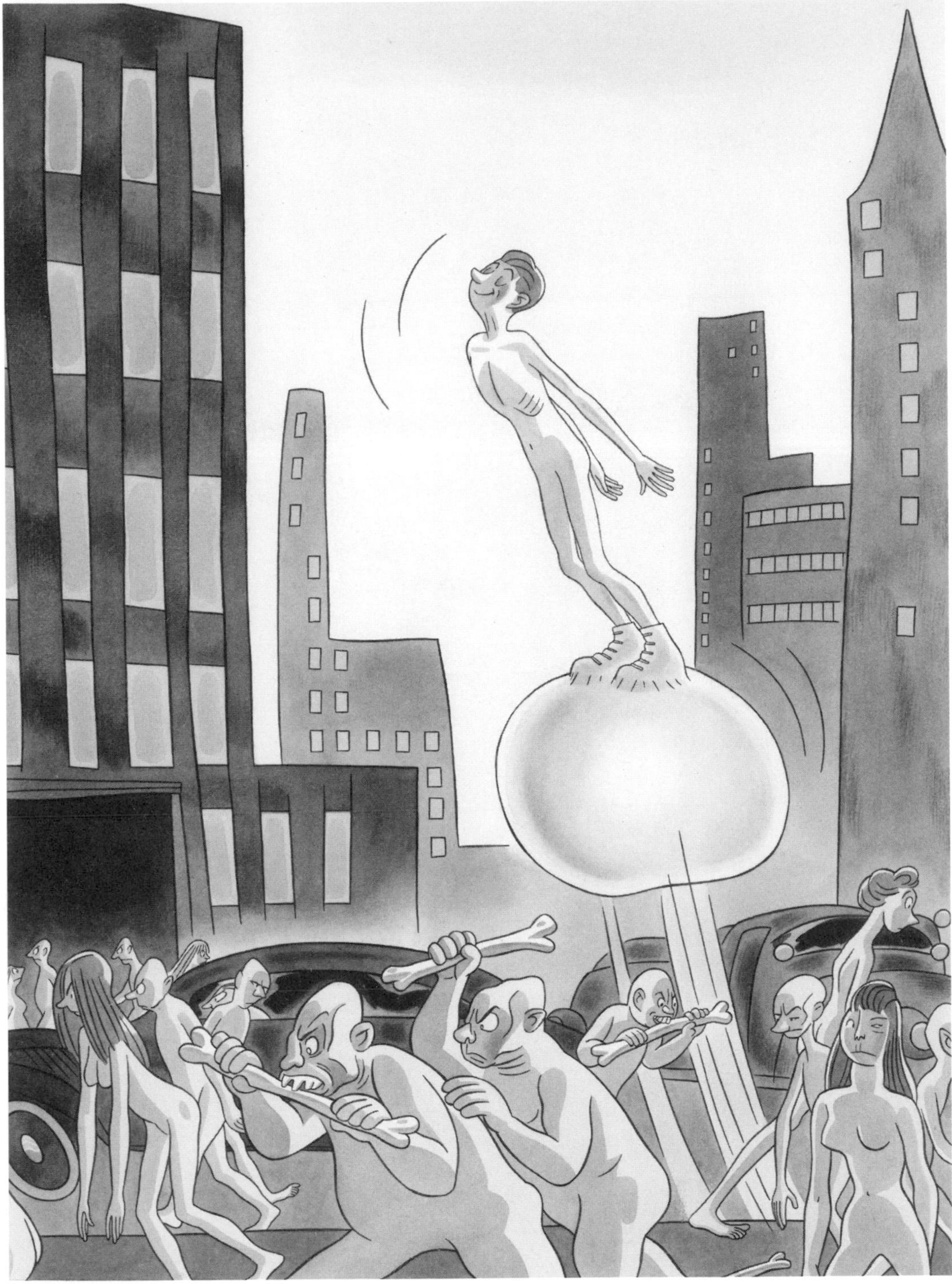

It takes only a little loving

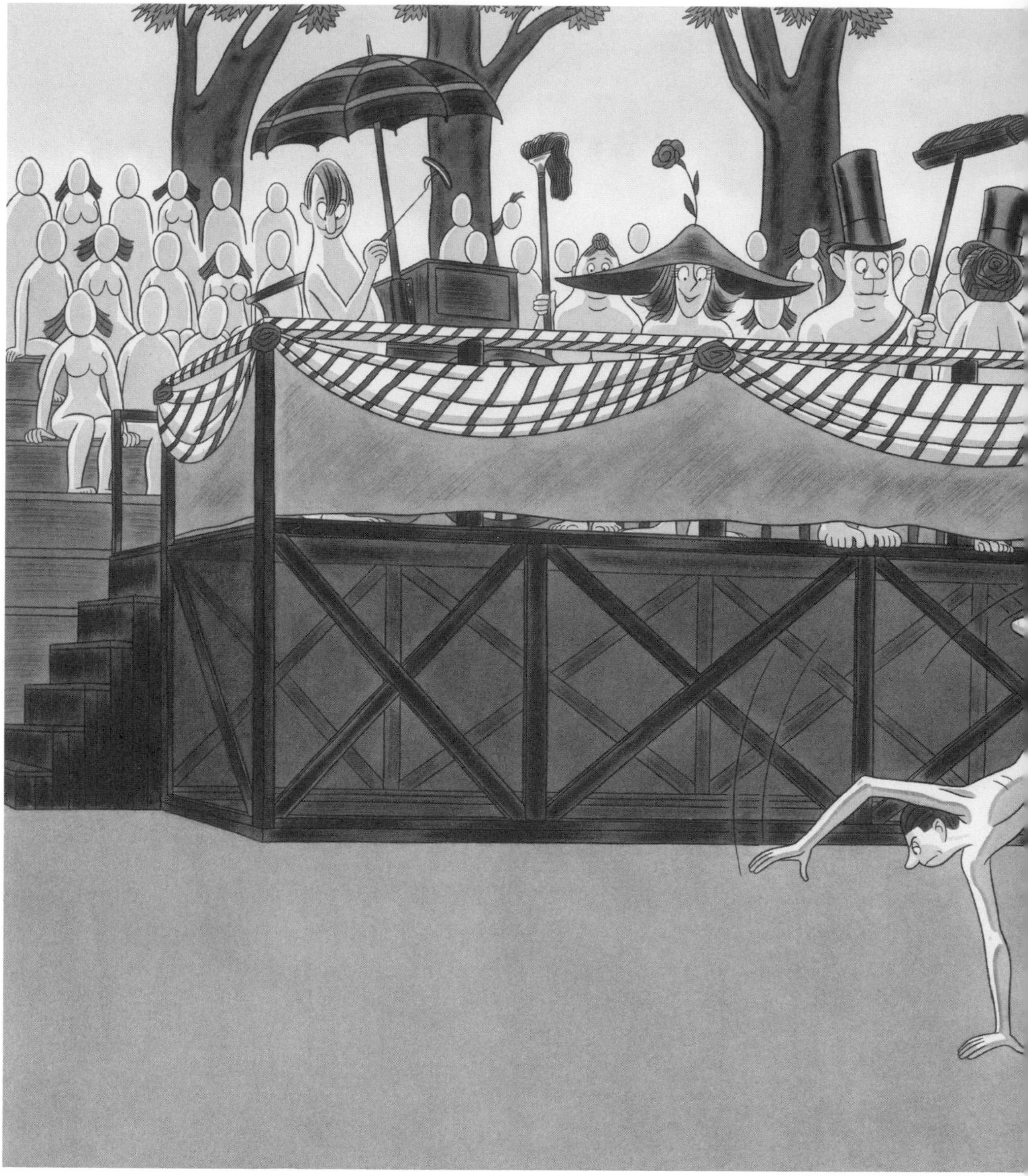

What am I doing here?

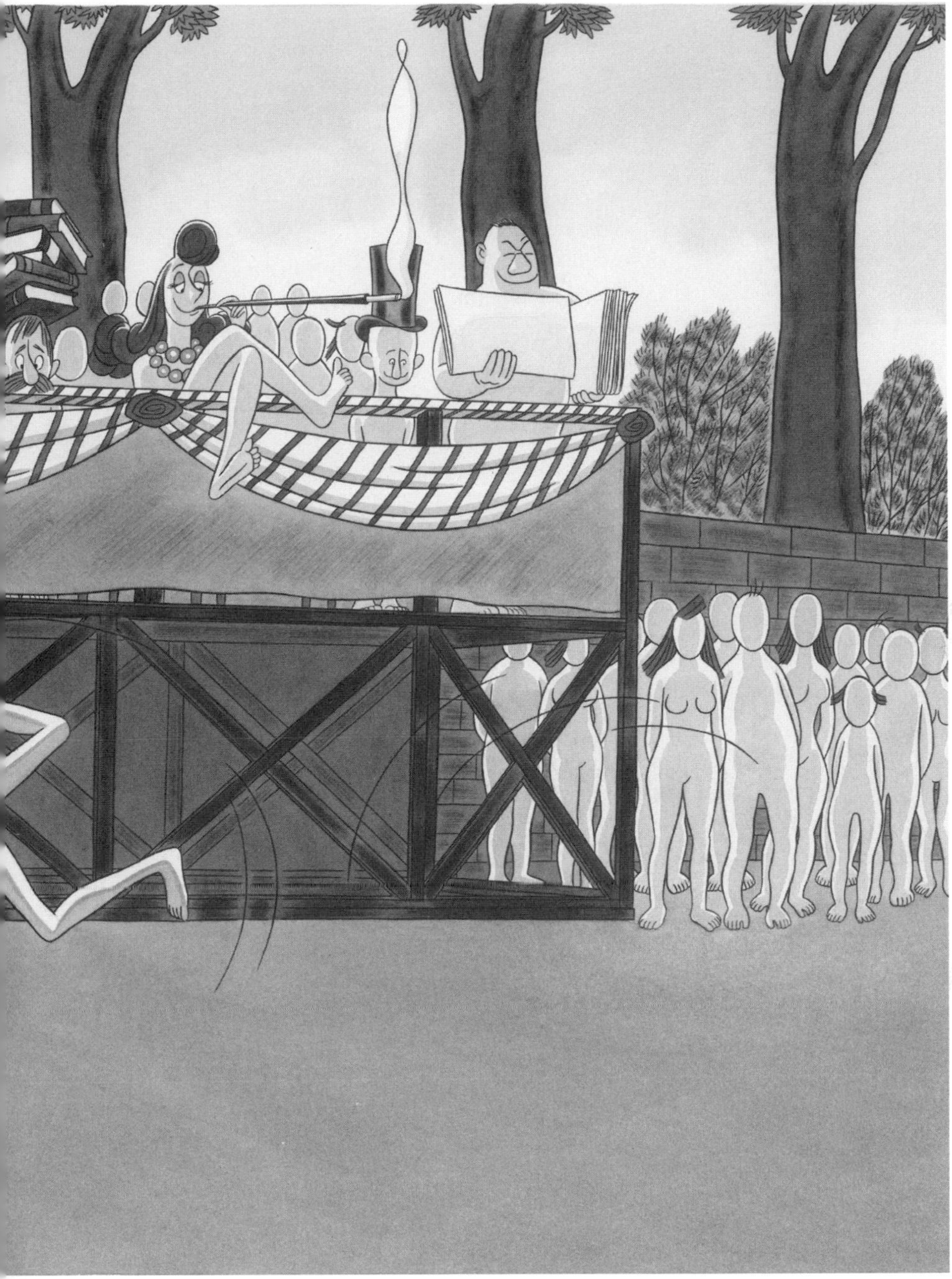

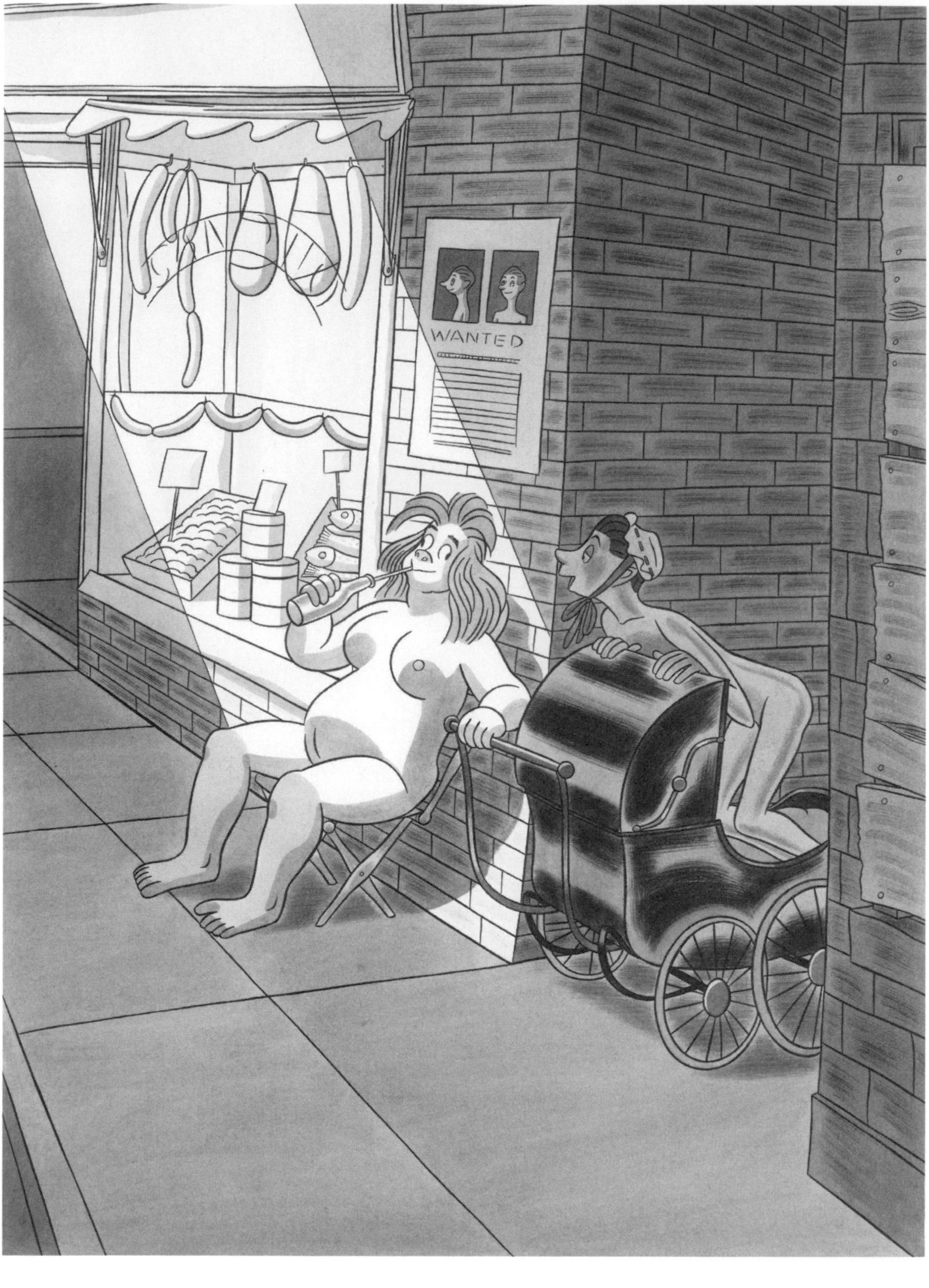
WANTED

Sing that song again

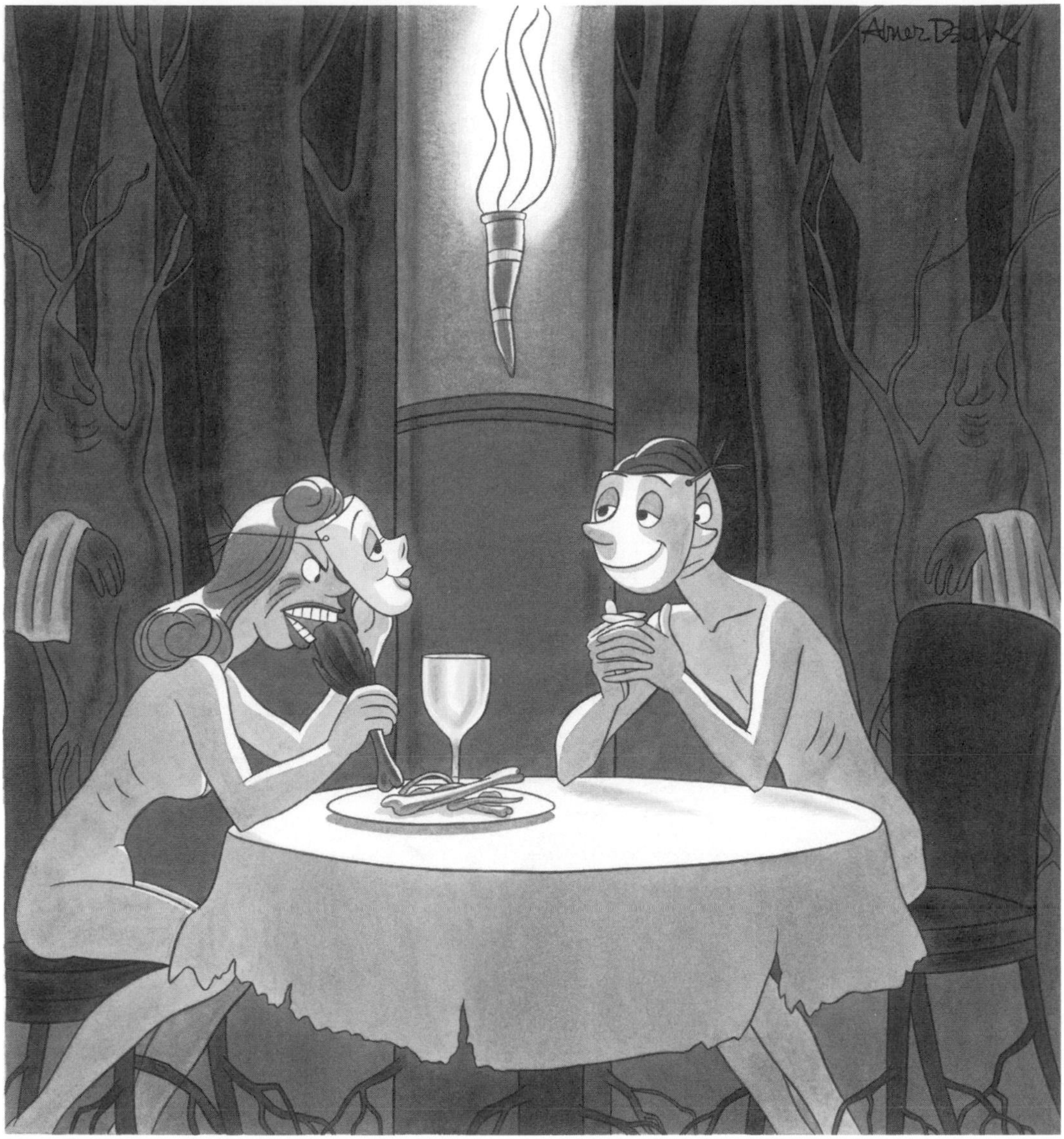

You've made me very happy

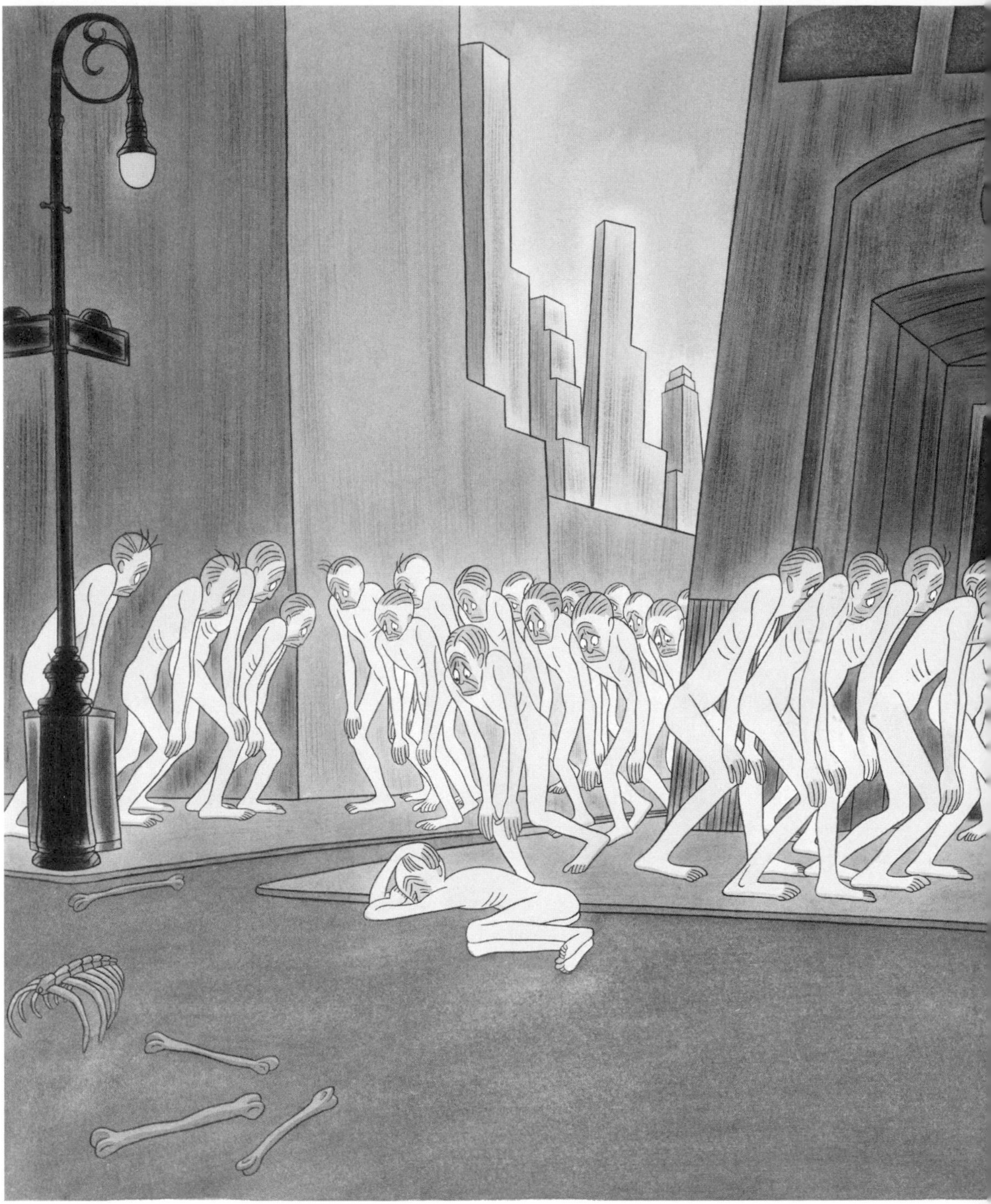

Nearer to the heart's desire

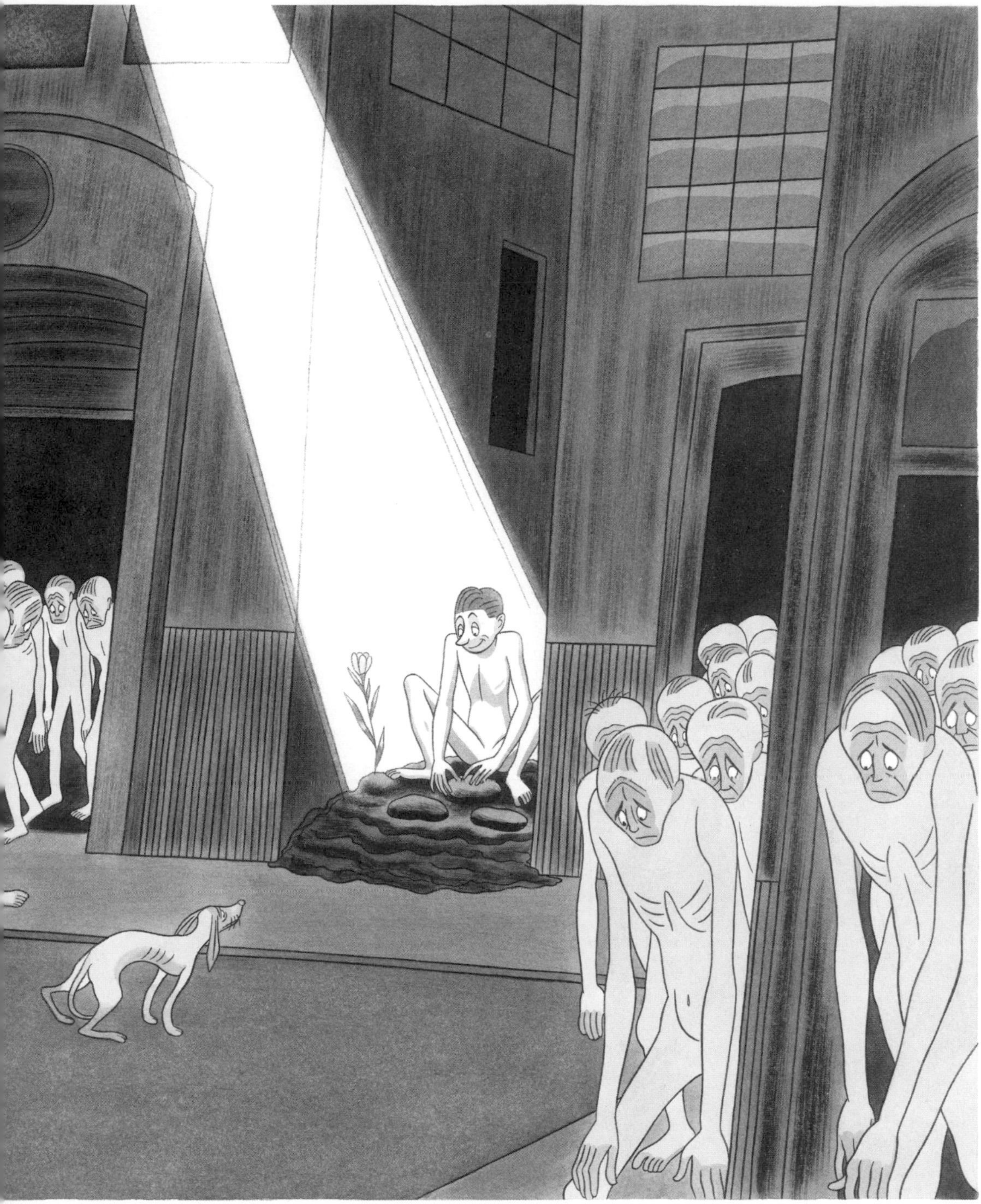

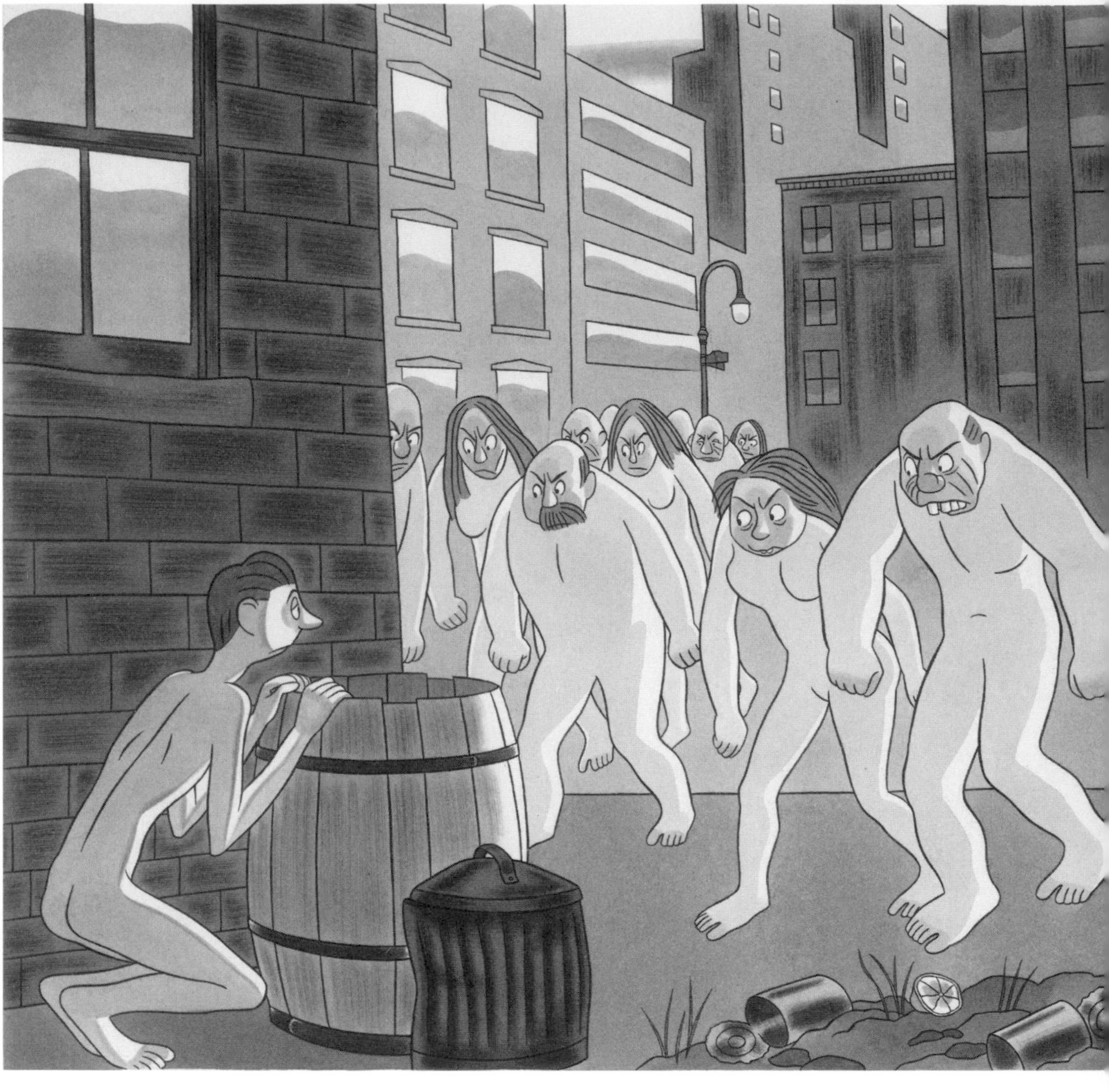

Somedays . . . everybody's looking for a fight

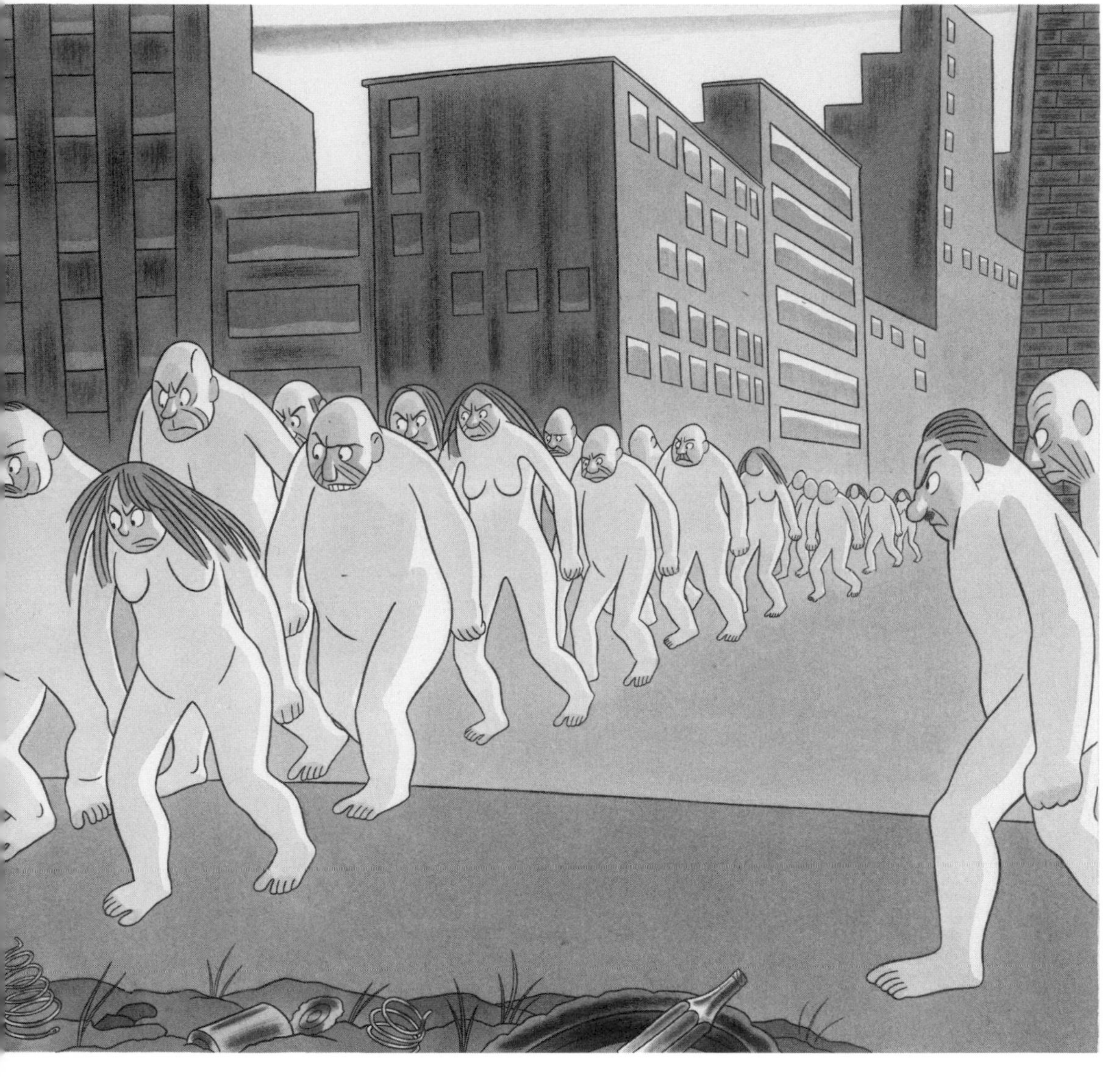

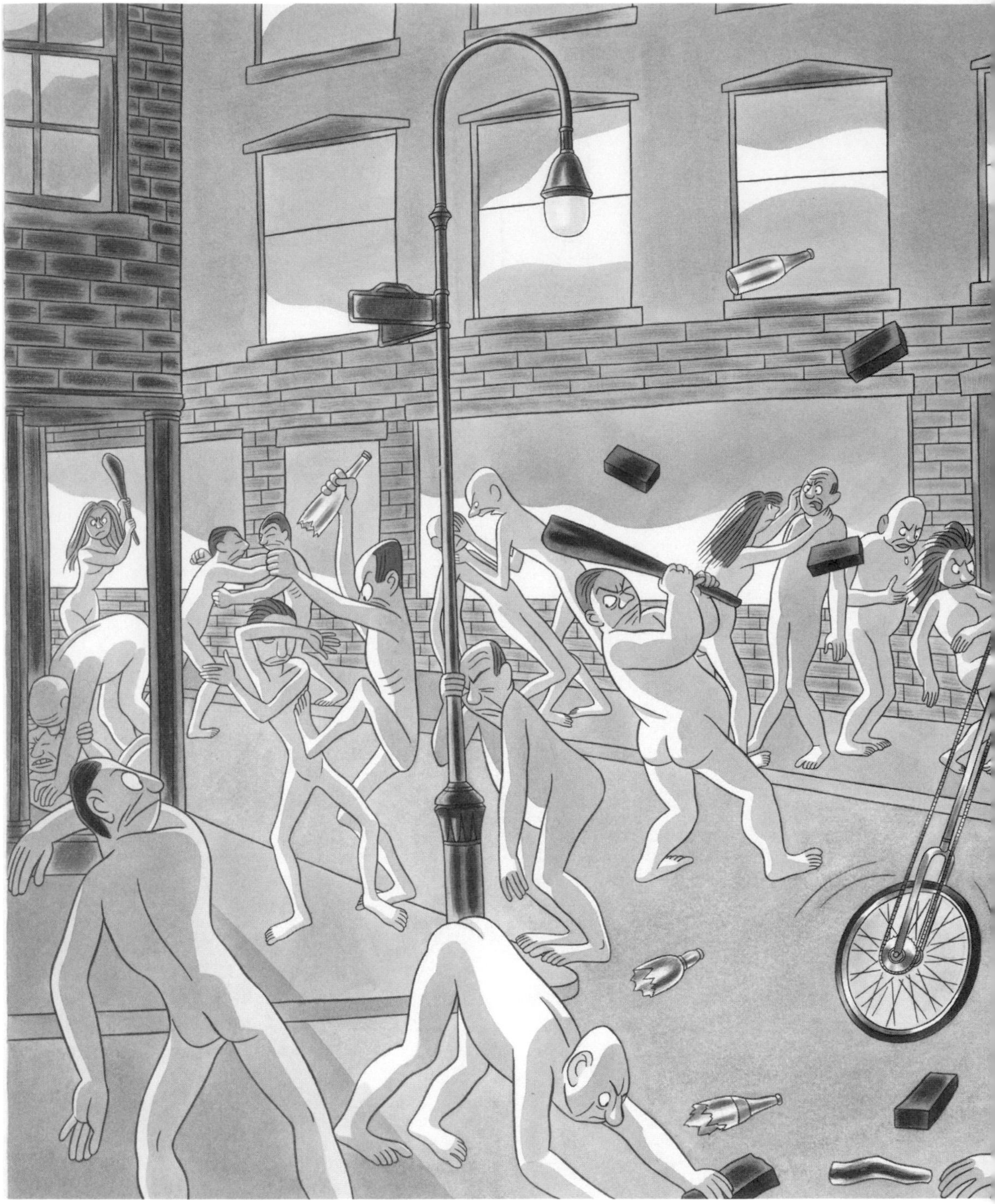

The trick is . . . not caring

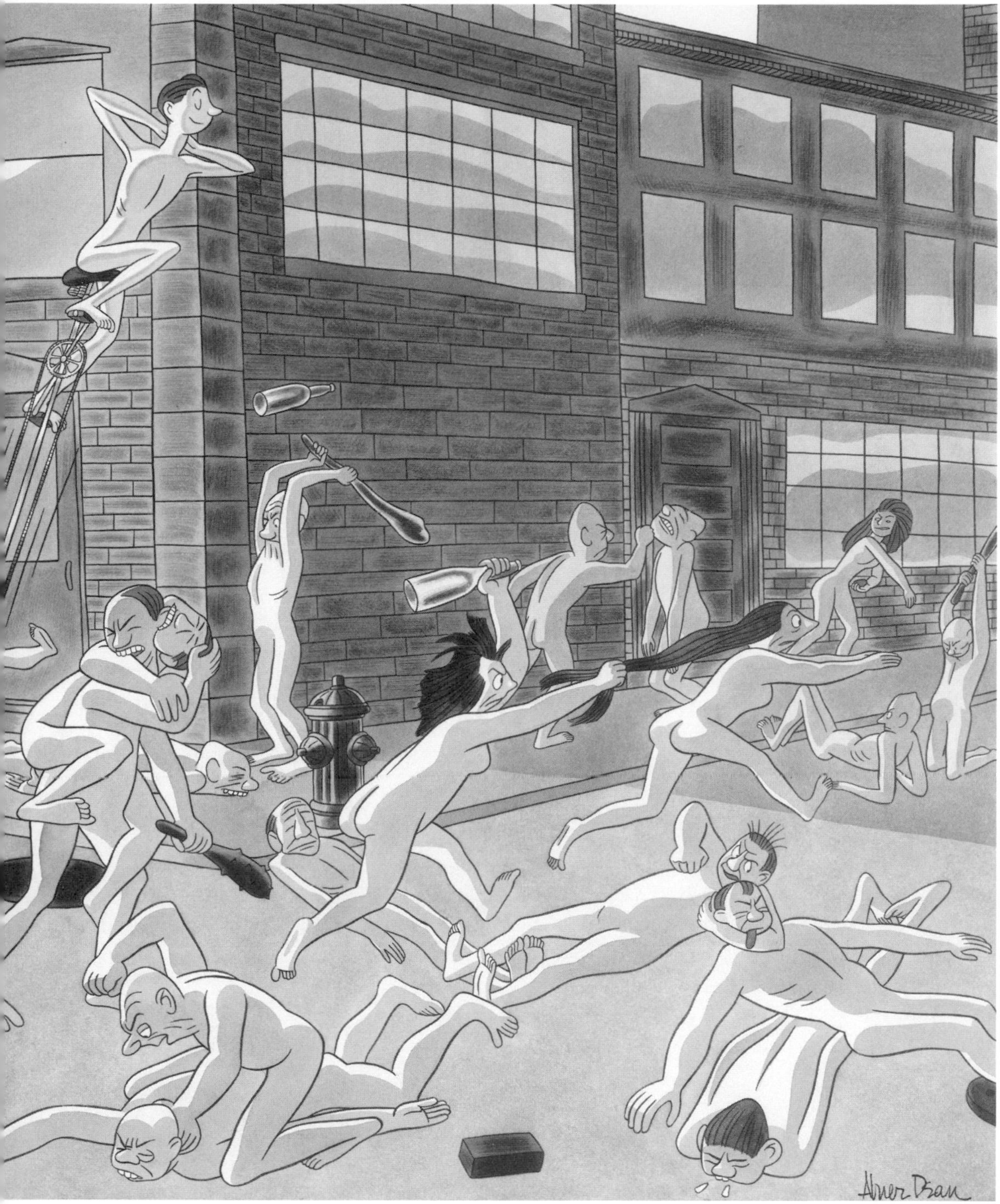
Abner Dean

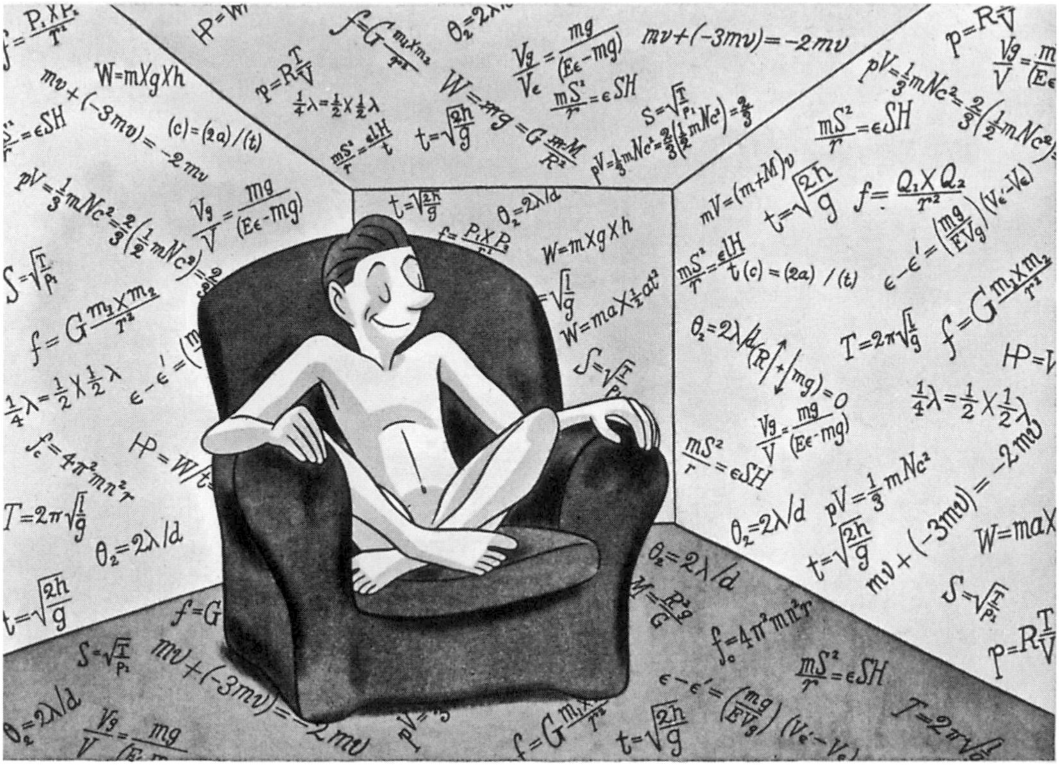
W=mXgXh
mv+(-3mv)=-2mv
W=mXgXh
T=2π√(l/g)
θ₂=2λ/d
t=√(2h/g)
f=G(m₁Xm₂/r²)
p=R(T/V)
mS²/r=εSH
W=maX½at²

No one can touch me

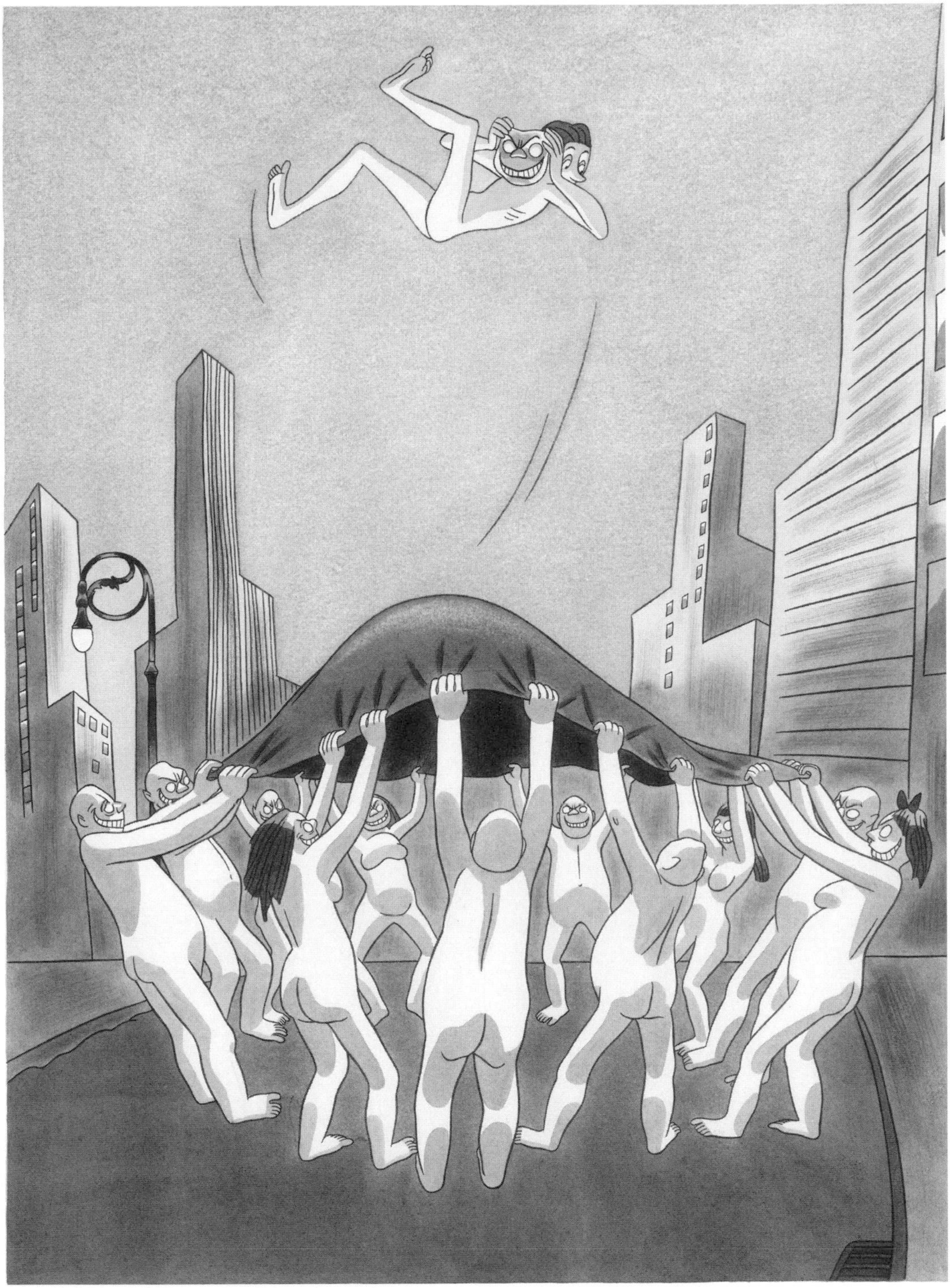

It's better to pretend

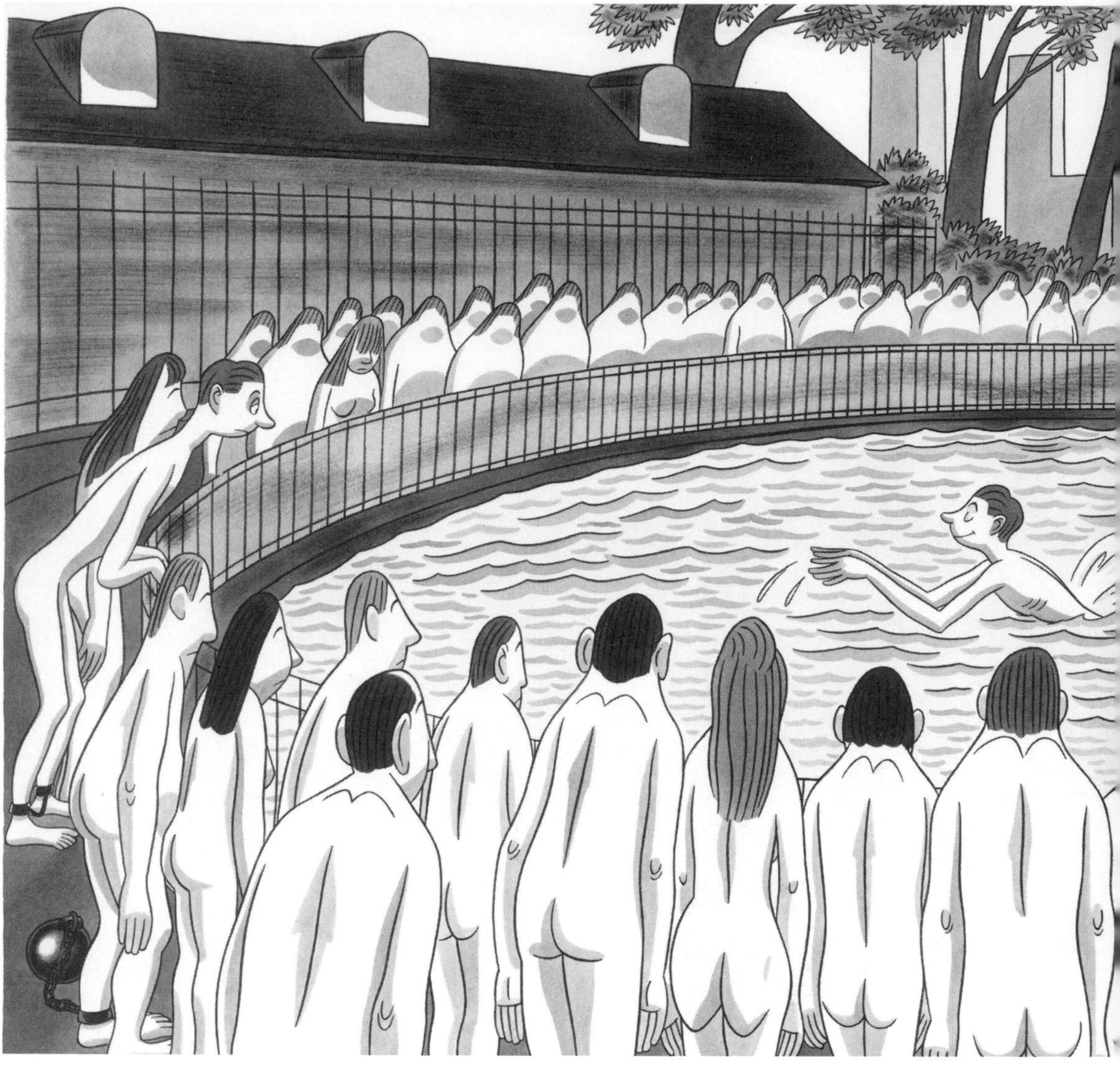

I wonder how it feels

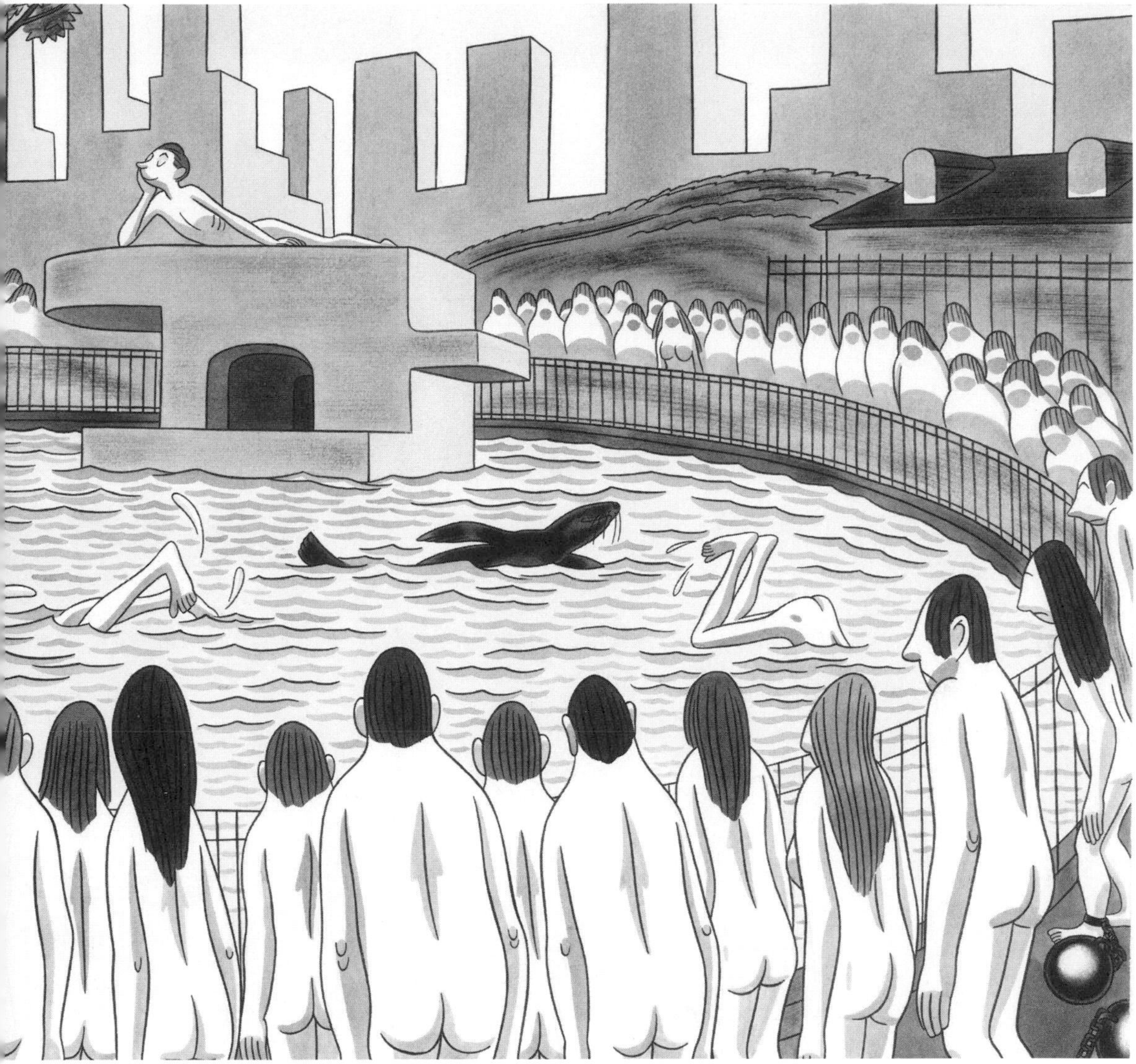

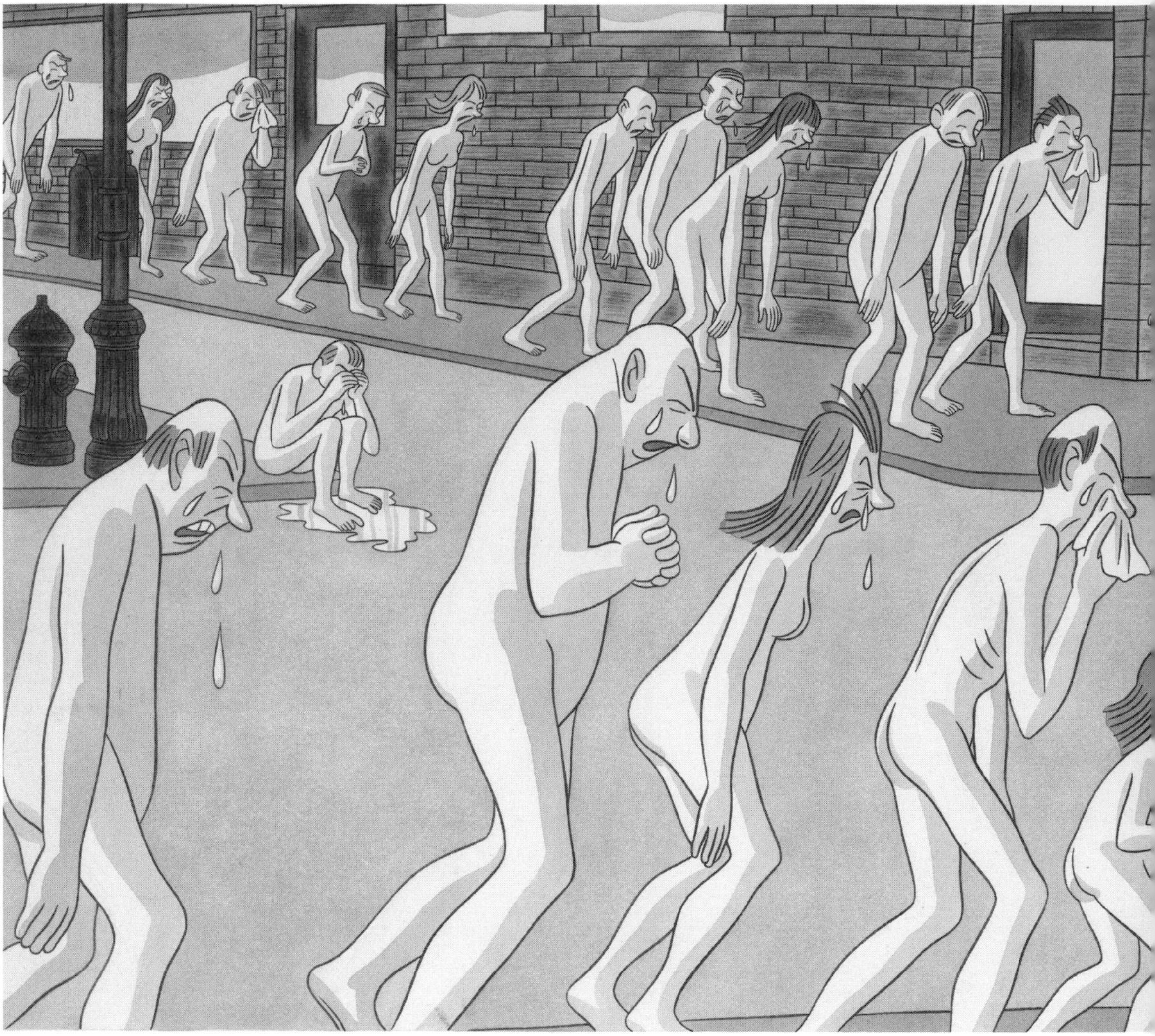

Can I help, maybe?

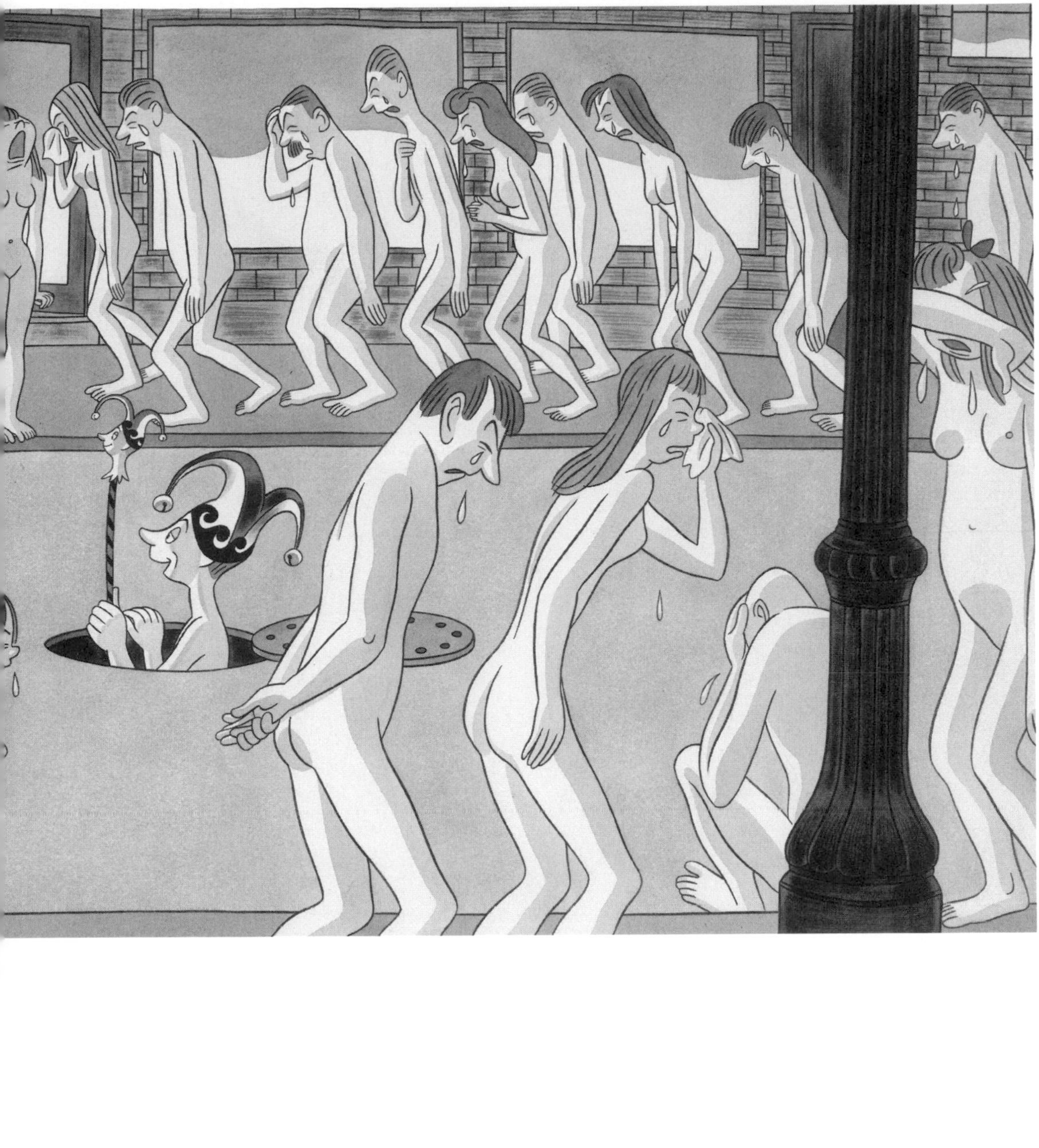

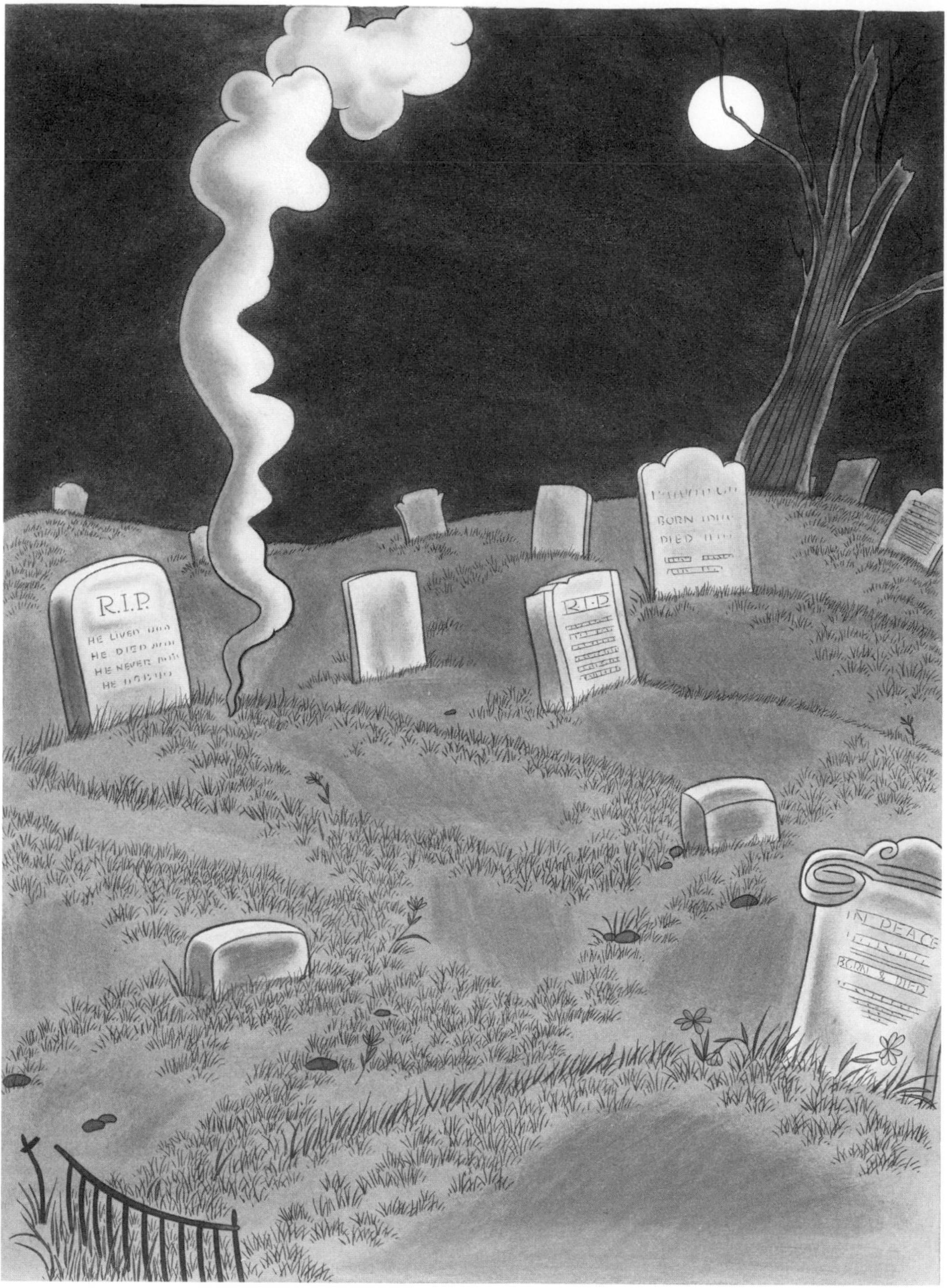
R.I.P.
HE LIVED
HE DIED
HE NEVER
BORN
DIED
R.I.P.
IN PEACE
BORN & DIED

I smoke too much

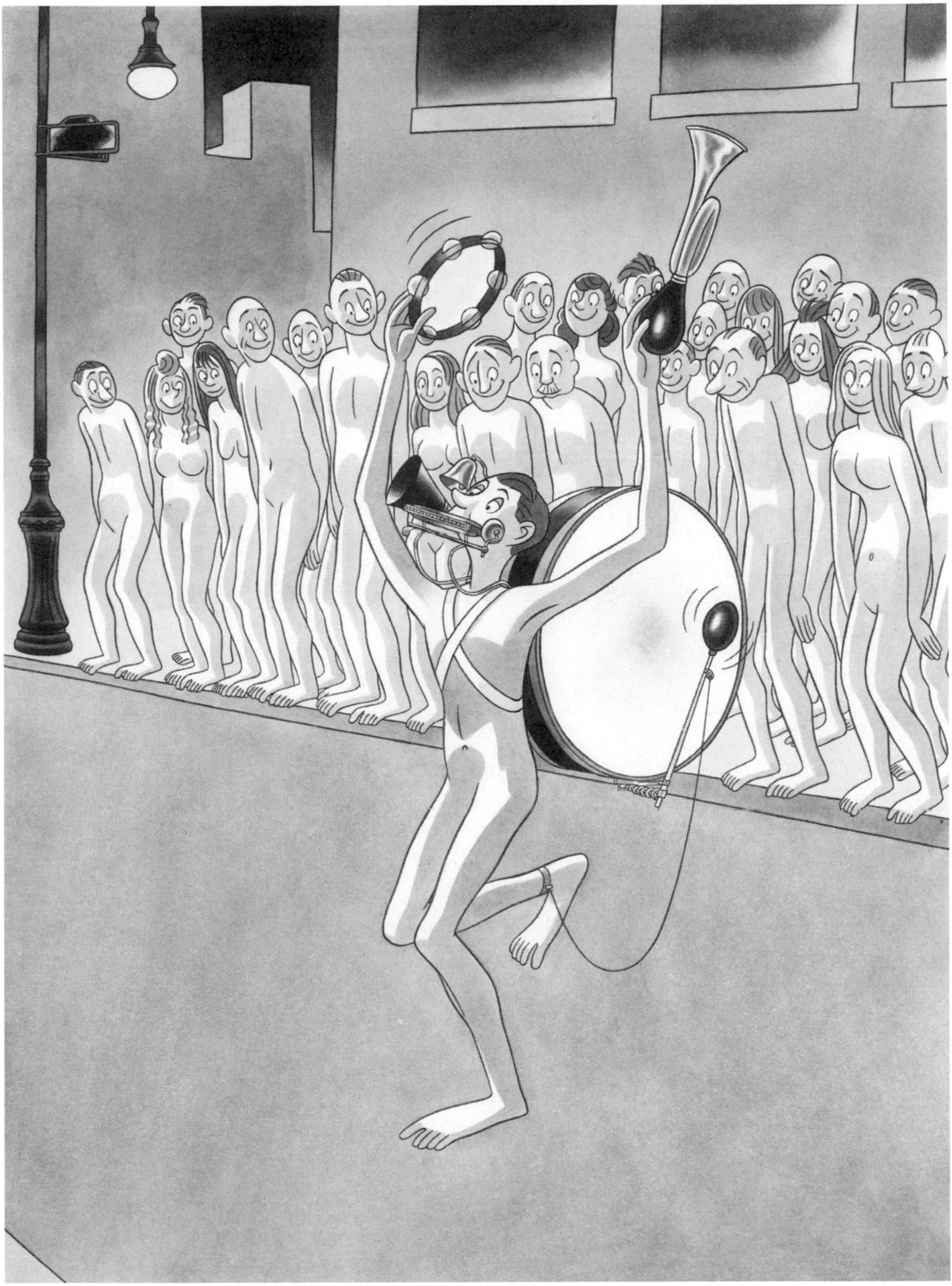

Act as though you believed in yourself

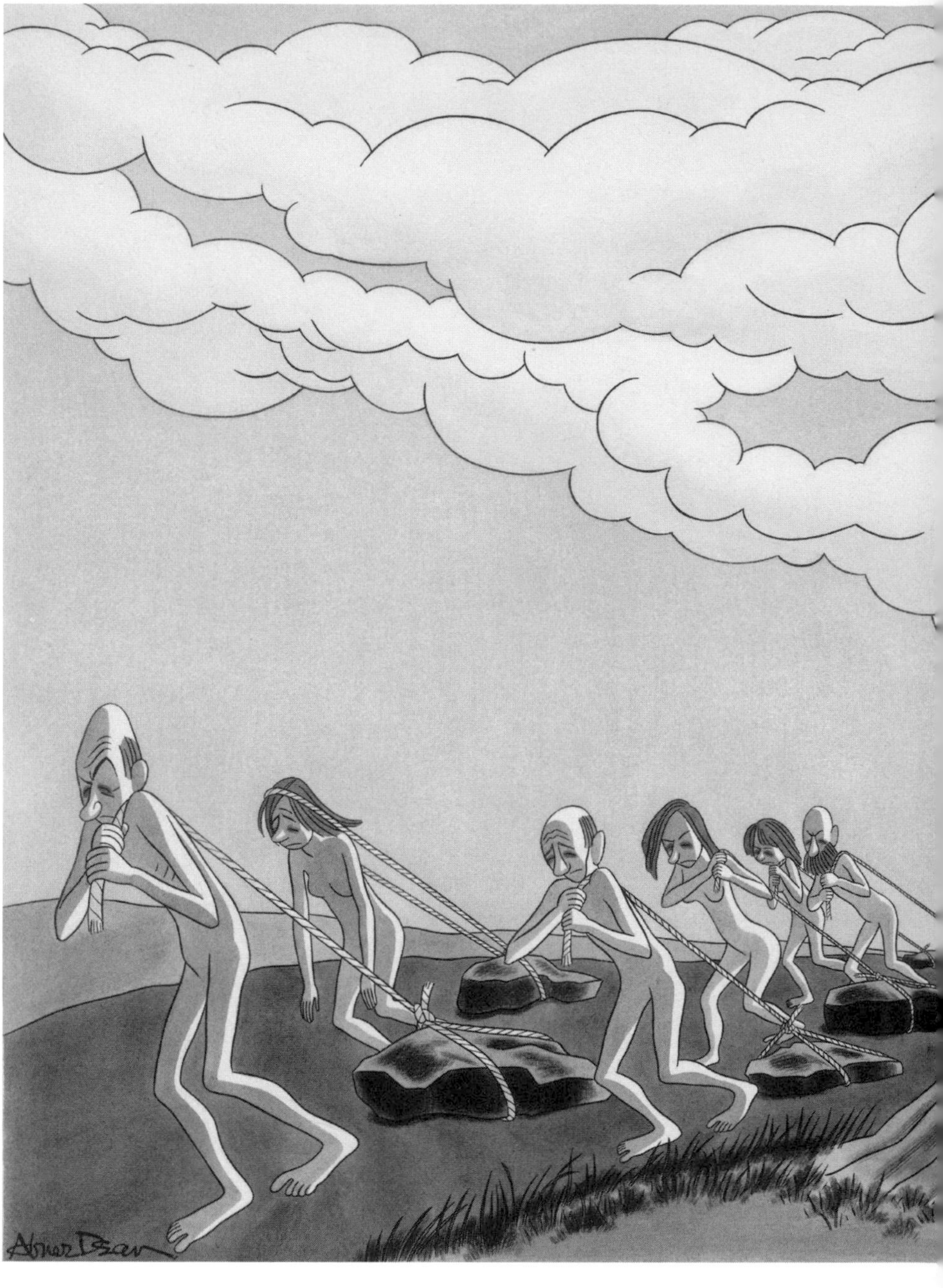
Abner Dean

I made this

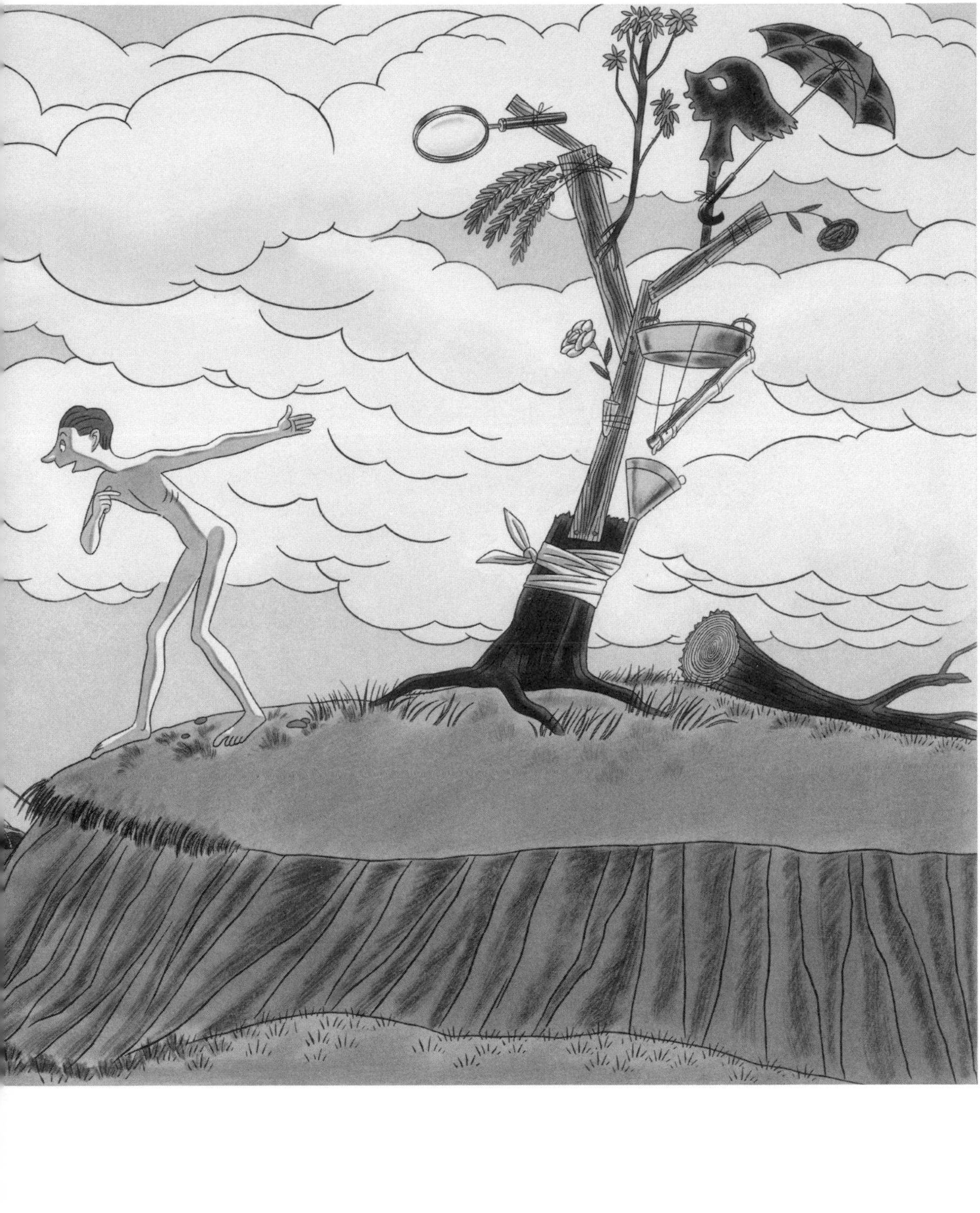

Where are you going?

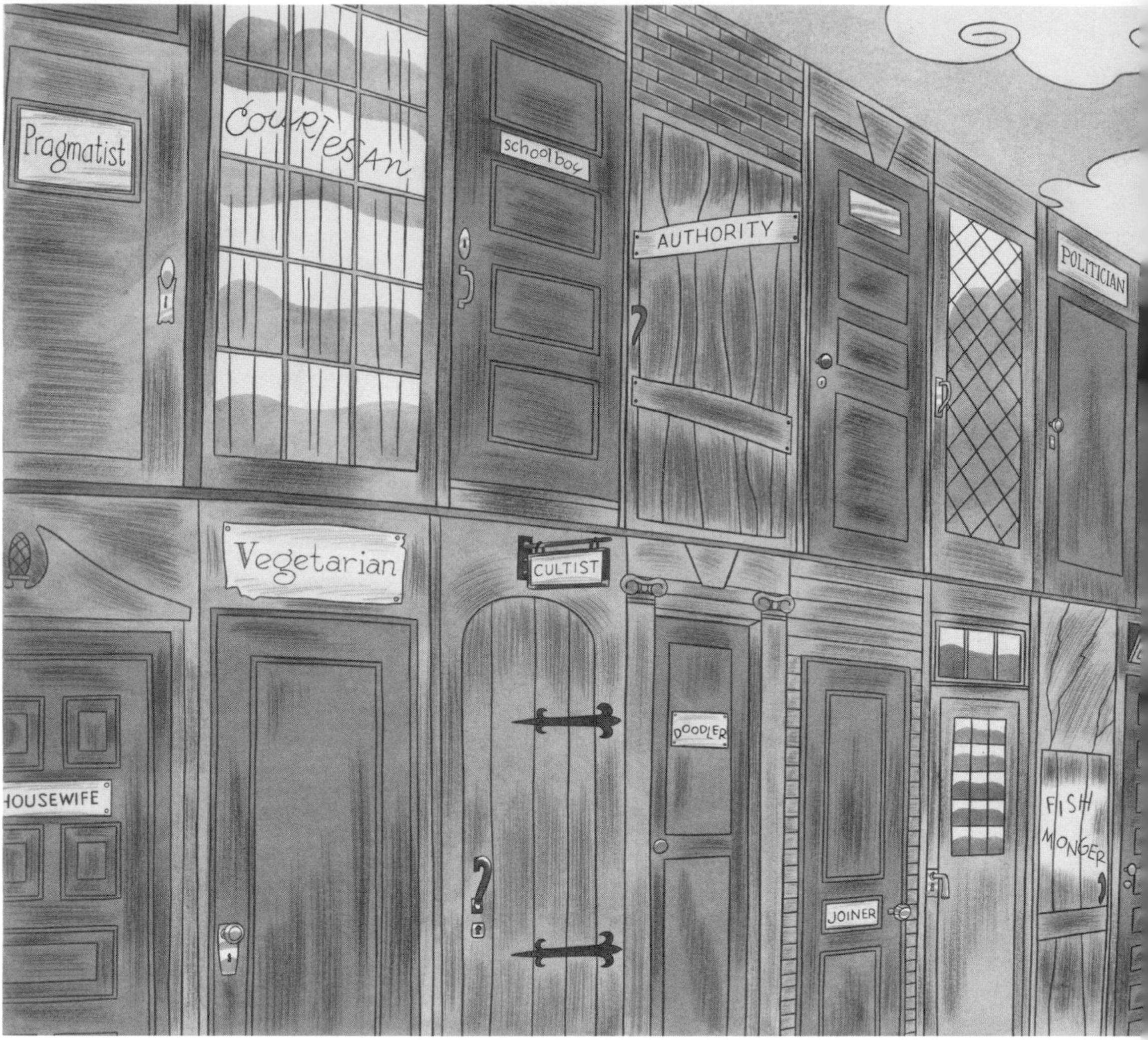
Pragmatist
COURTESAN
school boy
AUTHORITY
POLITICIAN
Vegetarian
CULTIST
HOUSEWIFE
DOODLER
JOINER
FISH MONGER

You missed life

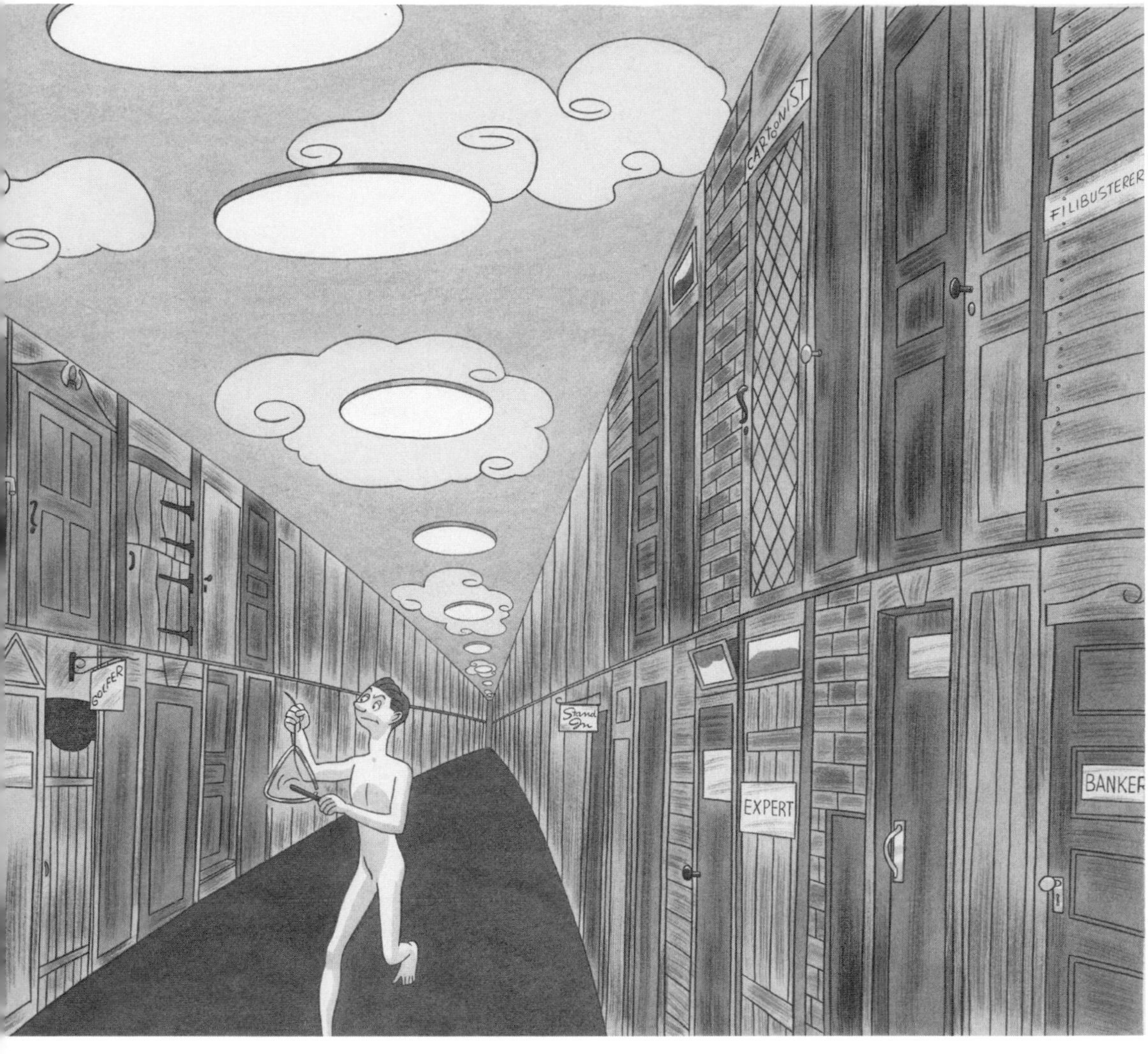
CARTOONIST
FILIBUSTERER
GOLFER
Stand In
EXPERT
BANKER

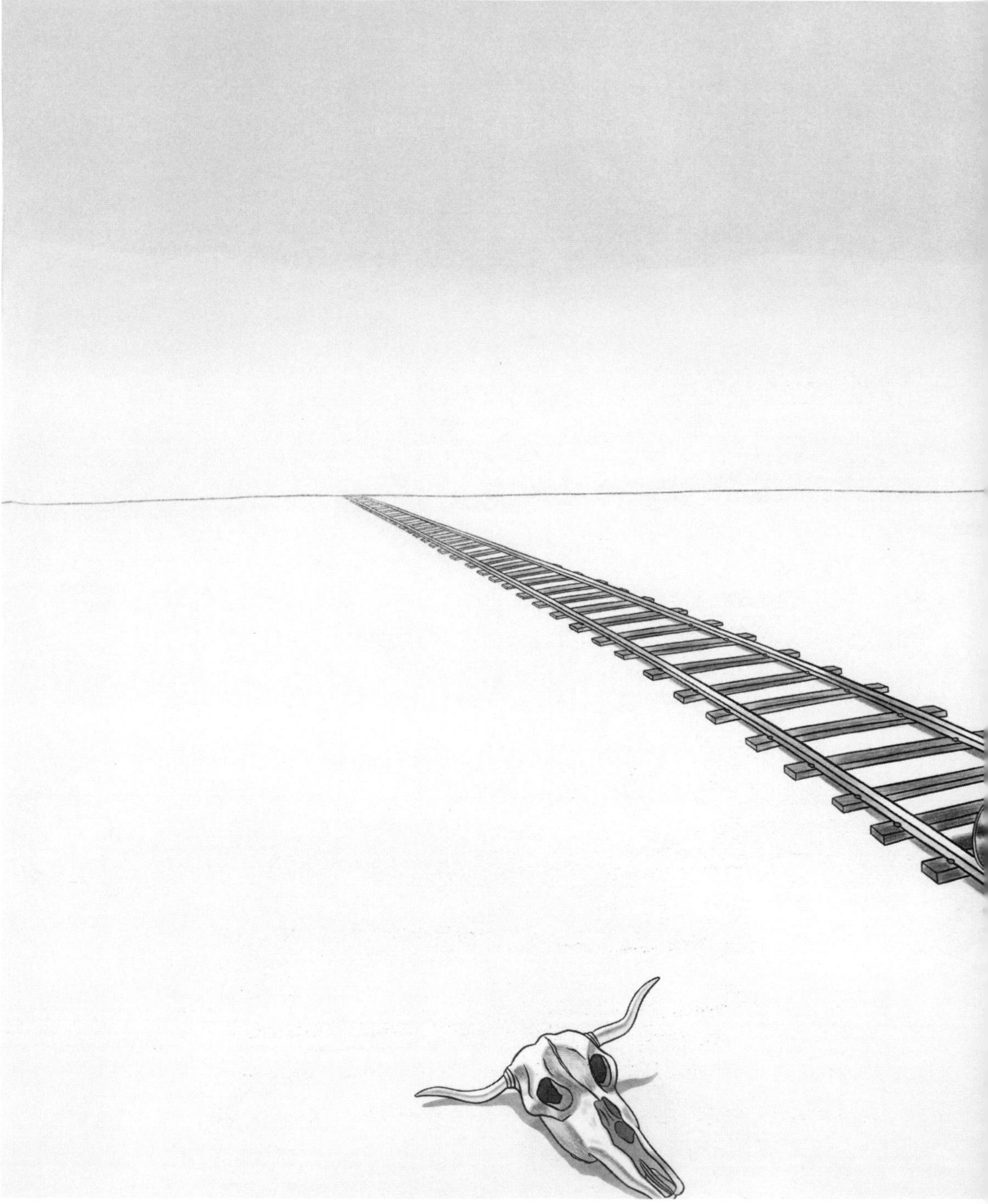

What am I doing here?

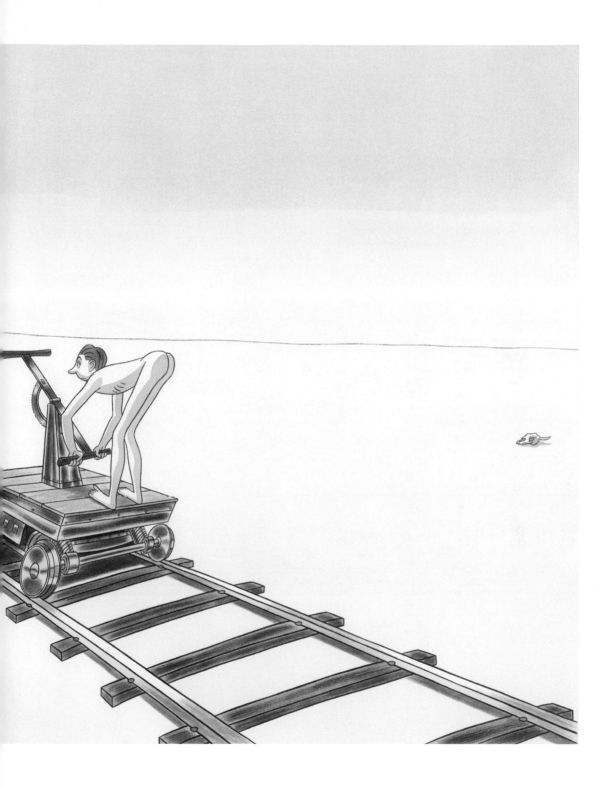

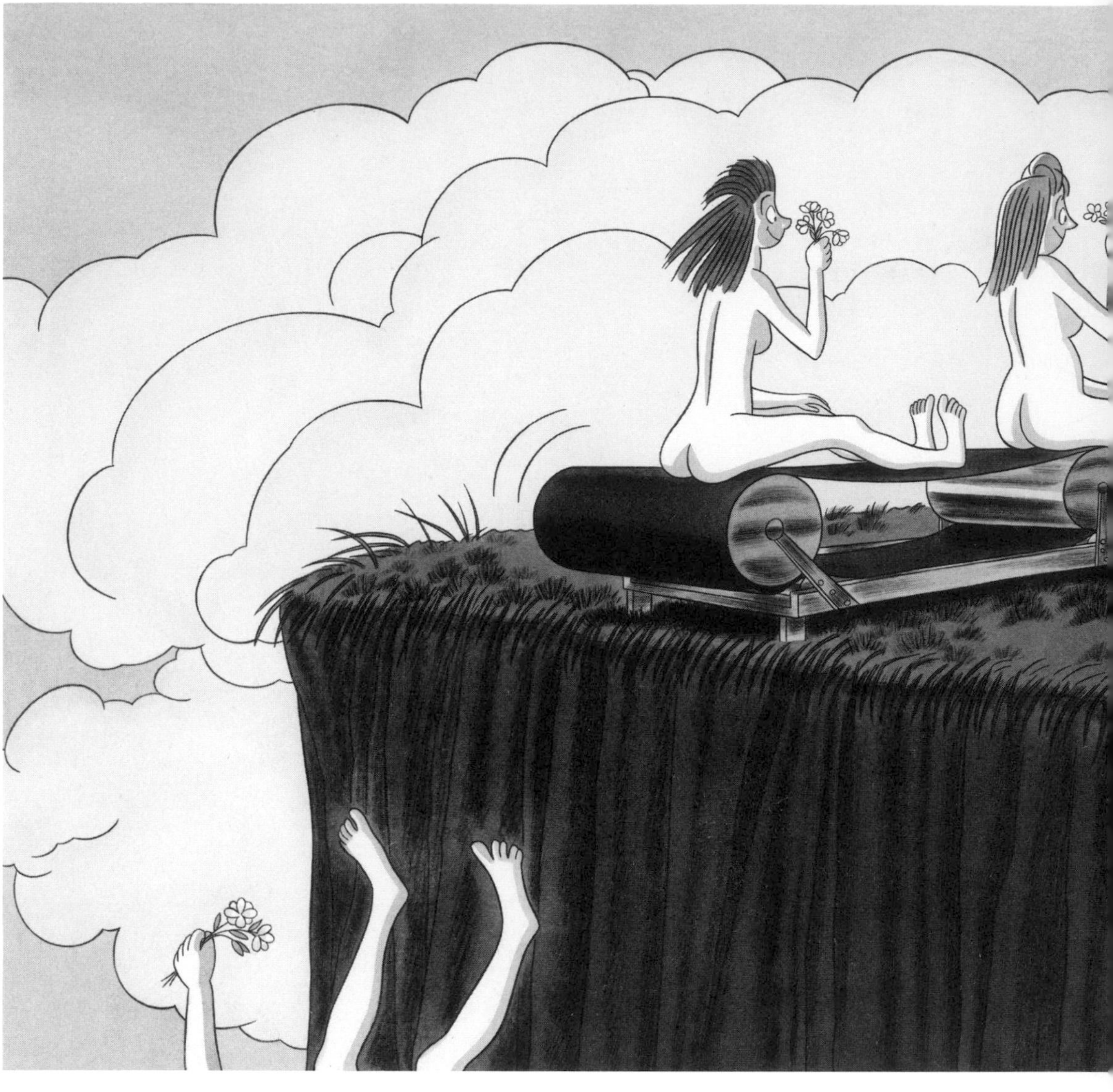

Forget-me-nots are foolish

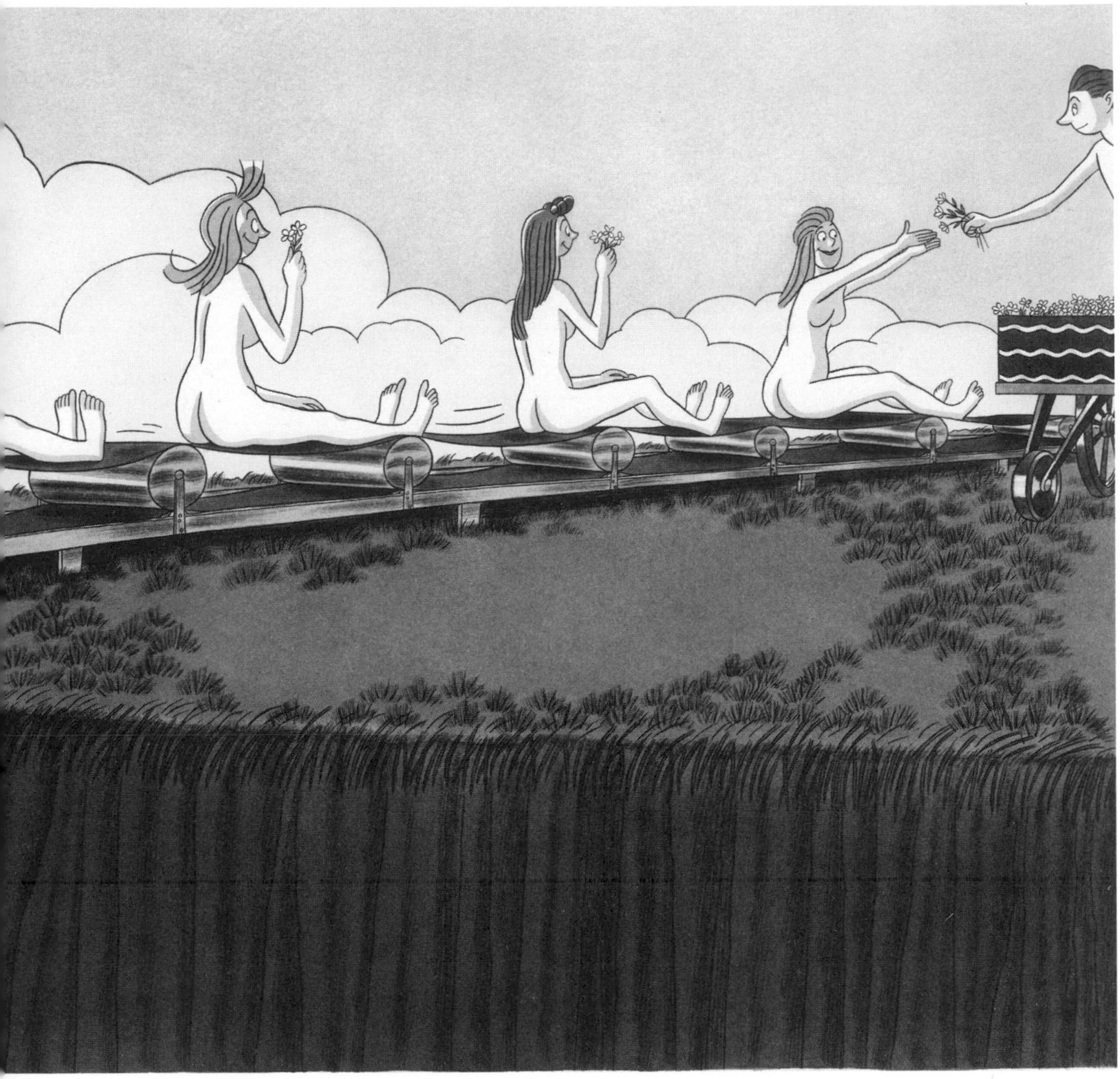

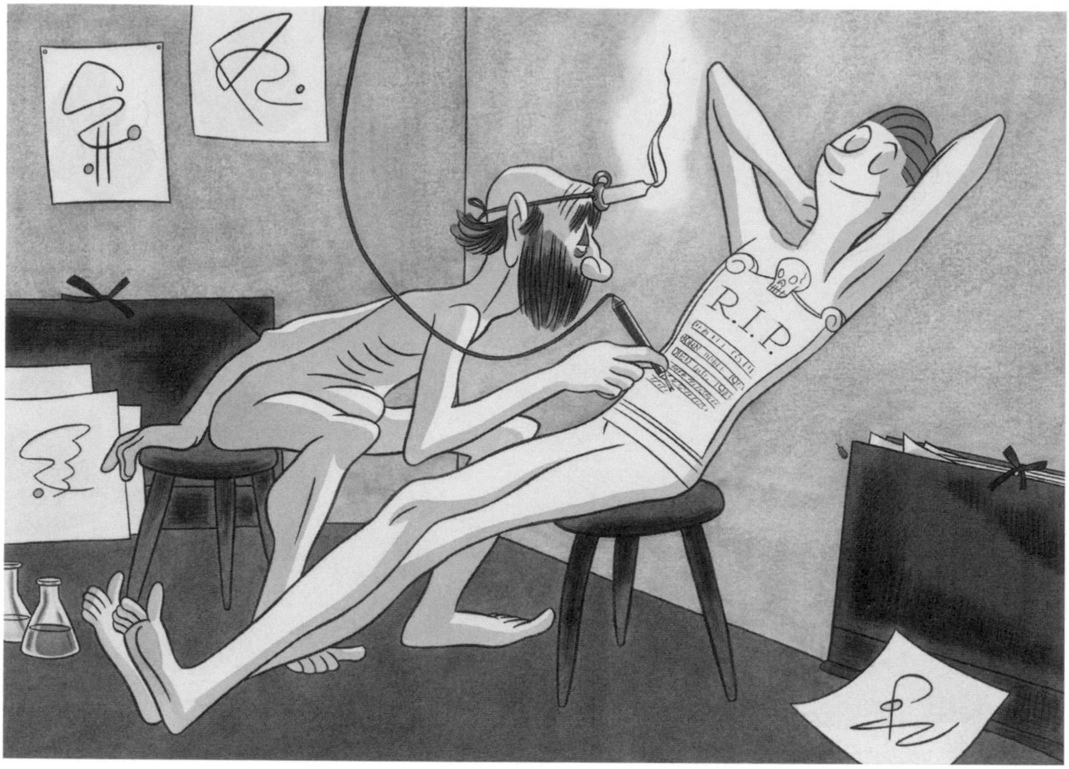
R.I.P.

. . . and then someday . . .

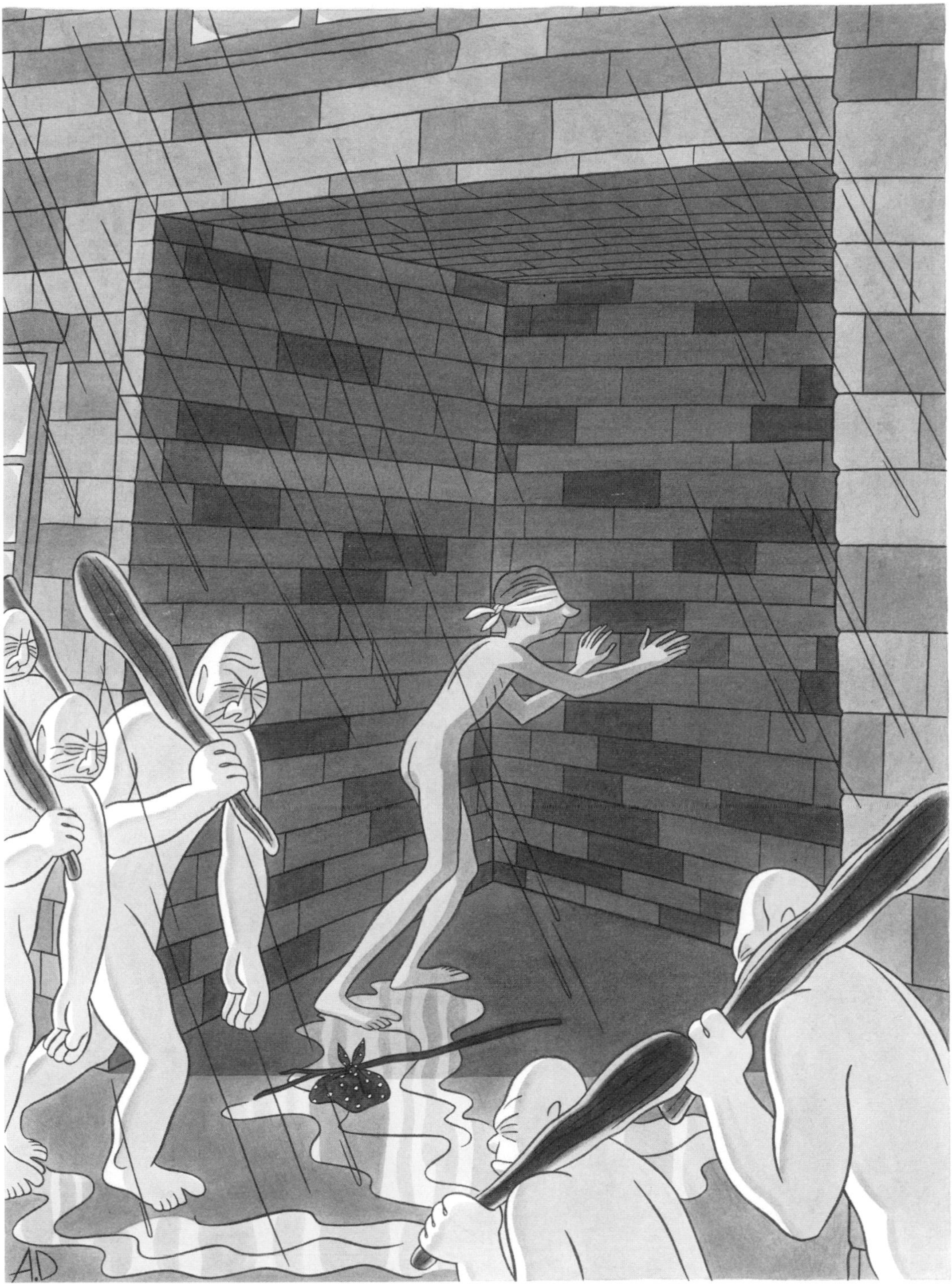
A.D

There used to be a door here

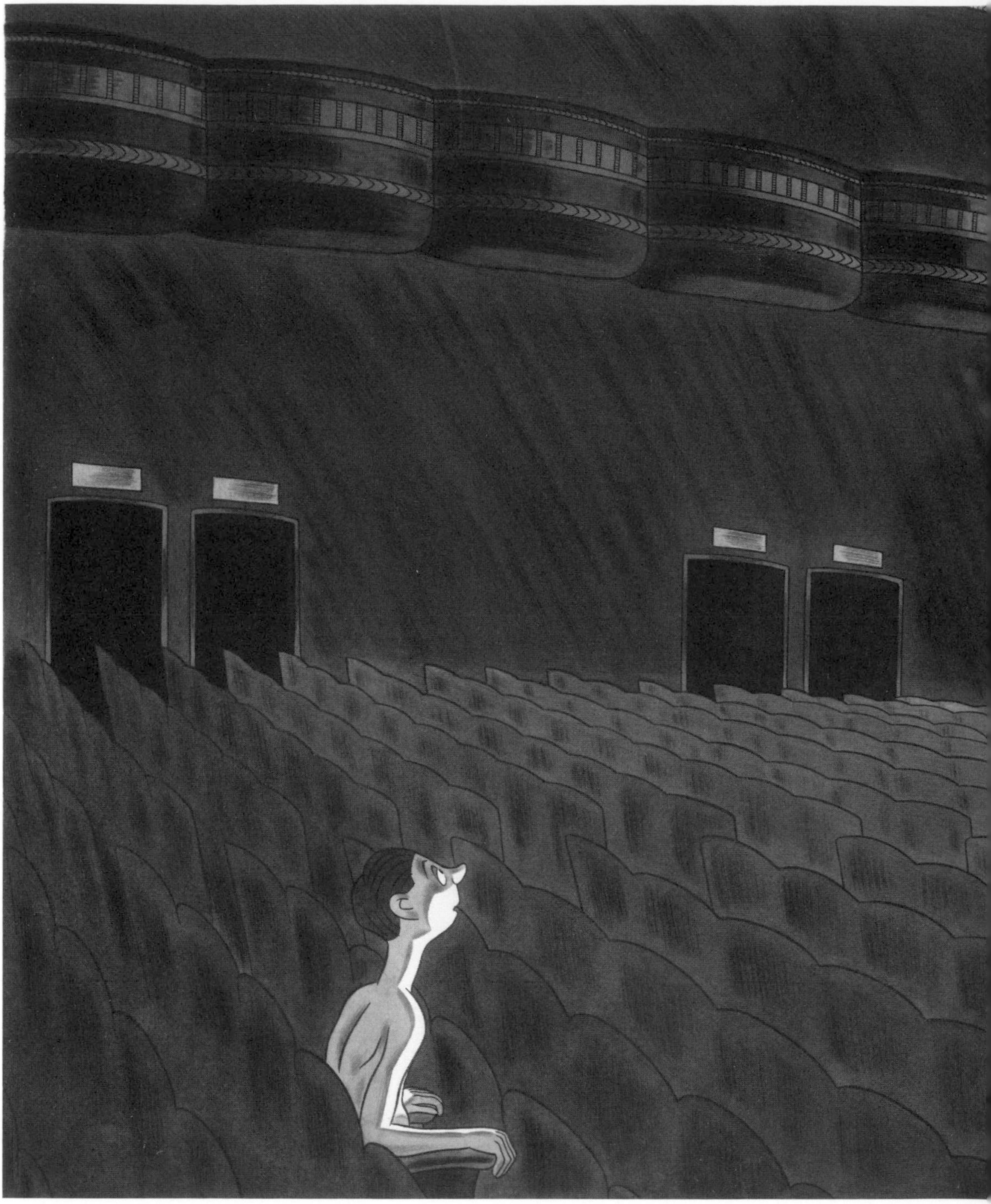

I always see her at a distance

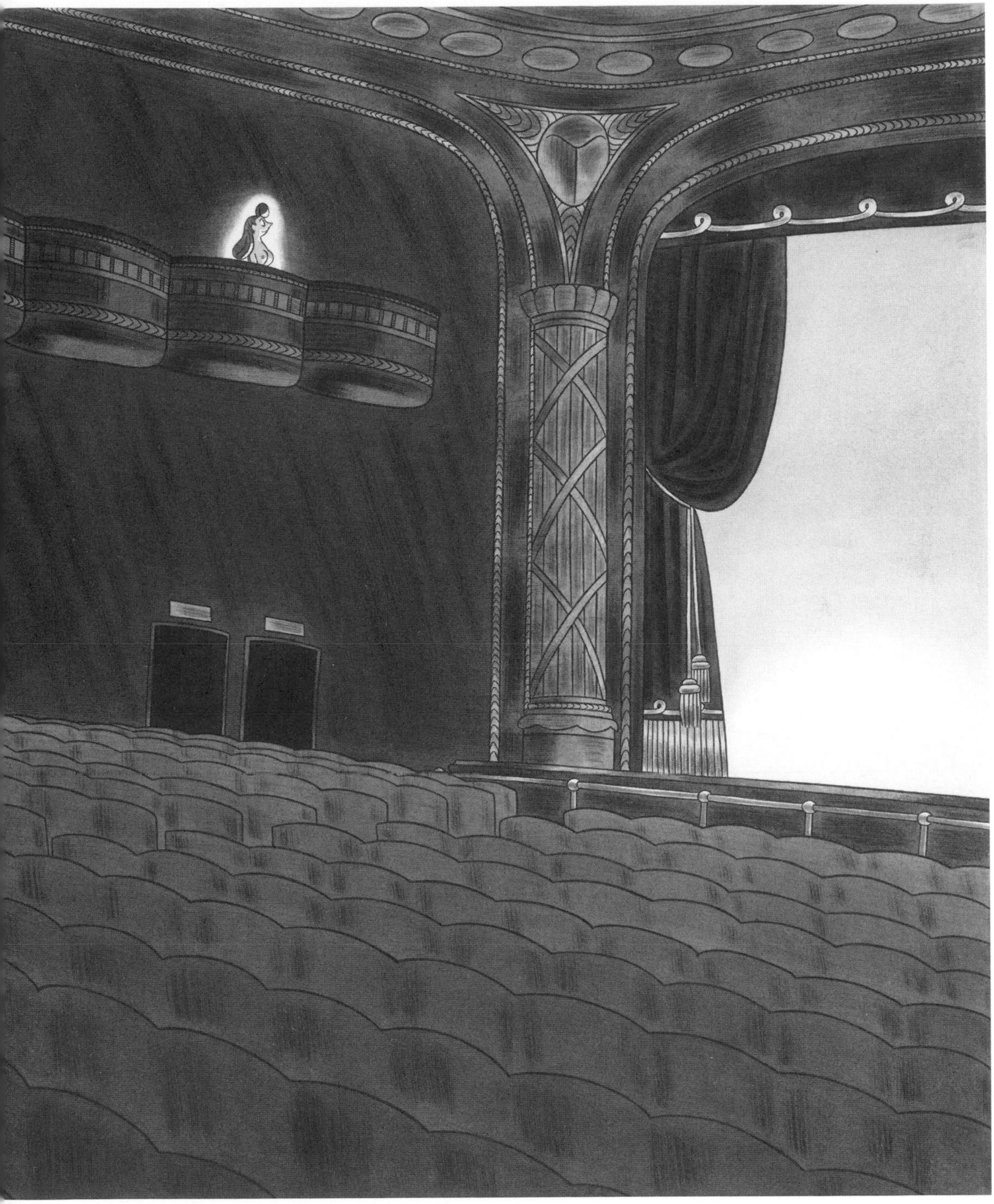

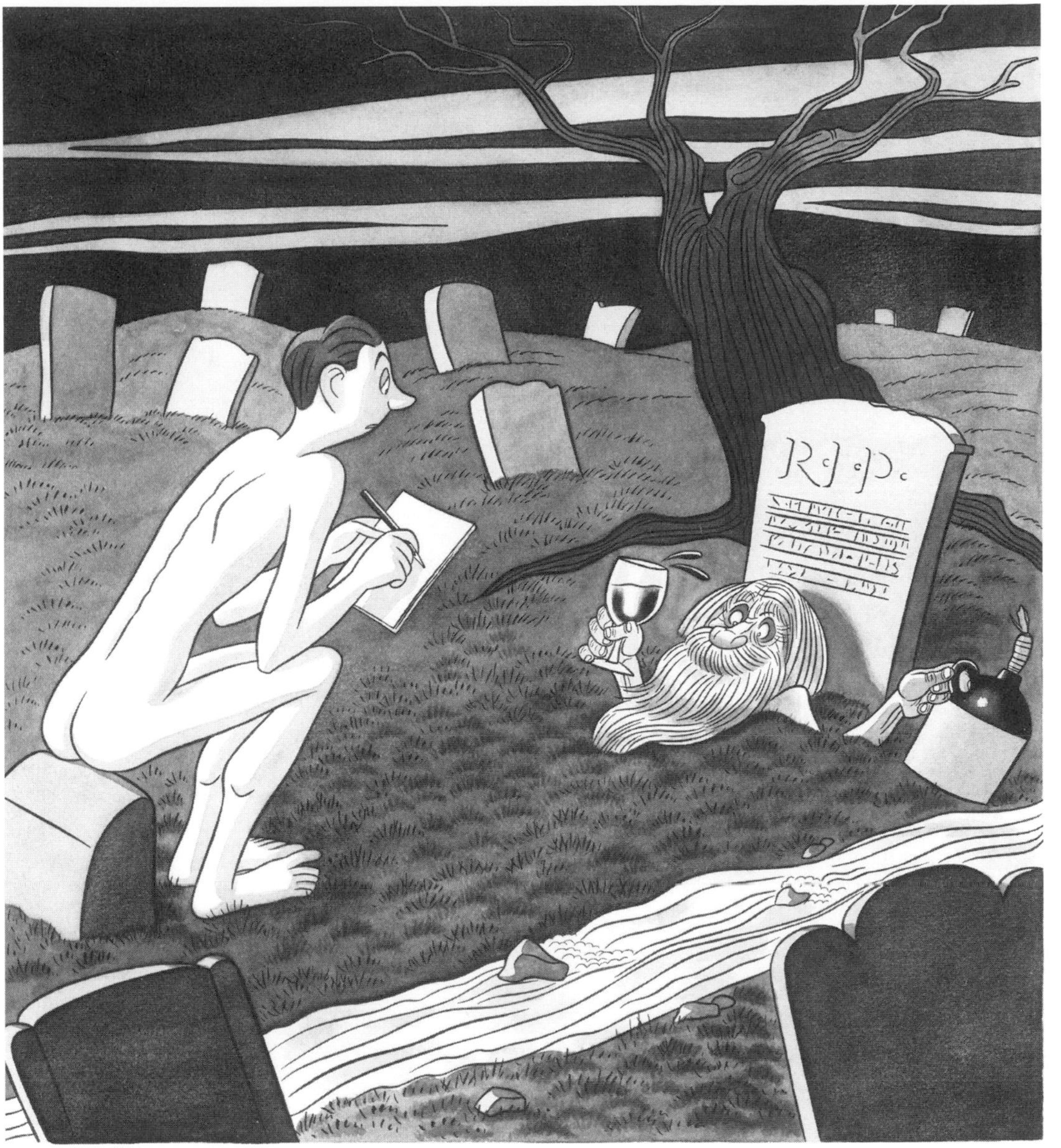
R.I.P.

Have you anything to teach me?

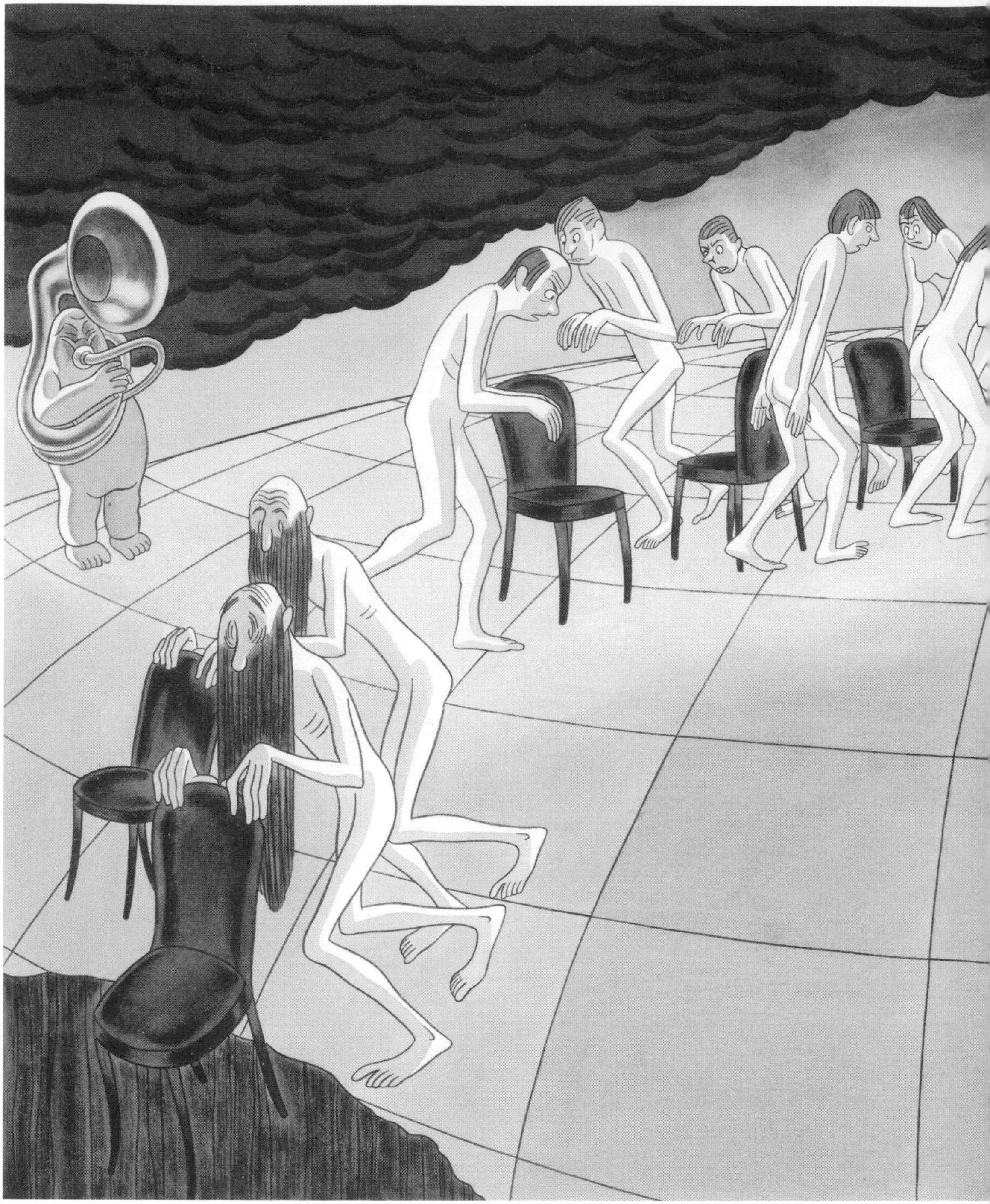

This is all there is

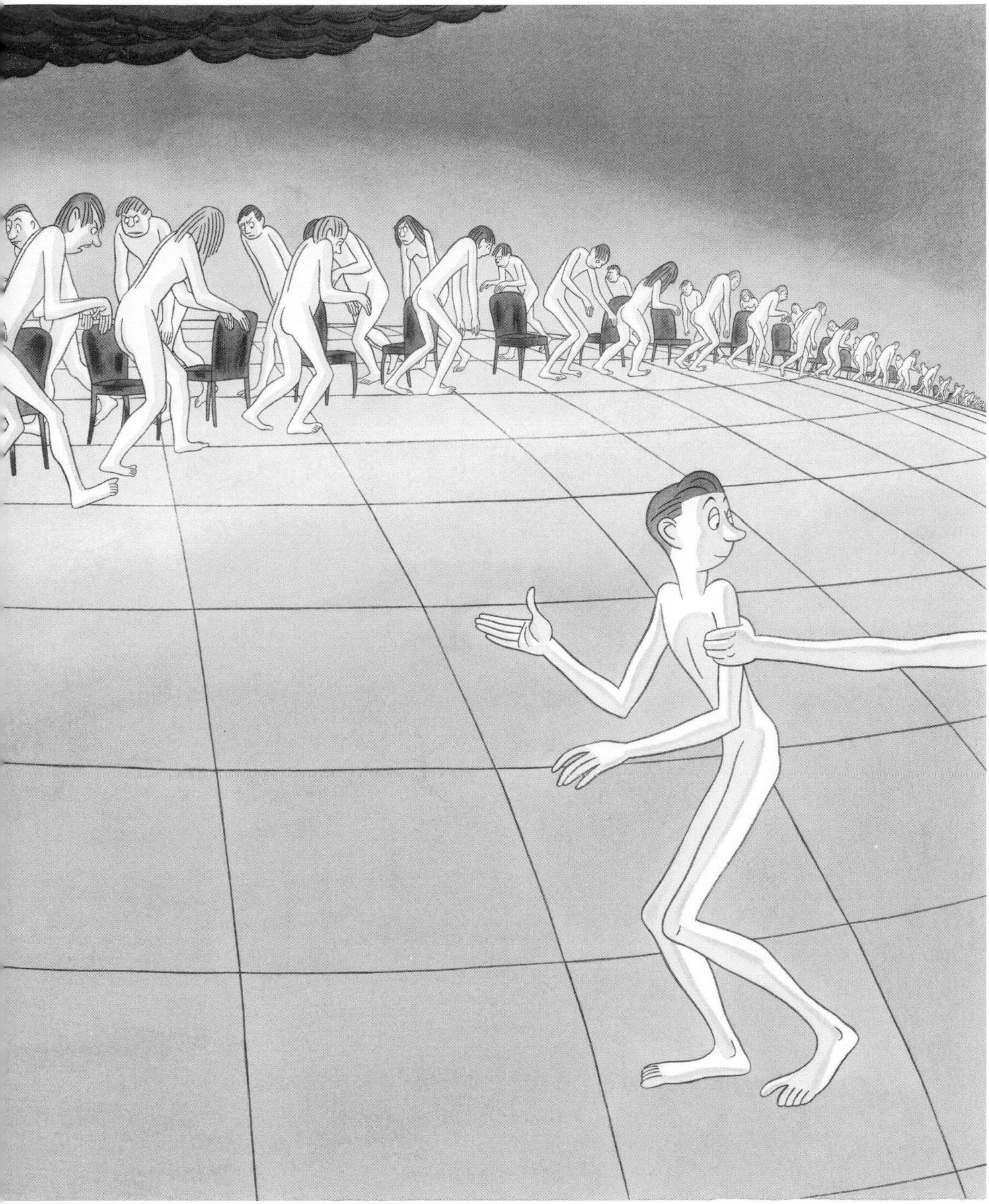

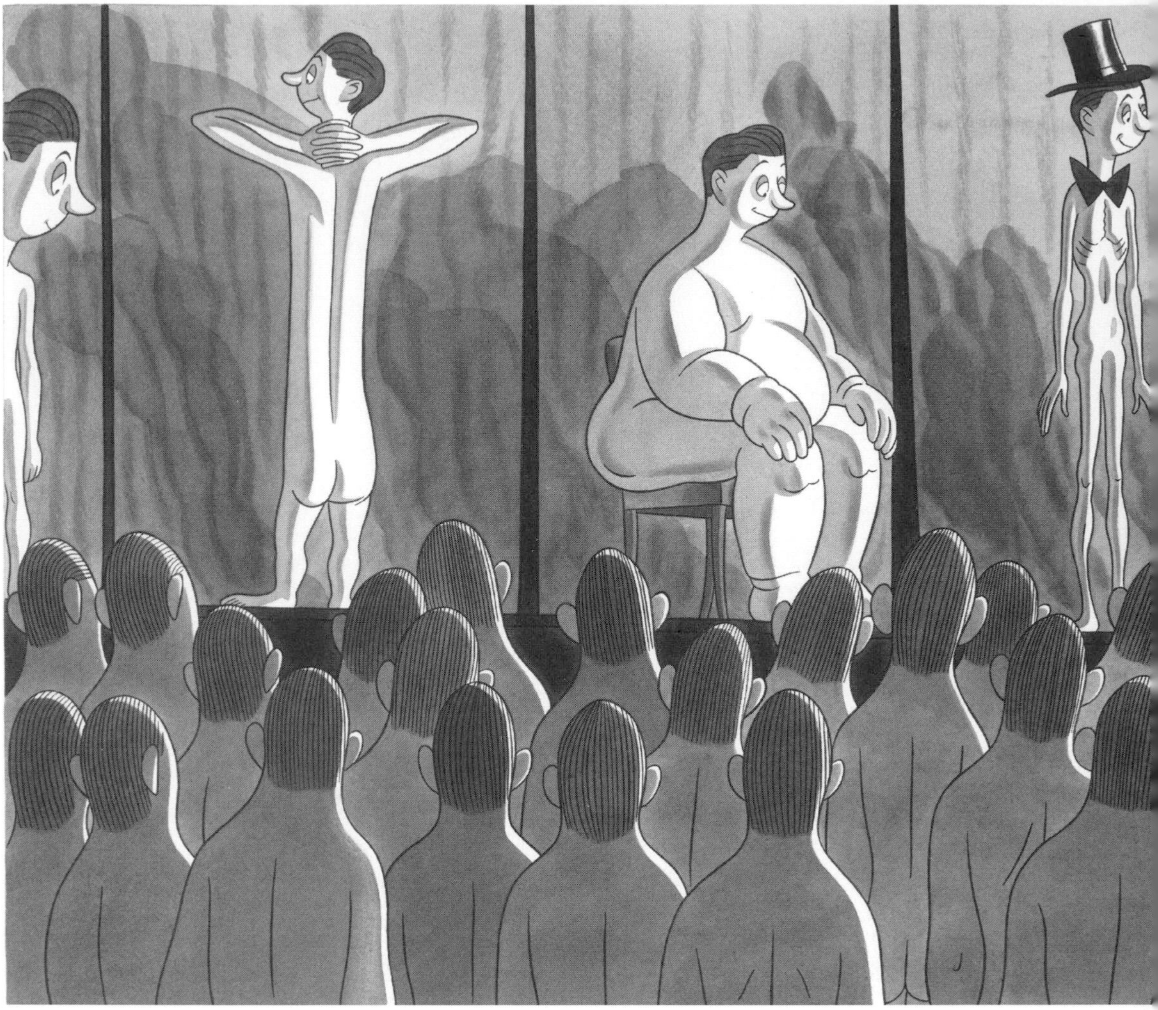

Look what I've done to my body

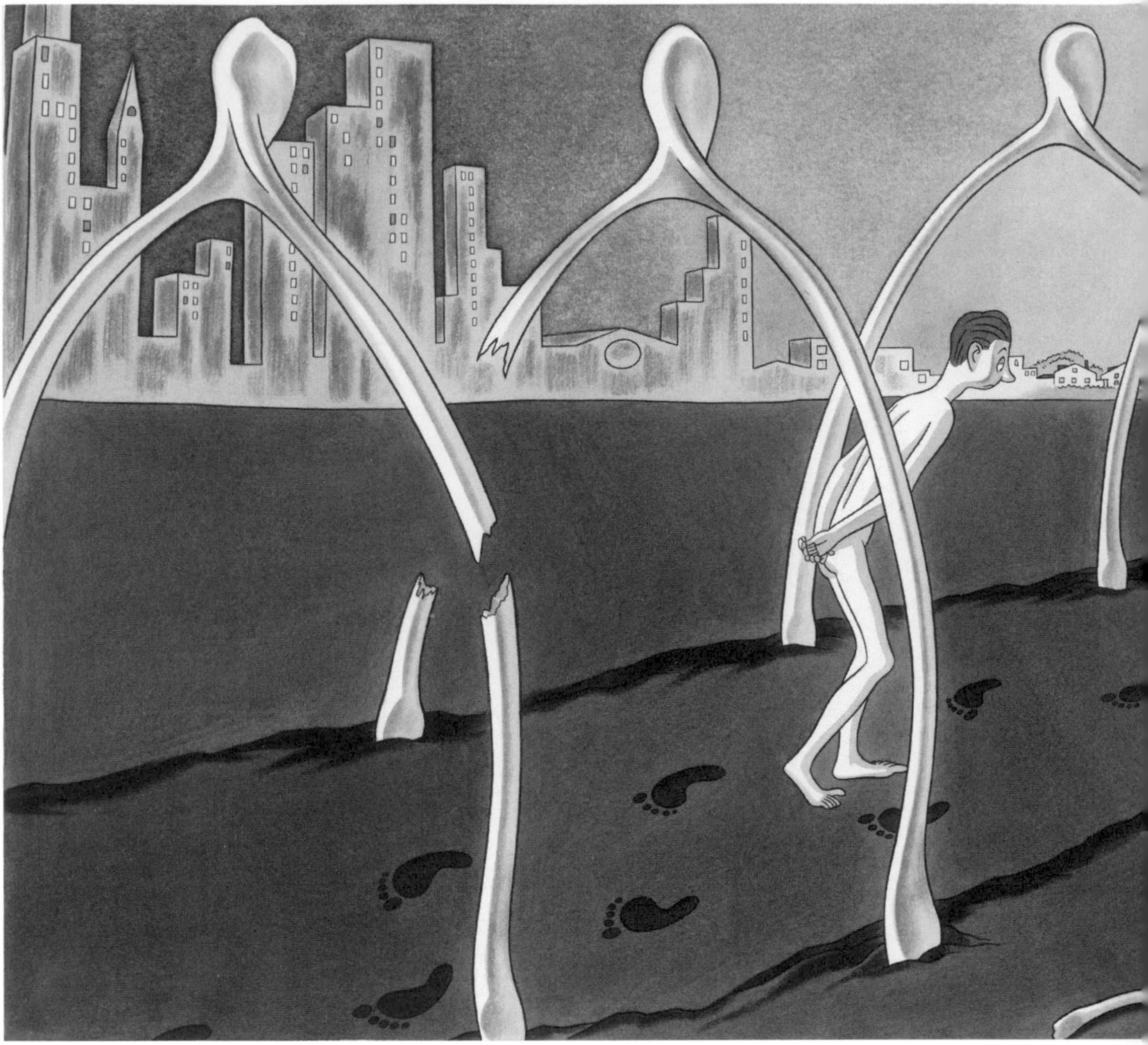

I've lost something

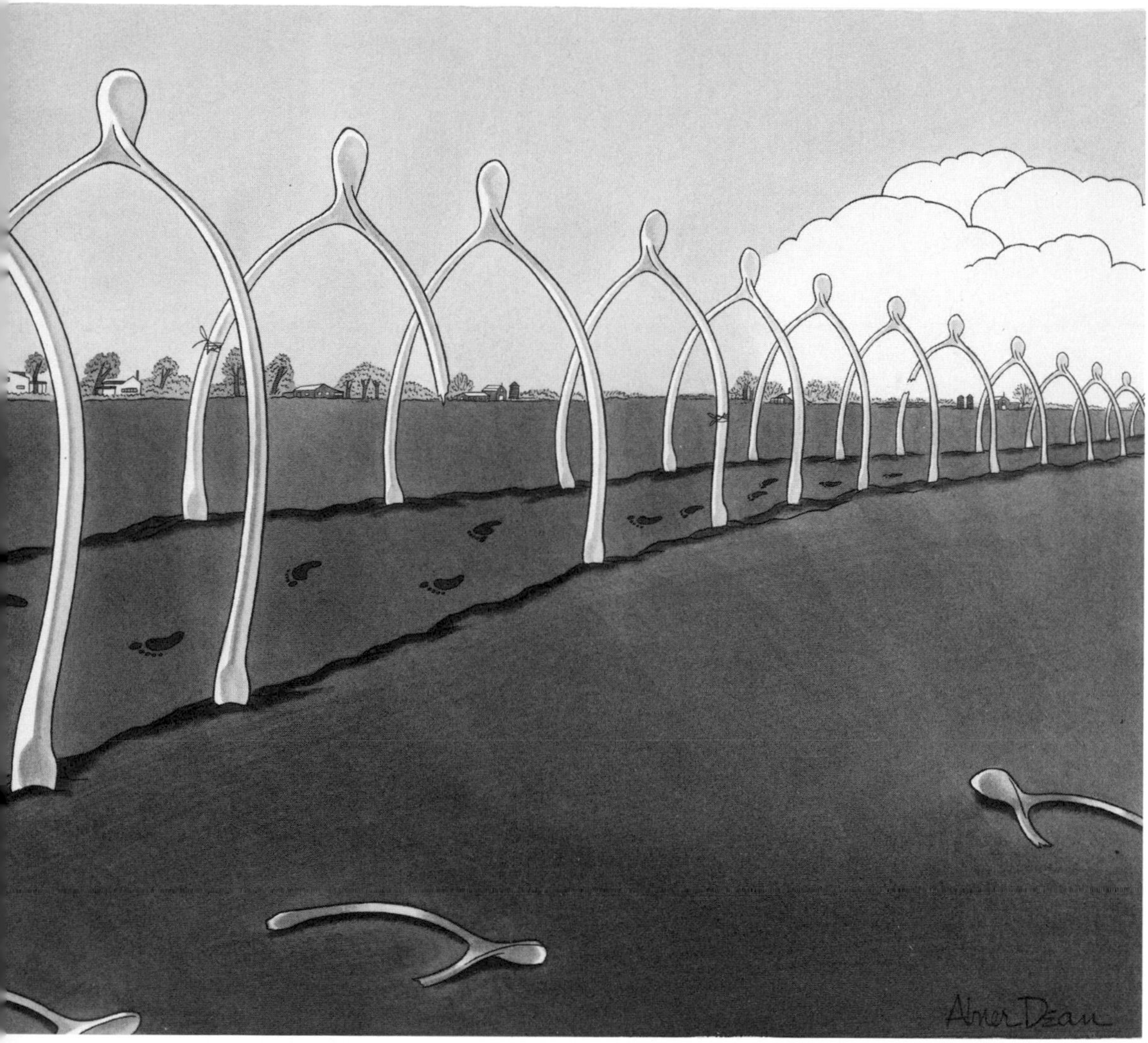
Abner Dean

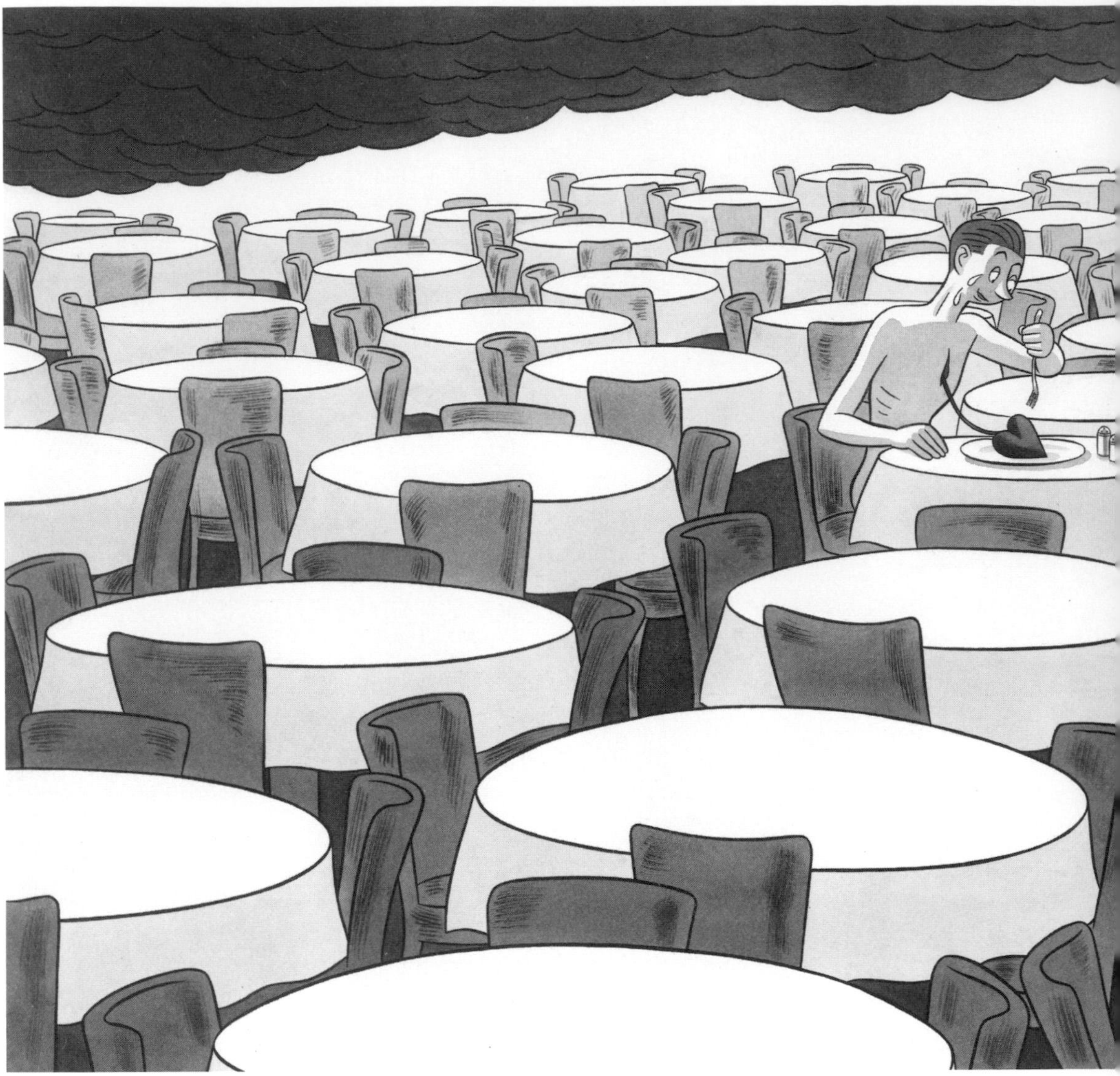

This is good food

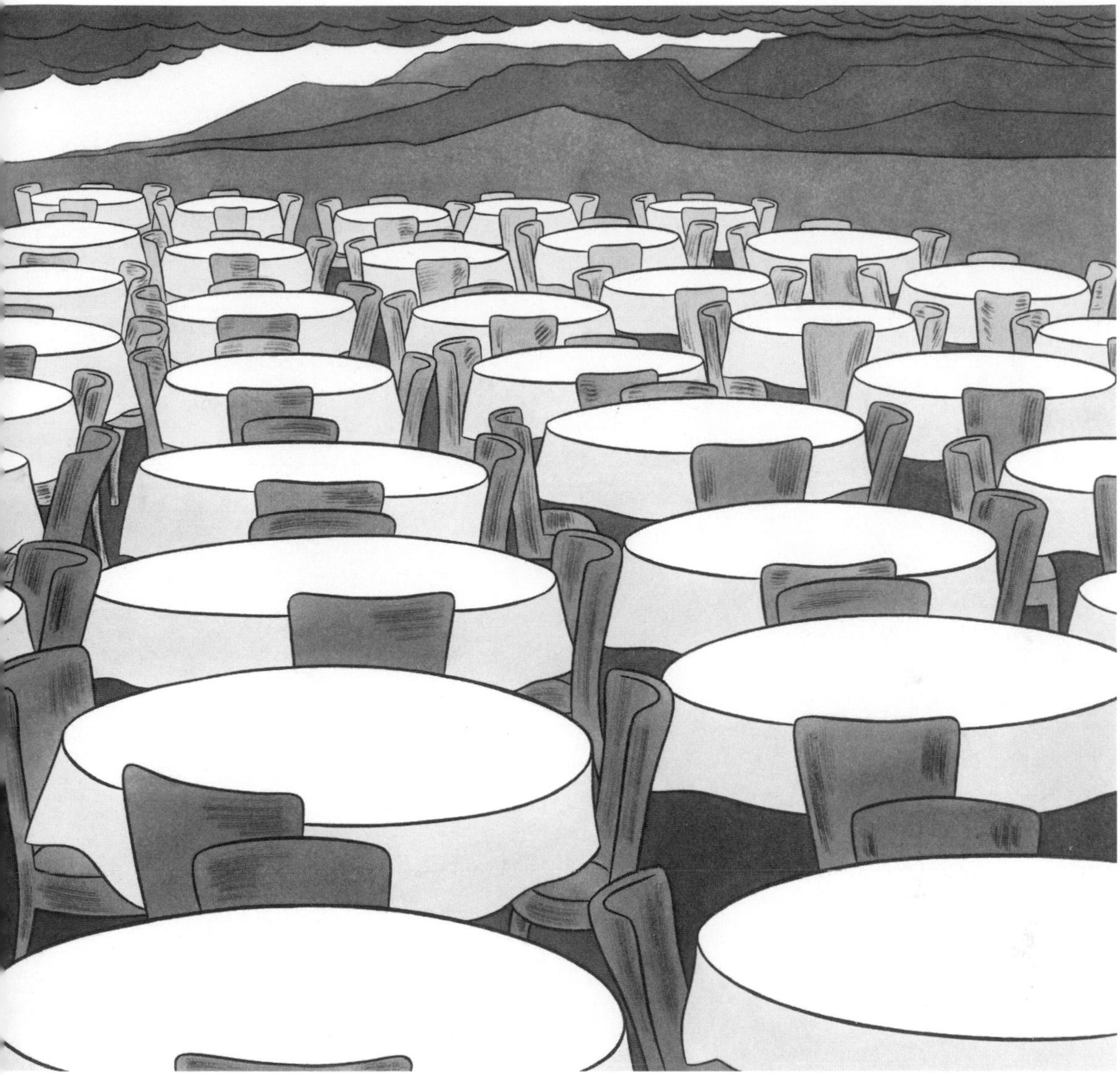

I won a prize once

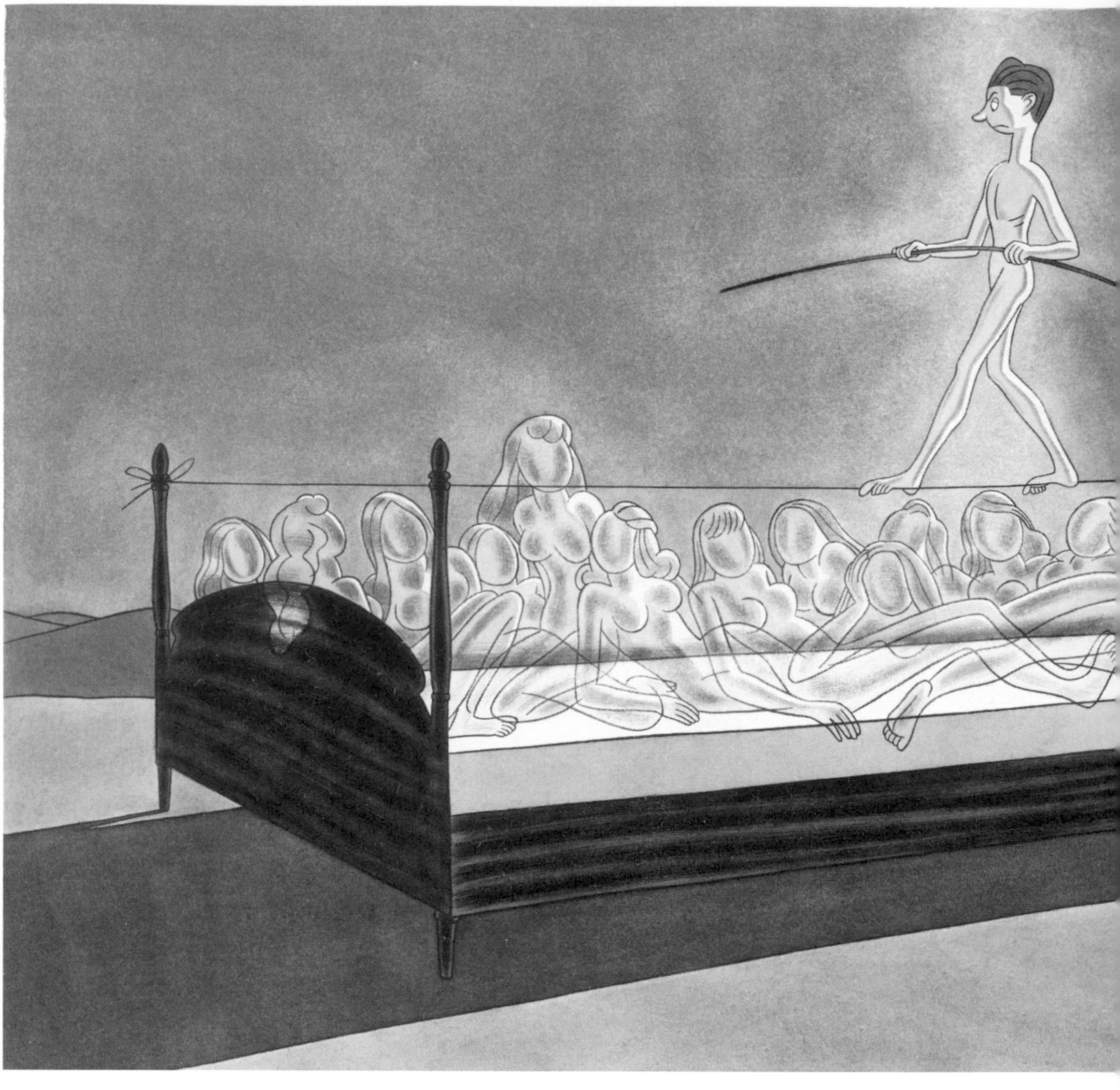

It's not always easy to fall asleep

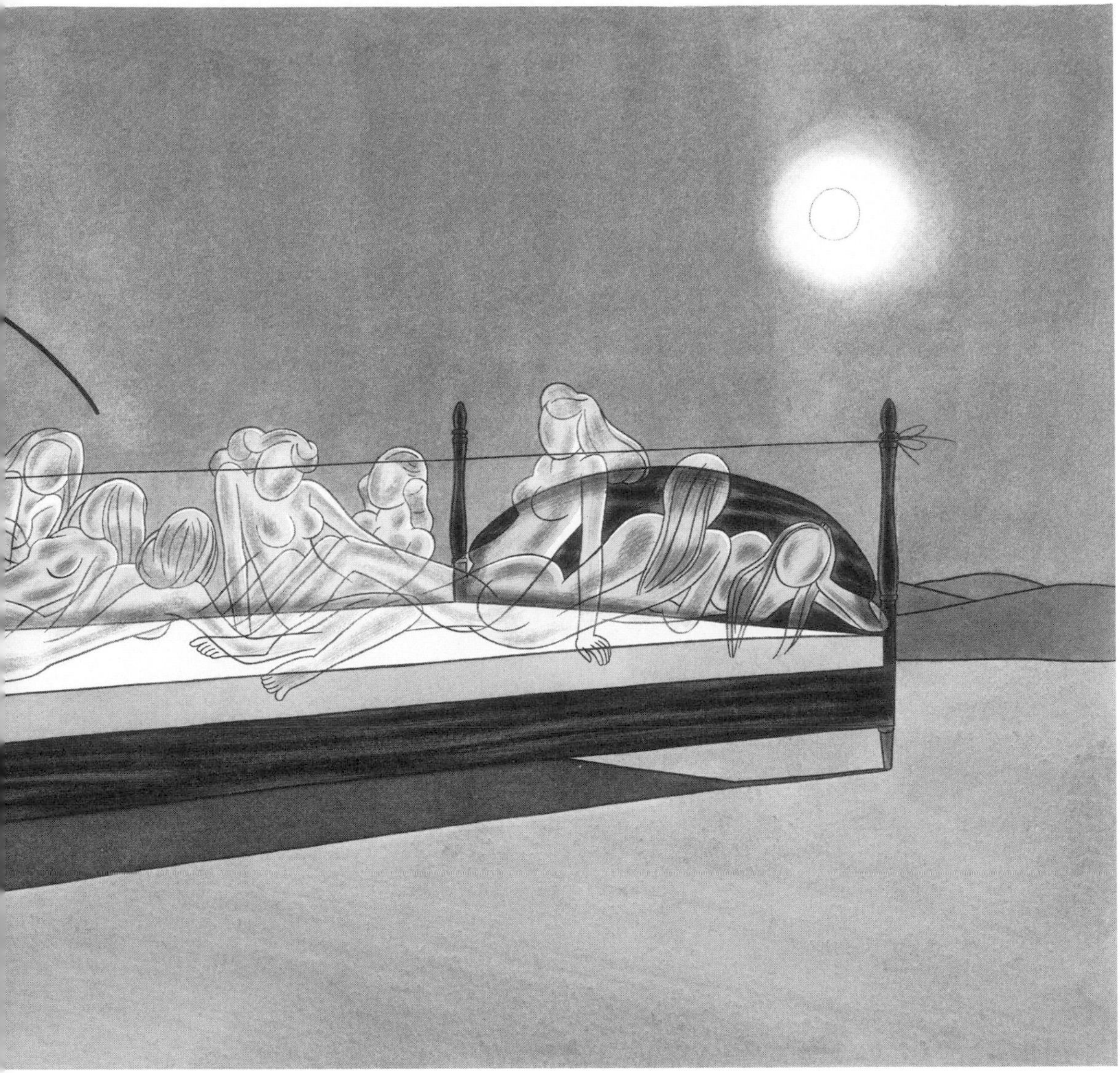

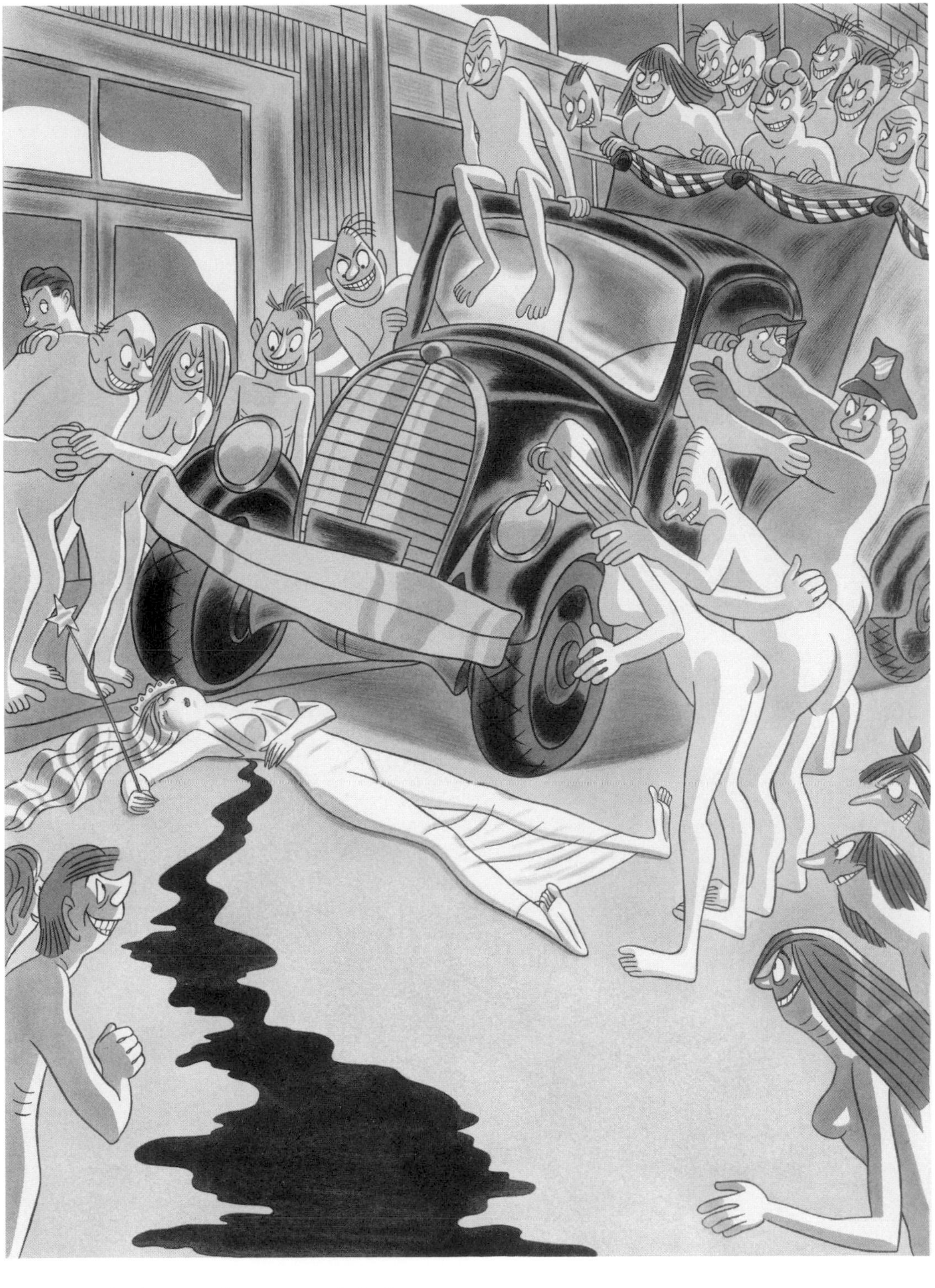

. . . and then the good fairy . . .

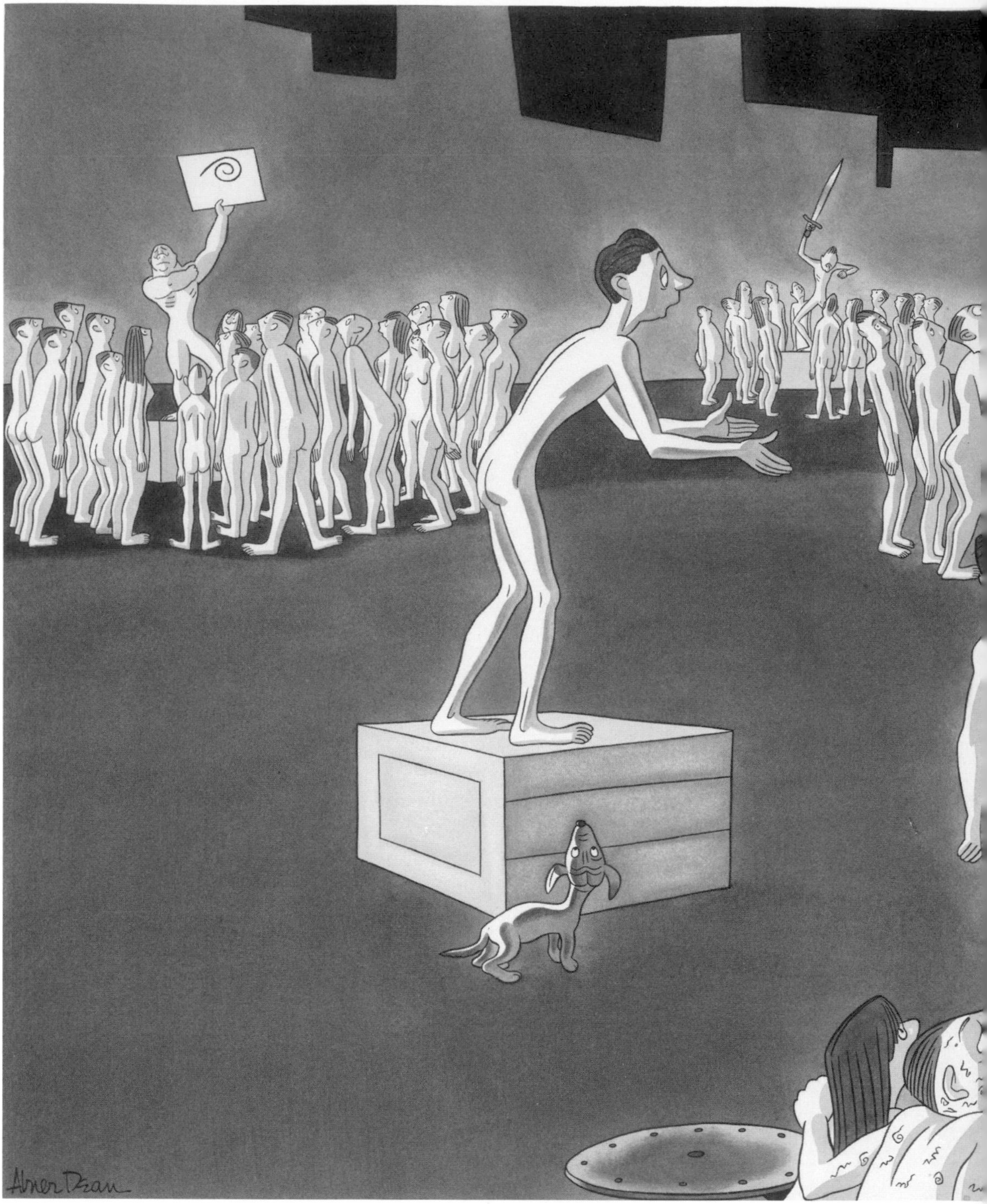
Abner Dean

I can cure you

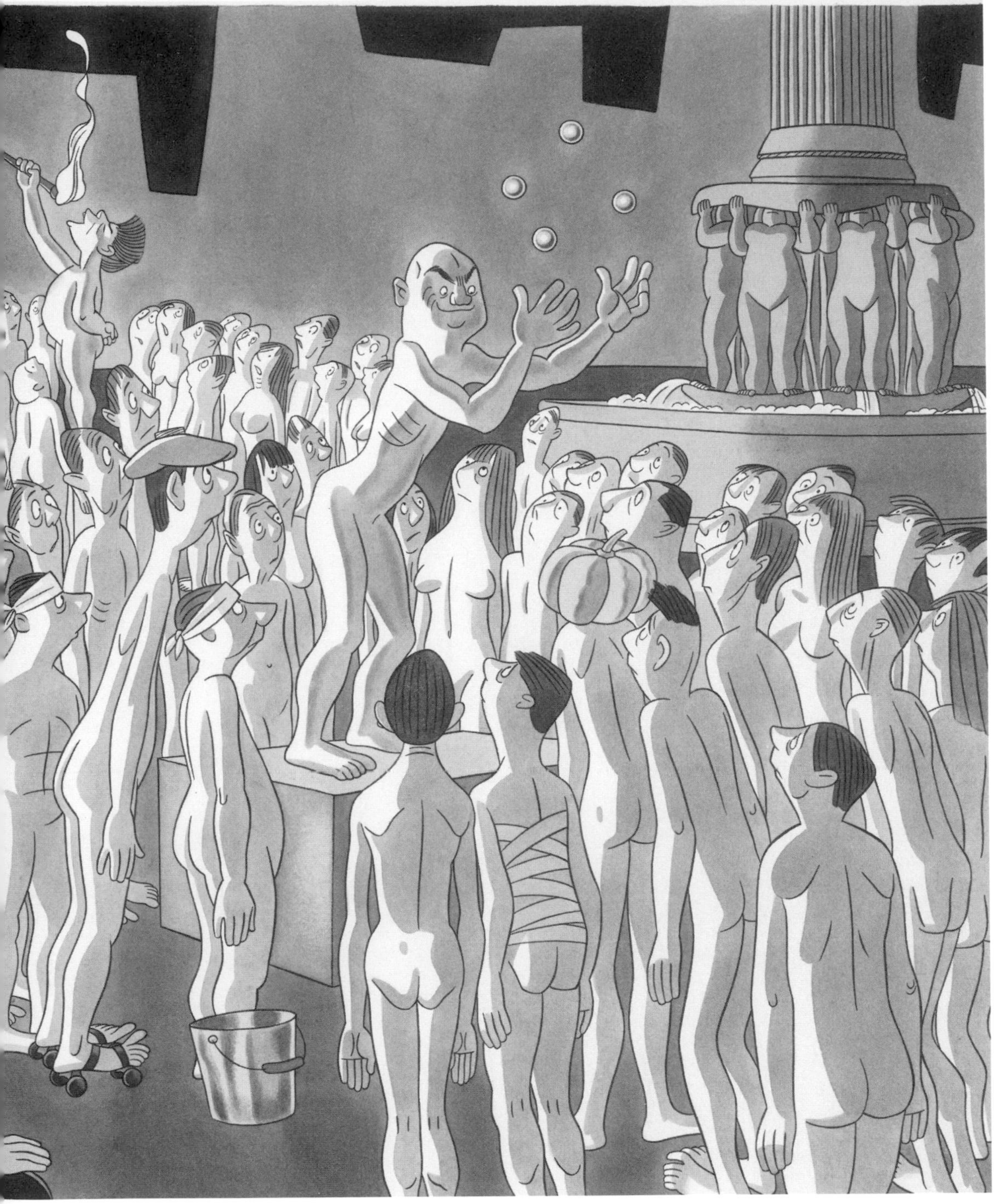

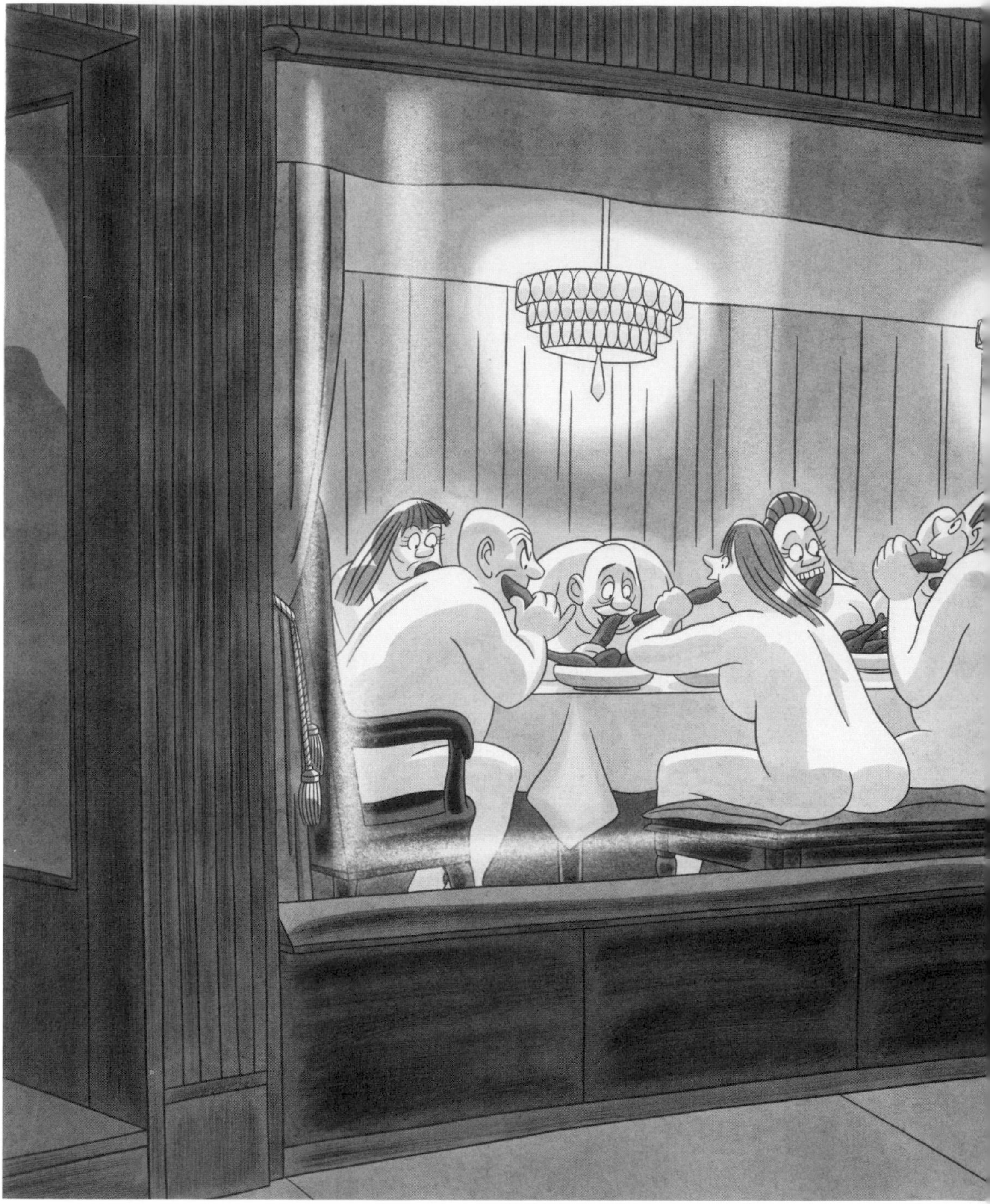

What am I doing here?

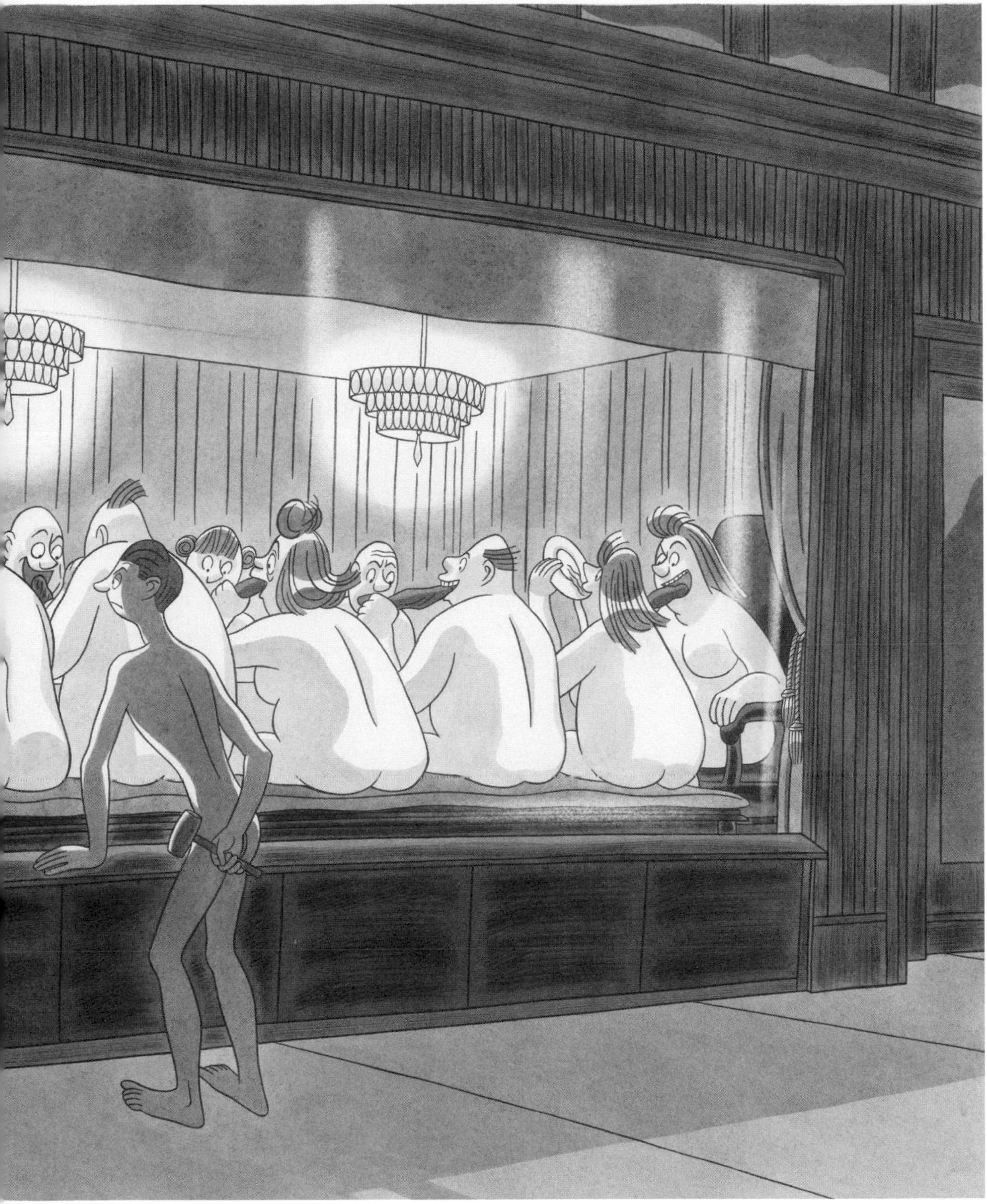

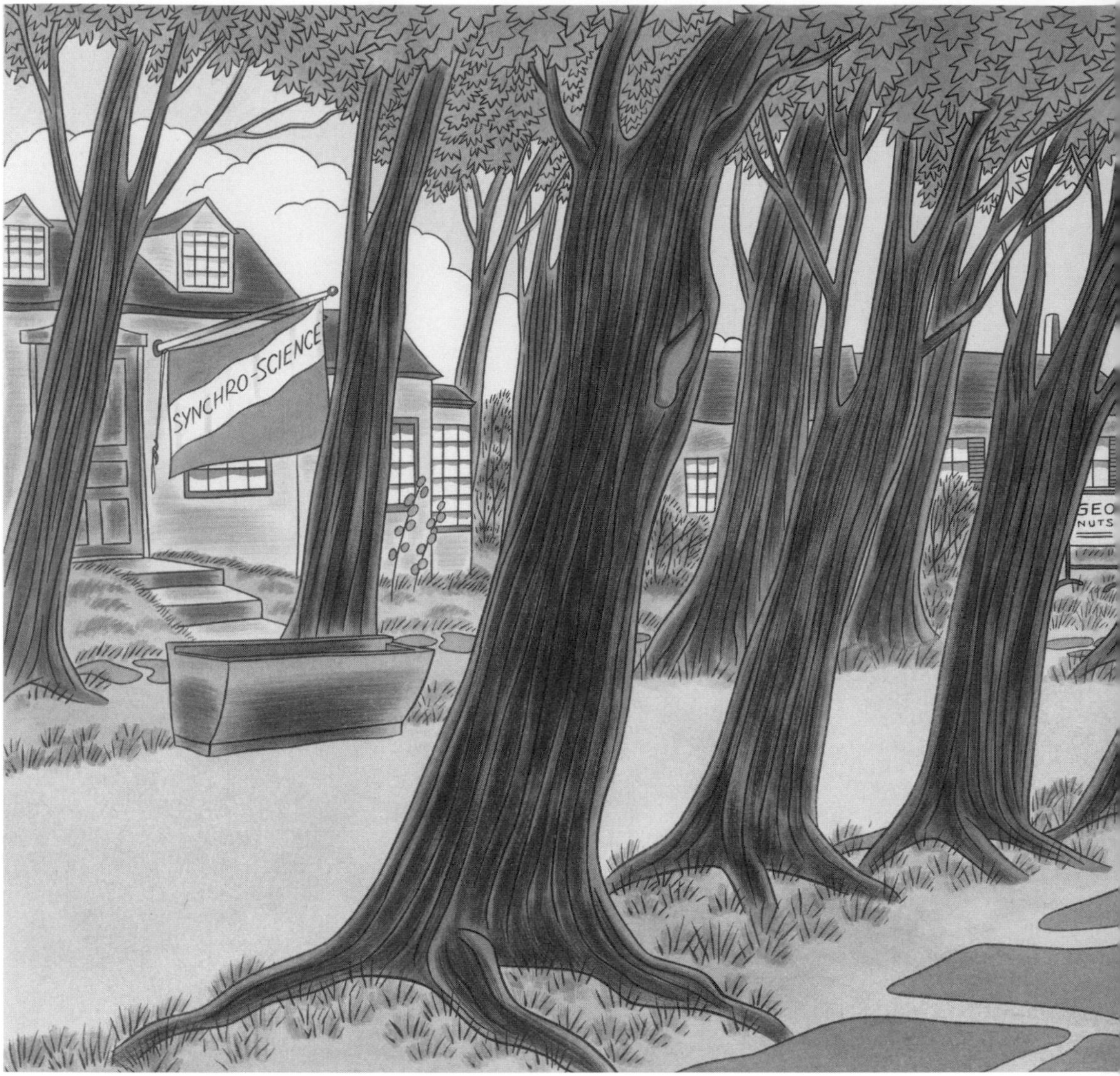
SYNCHRO-SCIENCE
GEO
NUTS

Facts are consoling

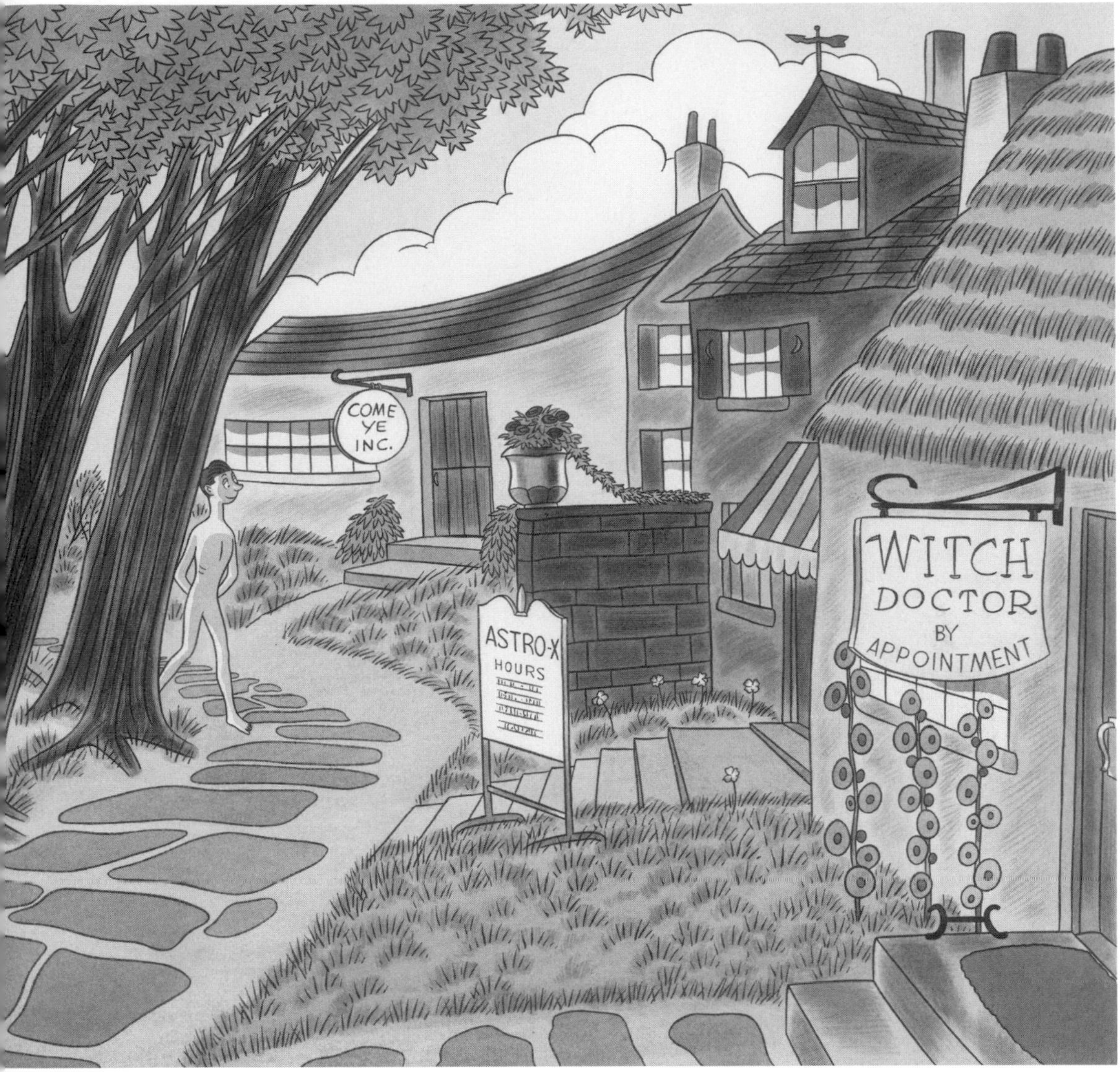
COME
YE
INC.
ASTRO-X
HOURS
WITCH
DOCTOR
BY
APPOINTMENT

Sometimes we give up too soon

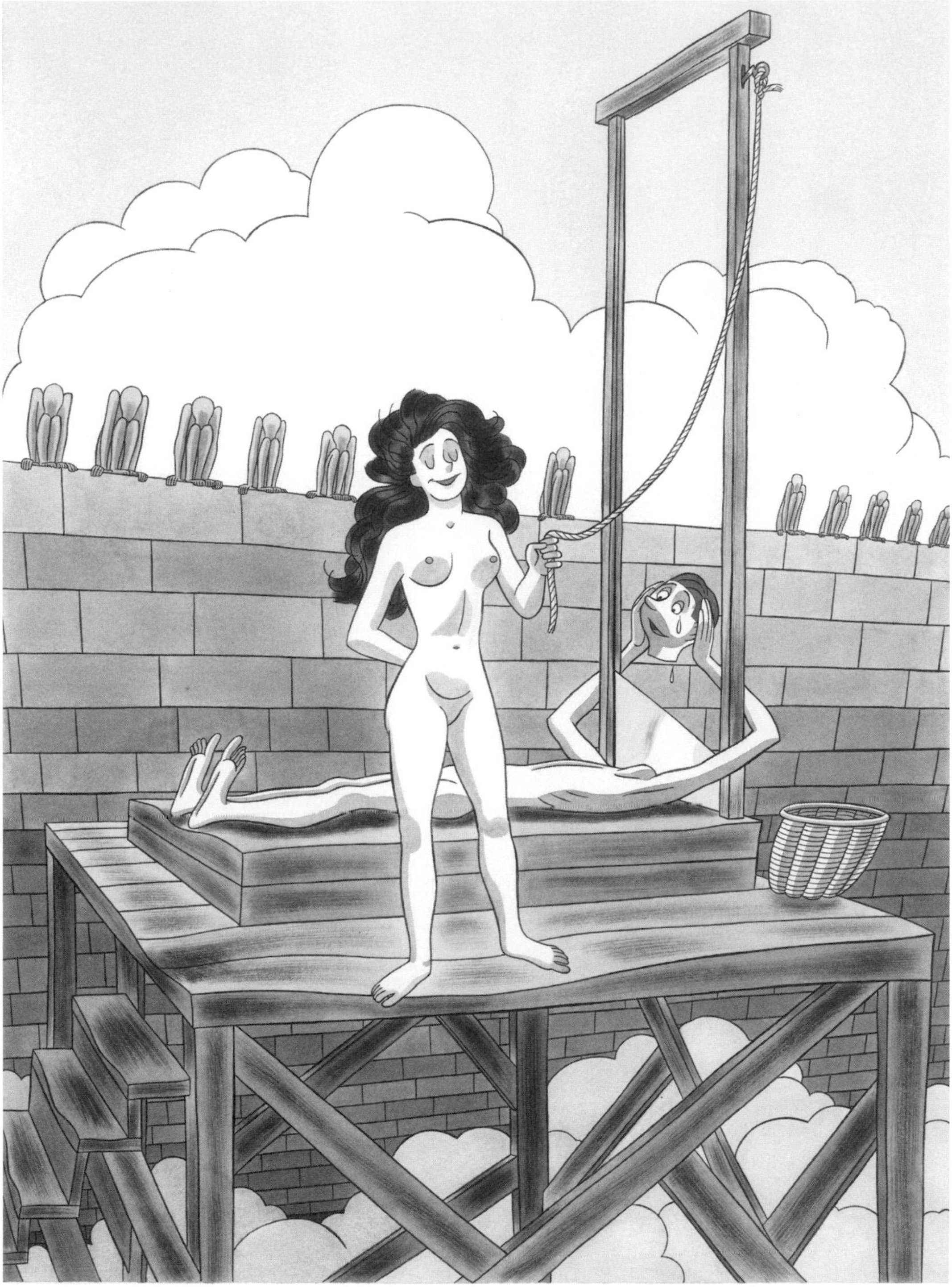

Give me one more chance, please

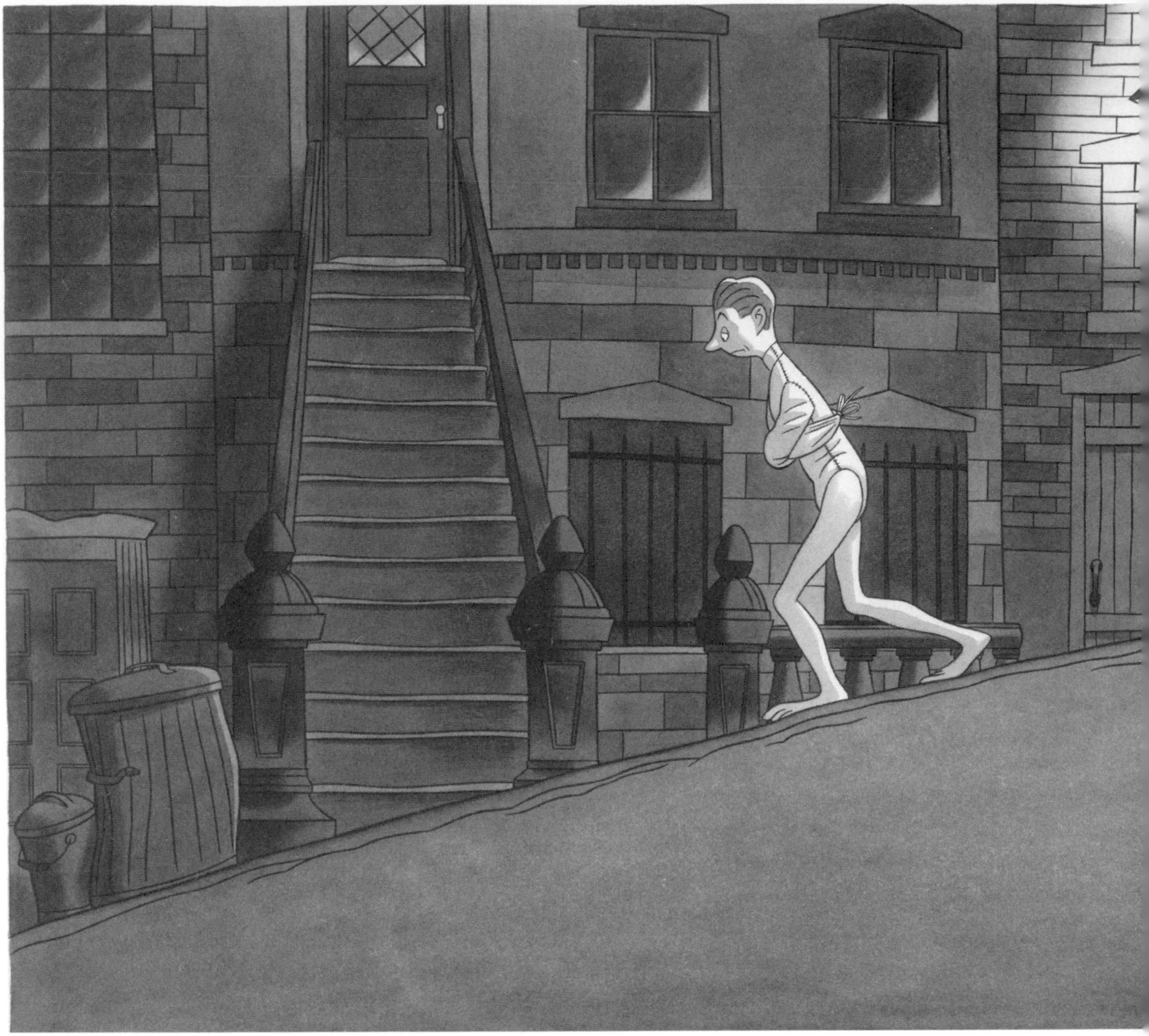

I miss good old . . . what?

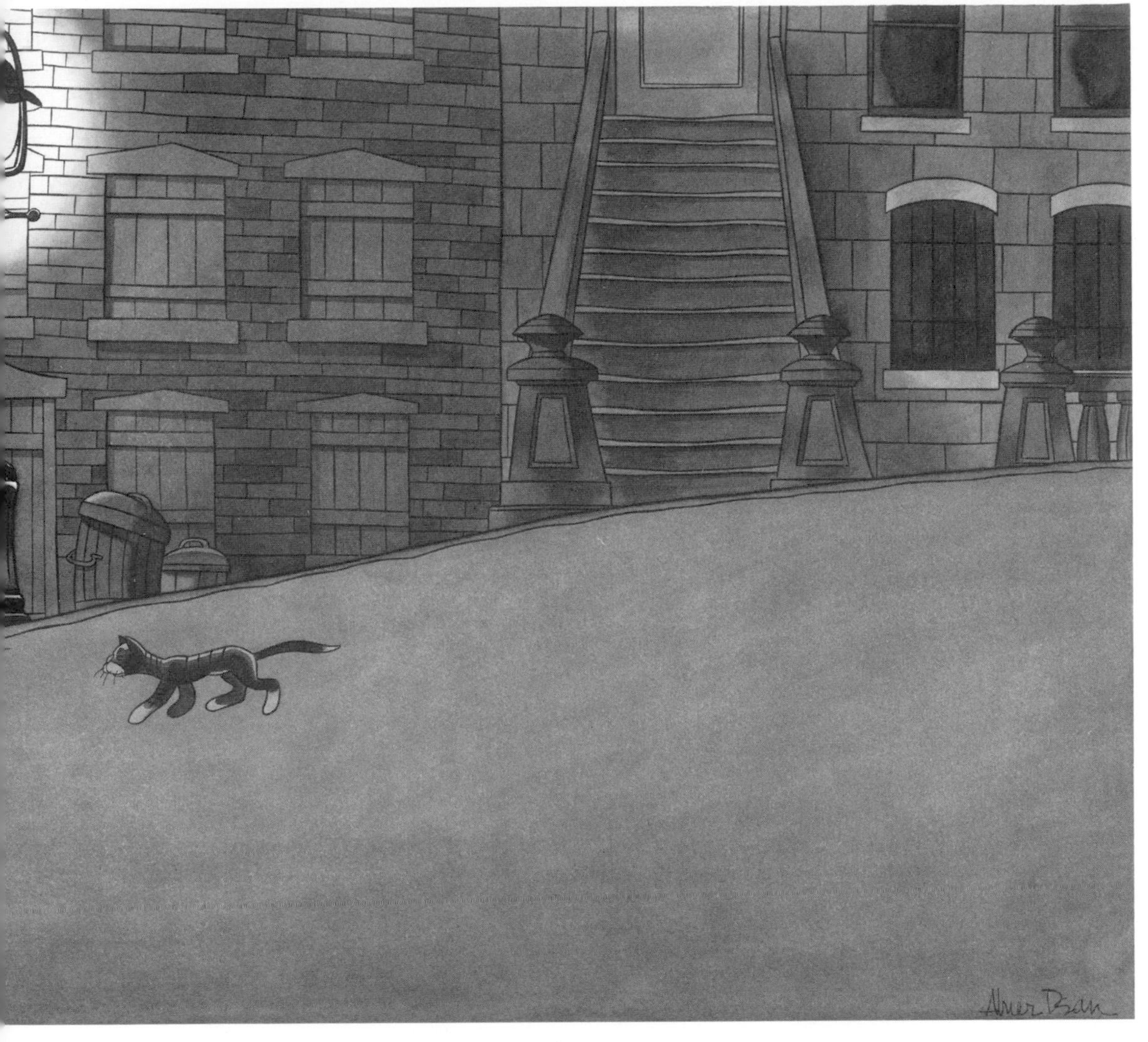
Abner Dean

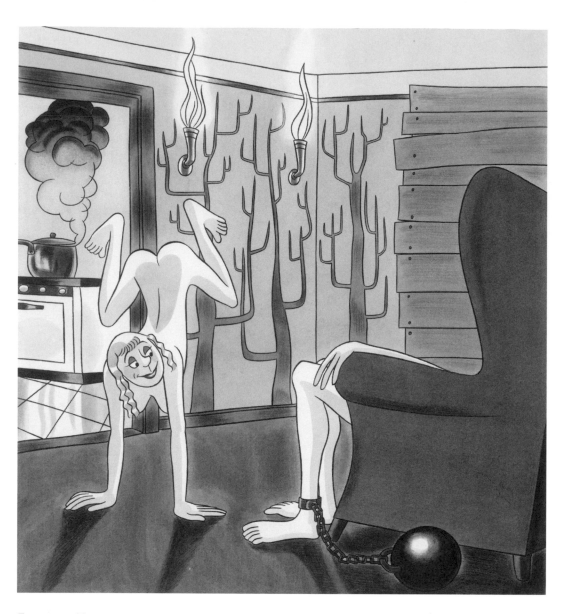

Just talk to me

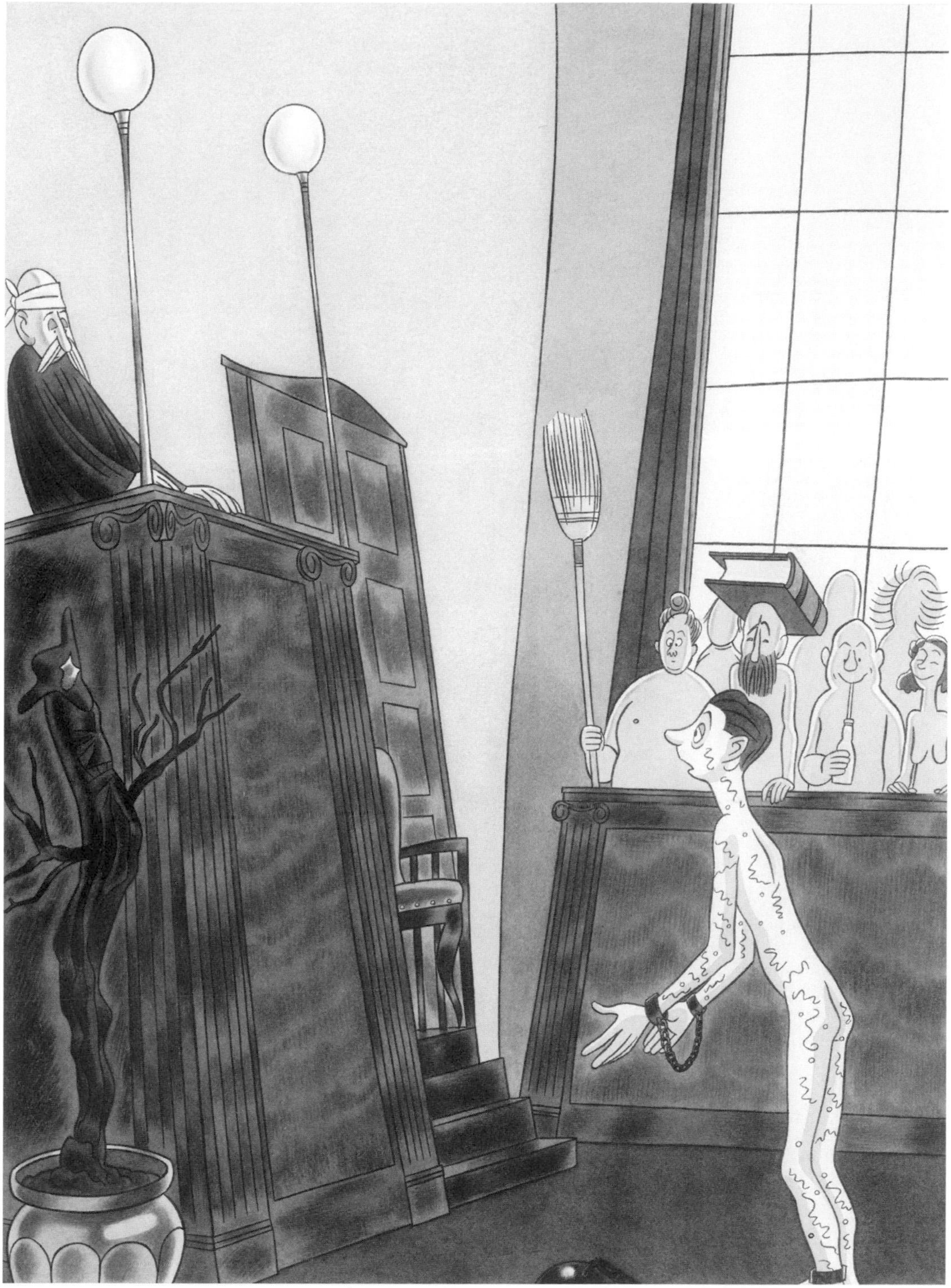

It's only a germ . . . not me

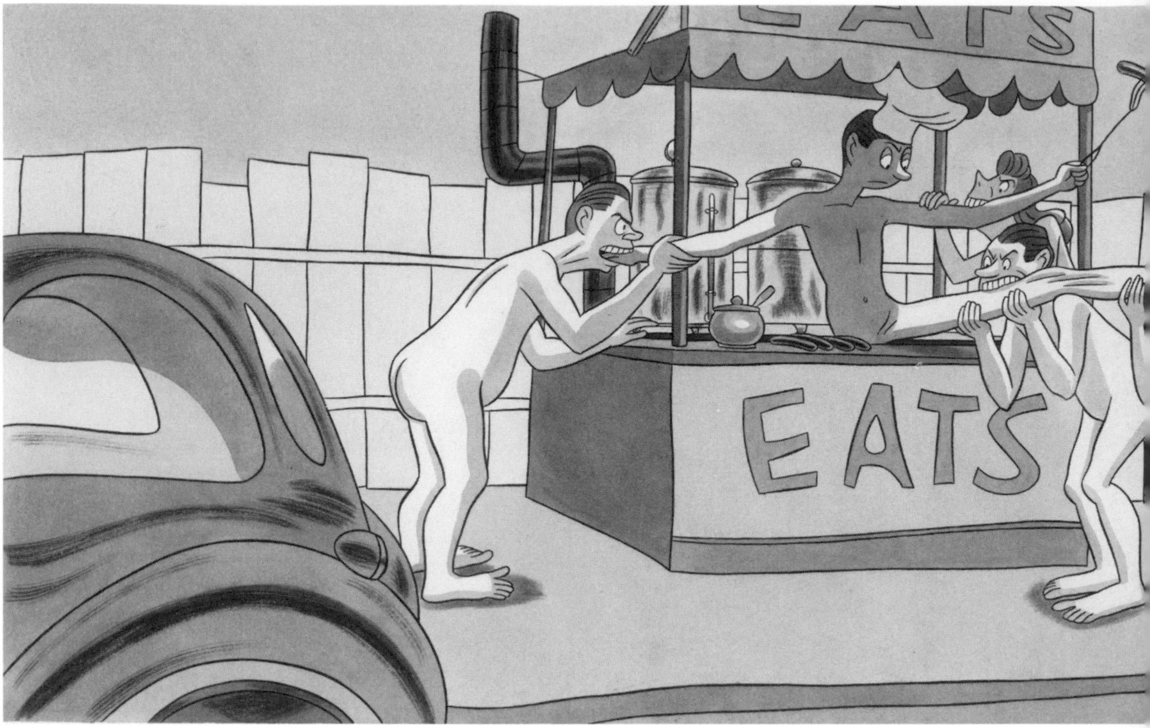
EATS
EATS

You can give too much of yourself

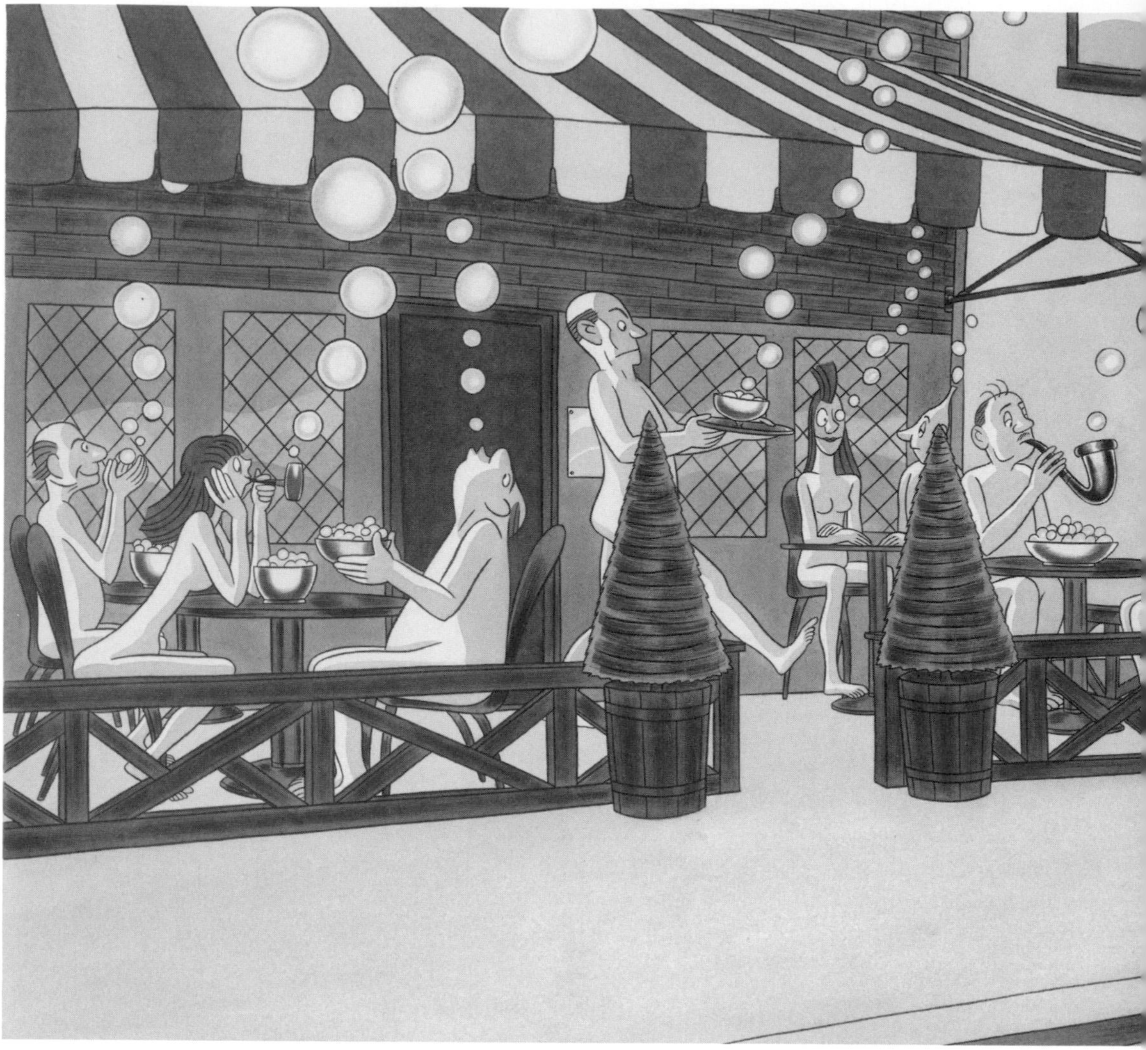

Each one to his own device

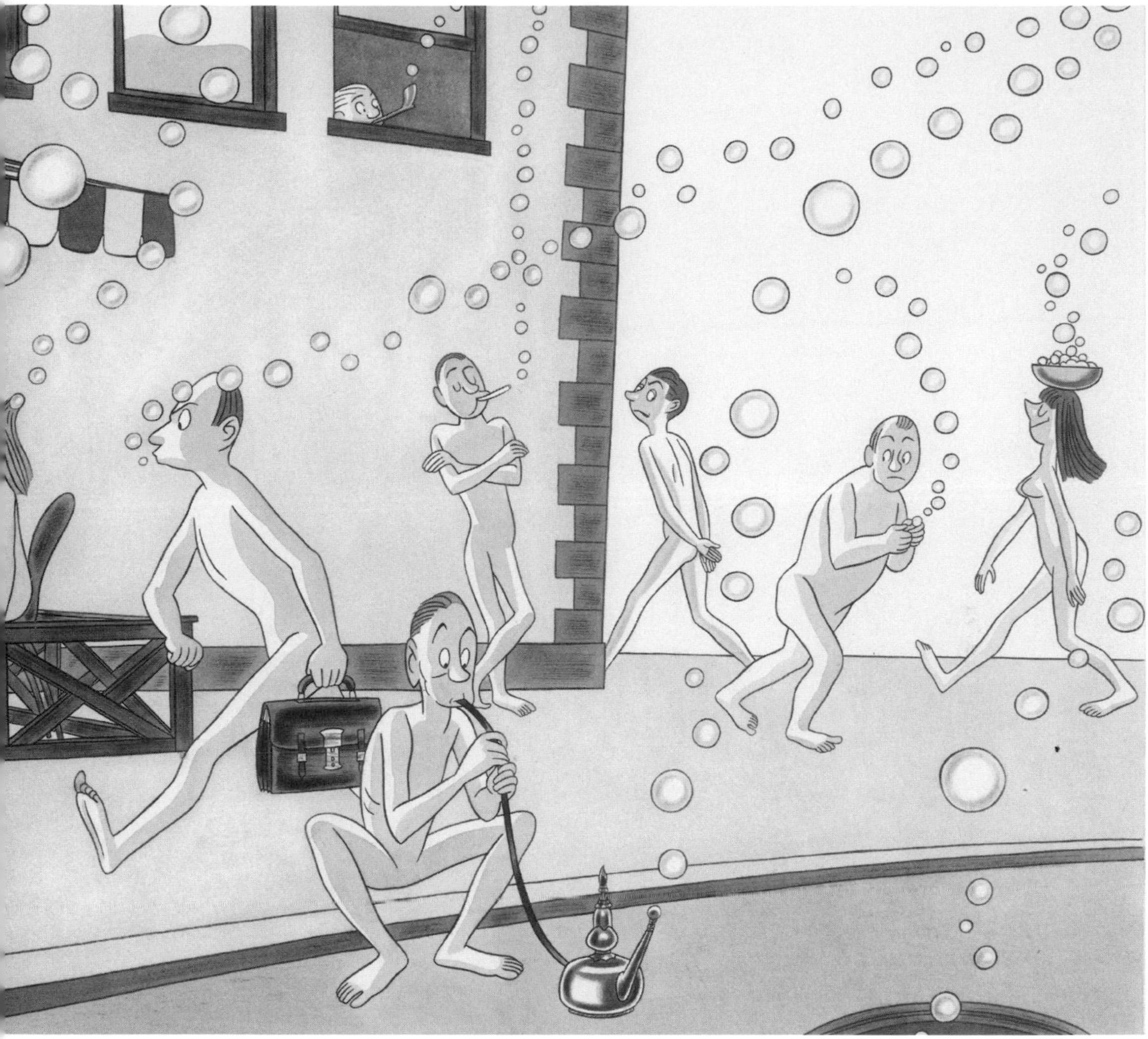

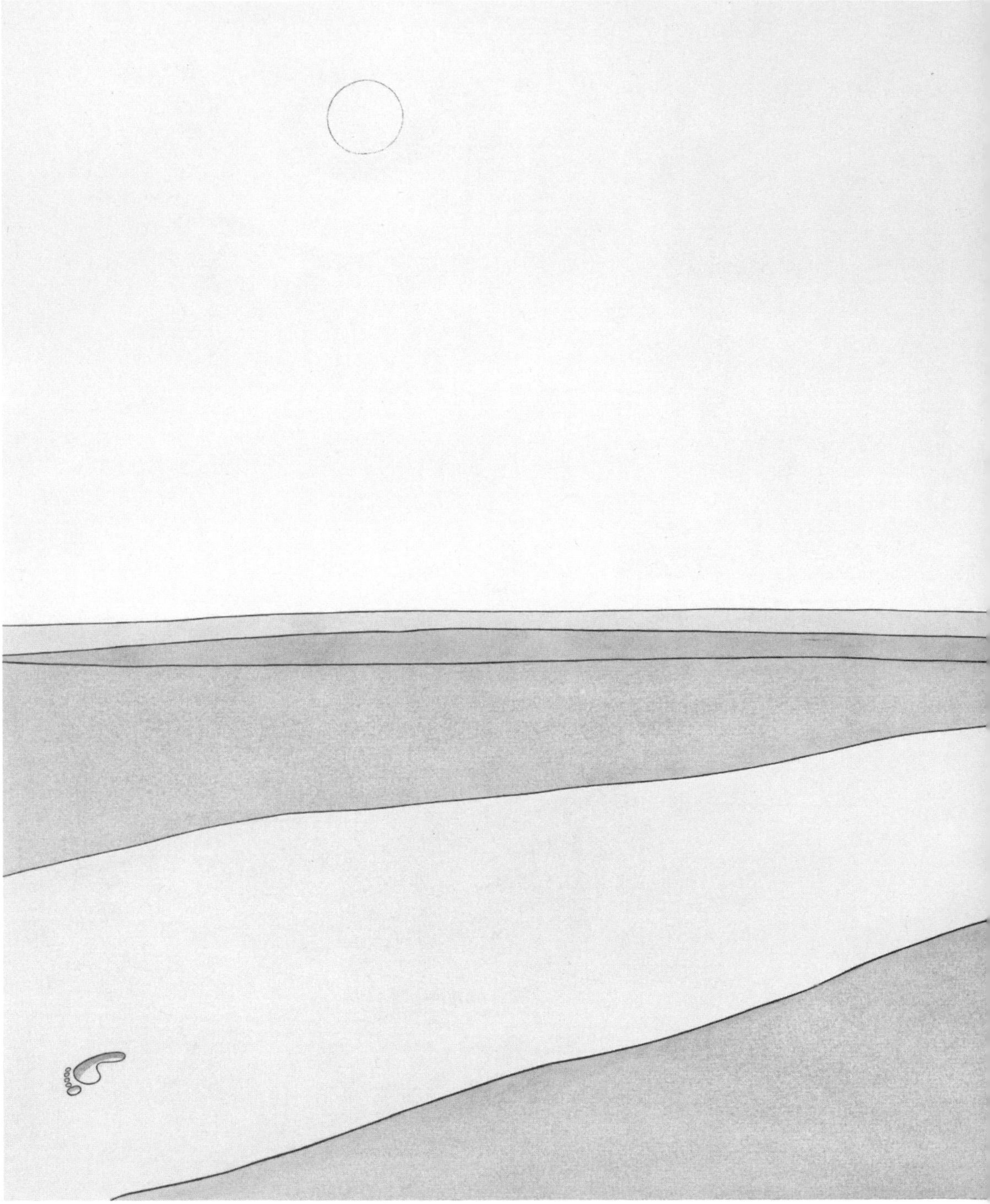

She had raven hair

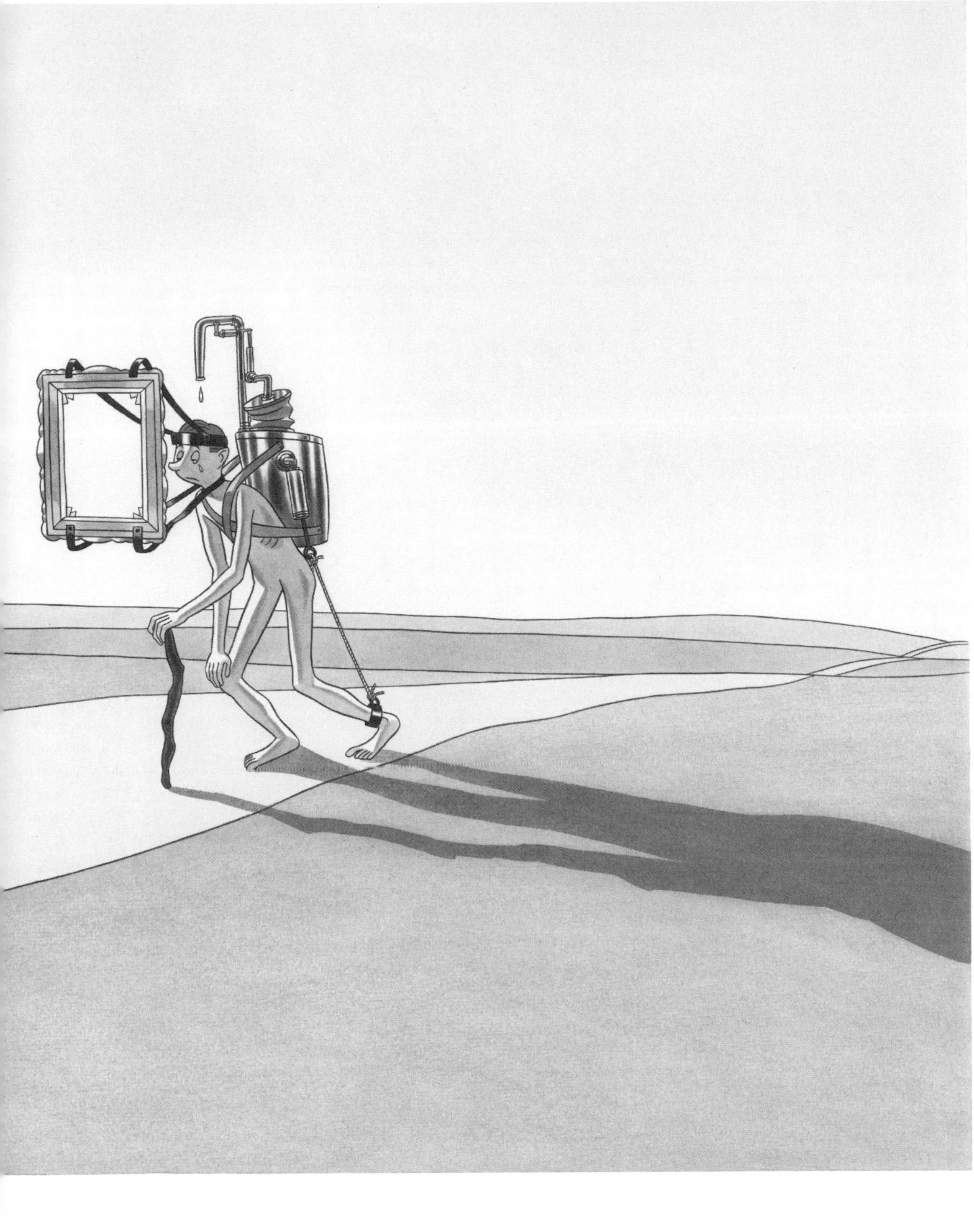

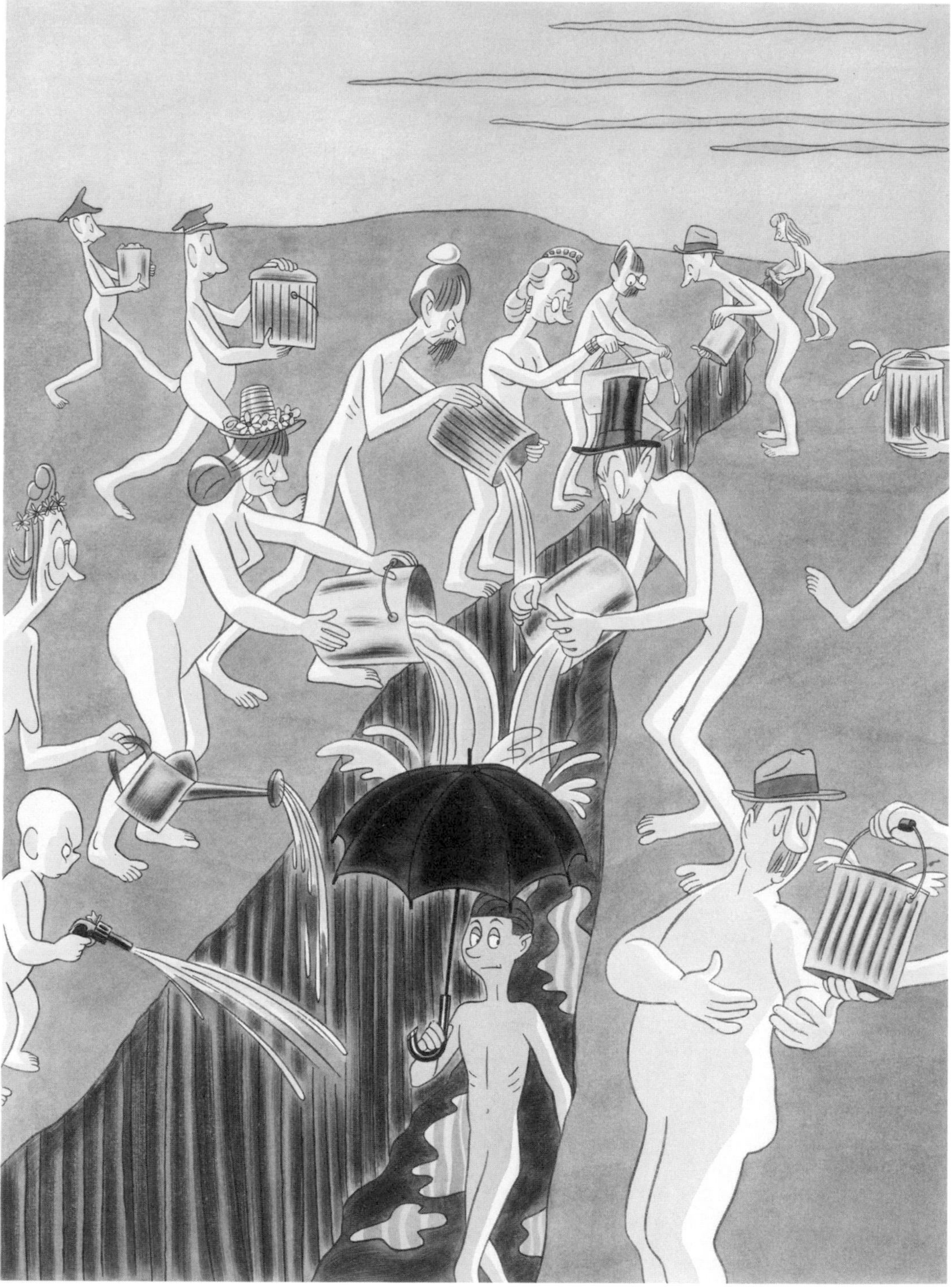

Always be charitable

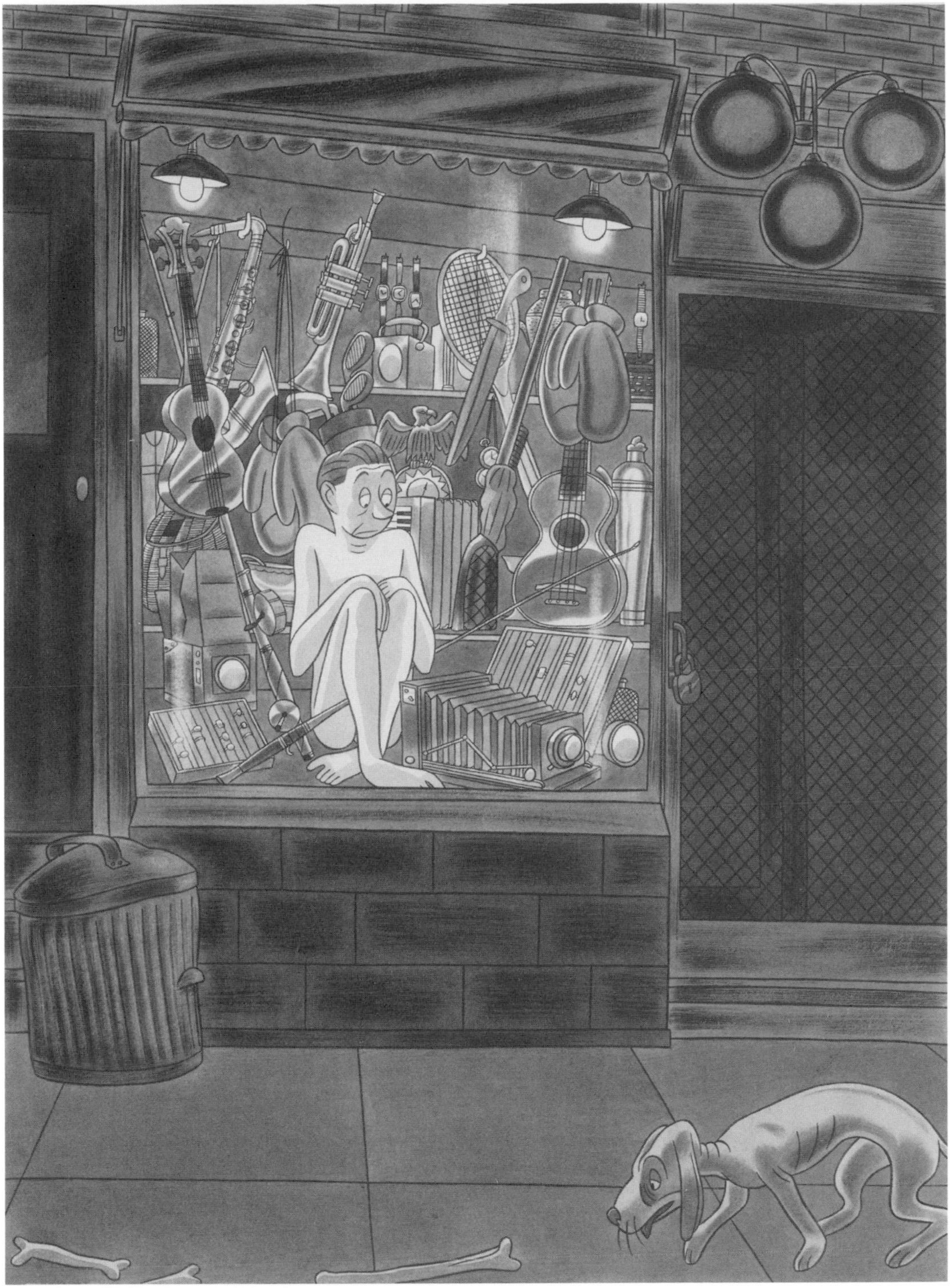

I suddenly feel very old

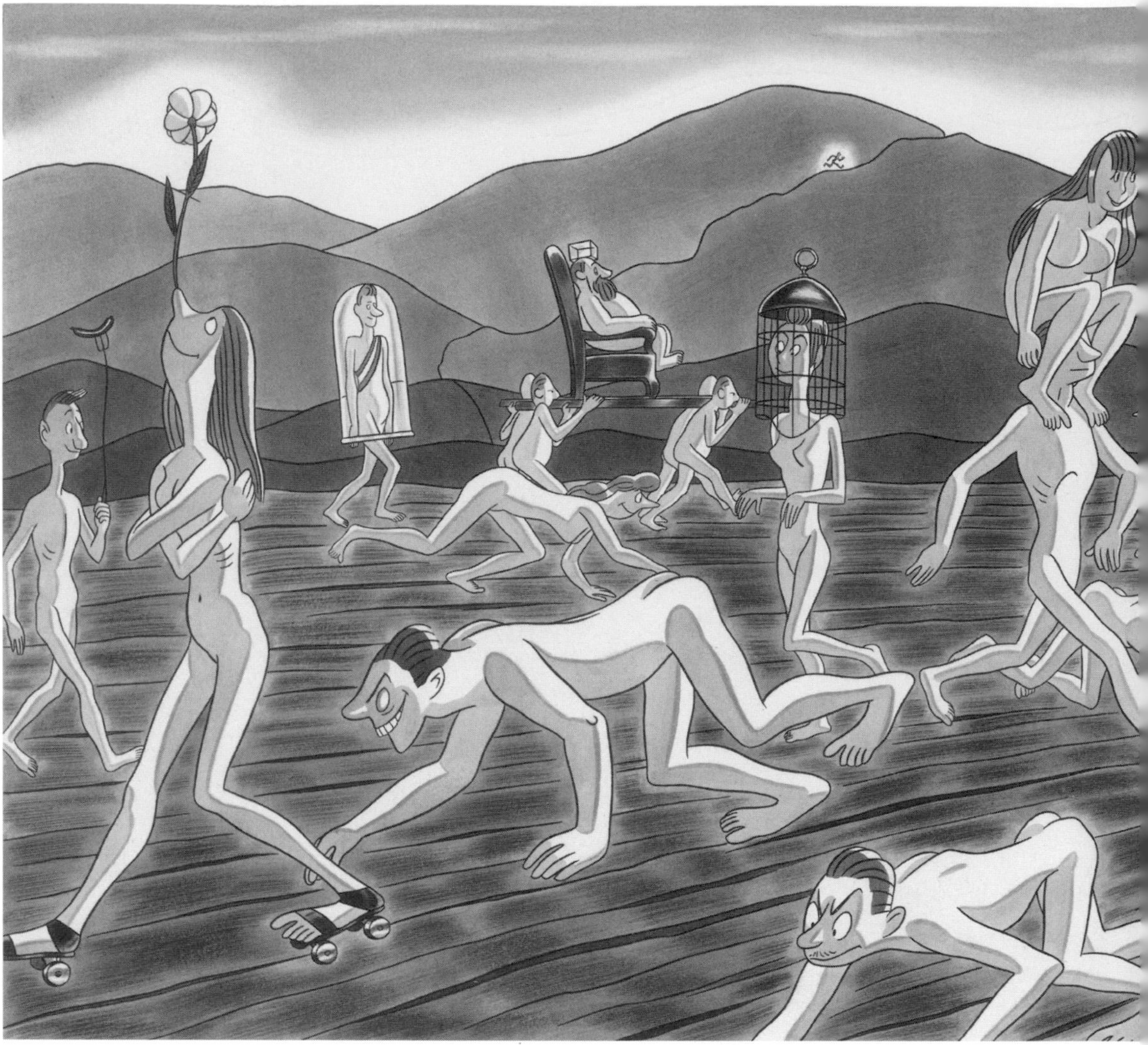

There must be some room for improvement

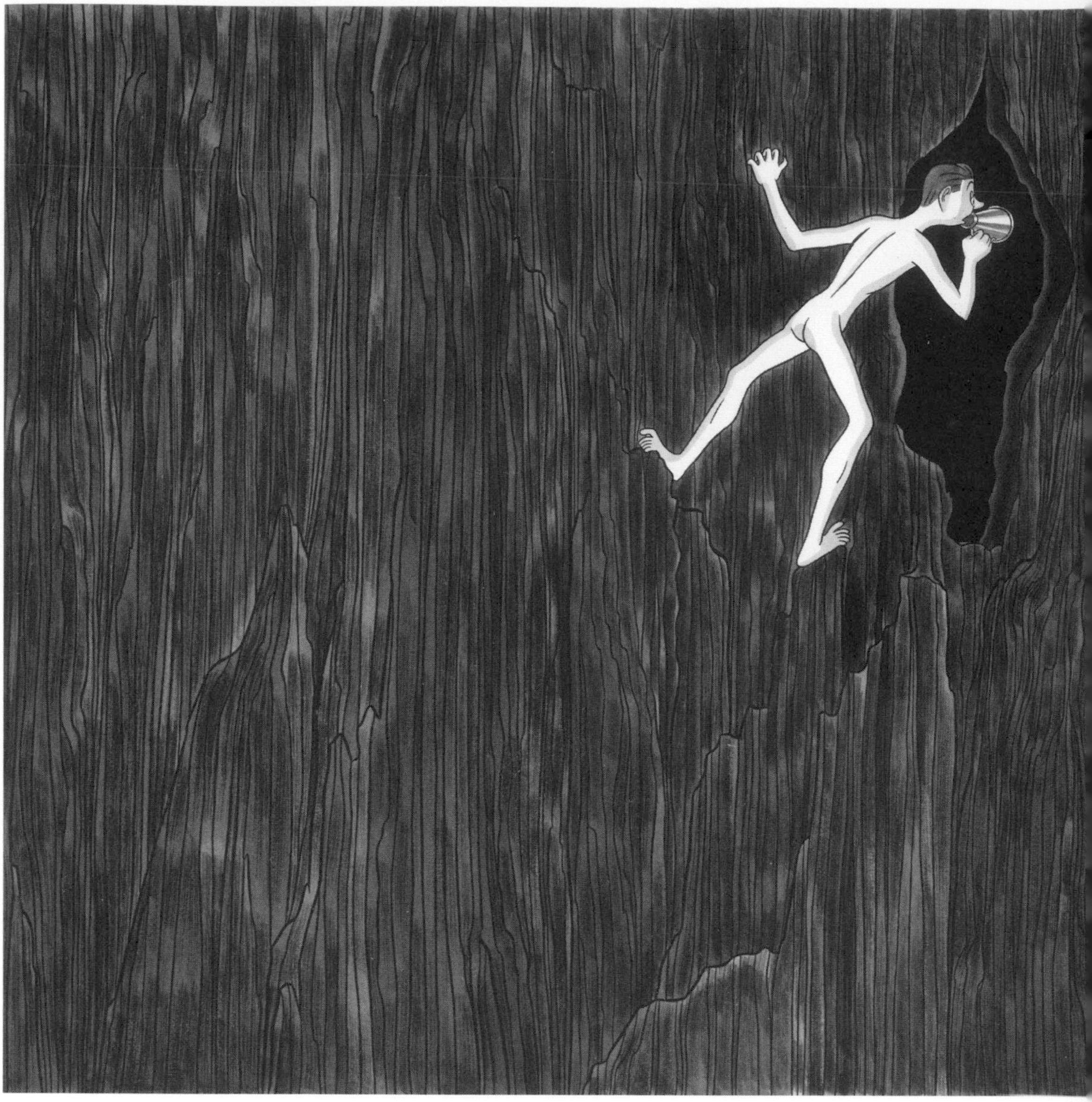

Will the three wise men please step forward

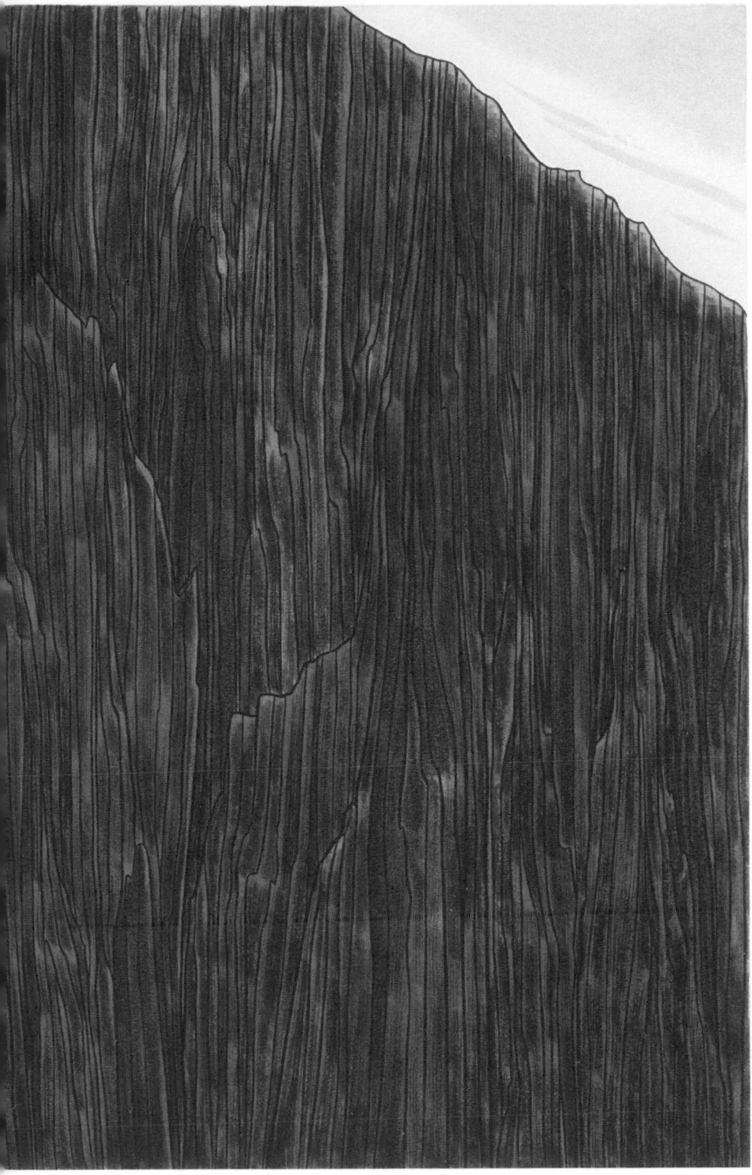

NEW AND FORTHCOMING TITLES
FROM NEW YORK REVIEW COMICS

AGONY
Mark Beyer

PEPLUM
Blutch

ALMOST COMPLETELY BAXTER
Glen Baxter

SOFT CITY
Pushwagner

PRETENDING IS LYING
Dominique Goblet